Hooked on Heroin

Hooked on Heroin

Drugs and Drifters in a Globalized World

Philip Lalander

Oxford • New York

First published in 2003 by
Berg
Editorial offices:
1st Floor, Angel Court, 81 St Clements Street, Oxford, OX4 1AW, UK
838 Broadway, Third Floor, New York, NY 10003-4812, USA

© Philip Lalander 2003

Berg is an imprint of Oxford International Publishers Ltd.

Library of Congress Cataloging-in-Publication Data
Lalander, Philip, 1965-
[Hela varlden èar din. English]
Hooked on heroin : drugs and drifters in a globalized world / Philip Lalander.
p. cm.
Includes bibliographical references (p.   ) and index.
ISBN 1-85973-762-5 (cloth) — ISBN 1-85973-767-6 (paper)
1. Heroin habit—Sweden—Norrkoping. 2. Subculture—Sweden—Norrkoping.
I. Title.
HV5822.H4H4313 2003
362.29′32′09486—dc21
2003010056

British Library Cataloguing-in-Publication Data
A catalogue record for this book is available from the British Library.

ISBN 1 85973 762 5 (Cloth)
1 85973 767 6 (Paper)

Typeset by JS Typesetting Ltd, Wellingborough, Northants.
Printed in the United Kingdom by Biddles Ltd, Guildford and King's Lynn.

www.bergpublishers.com

To my father, Folke

Contents

Preface

Sure, of course, no one wants to be a horser. When you're up at the Sergels Torg [a famous square in Stockholm] buying bags and see the wrecks hanging out up there, thirty to forty years of age, some of them only twenty-five, with no teeth, haven't had a shower in three weeks . . . It's not cool. It's no fun seeing them . . . And then you think, 'No one, just no one wants to become a heroin addict', that's just the way it is, not anything you dream of at all, so you start to think, 'Well, maybe just a little while more, one more fix . . .' (Steve, one of the 'new' heroin users in Norrköping)

In Norrköping (a Swedish town with a population of 122,000 inhabitants) in 1994 there were no heroin circles, and only four or five regular users of the myth-surrounded drug. By 2000, there were 248 opiate users to be found in the official statistics, and a well-established sales network. Police and social workers had a new problem requiring their attention, and parents had yet another danger to worry about. This book is based on interviews with twenty-five young heroin users and observations of close to forty, who were involved in the rapid development of a local heroin scene.

When this book was written, in late autumn 2000 and spring 2001, I was under a lot of psychological pressure. I felt I had to have it published as soon as possible in order to draw attention to the heroin problem in Norrköping so that maybe the authorities would do something. I was shaken by what I had seen, but also surprised by the warmth and engagement with which the young heroin users in Norrköping received me. I had not thought it would be as easy to make contact with them, and this turned out to be the case. I made many friends with whom I am still in touch, mostly heroin users, some now former heroin users, but also social workers. I believe my emotional engagement caused the book to be written rather quickly; I could seldom stop thinking about Norrköping's young heroin users.

However, this book is not merely a translation, but rather a reworking of the book entitled *Hela världen är din – En bok om unga heroinister* (*The Whole World is Yours – A Book about Young Heroin Users*). The first part of the title is from the cult film *Scar Face* from 1986 where 'the whole world is yours' is a theme throughout the film. Tony Montana, played by Al Pacino, tries, through crime, to create respectability and a name for himself. I saw certain Tony Montana characteristics among the young heroin users, including a wish to create a form of respectability in a capitalist society via consumer goods, and so the book got its name.

When I wrote the Swedish book I left out certain specifics, not least because those involved and mentioned in the book were still subject to police scrutiny. I did not want my book to contribute to putting them in prison, in particular because Swedish prisons to a great extent have no care or treatment facilities. I was also ambivalent about what I had seen in the field. On the one hand I believed that it was important to carry out this sort of research – otherwise I would not have undertaken it. I have, on the other hand, been raised in a culture where I have learnt that it is every citizen's duty to report all drug-related crimes, and that drug-related crime is a very serious phenomenon. Bengt Svensson, researcher and close friend, wrote the following in the preface to the Swedish book:

> But is it legitimate for a researcher to watch, without intervening, when people are doing something as destructive as using heroin? Isn't it his moral duty to try to influence the young men and women to stop using narcotics and leading lives of crime? Should he not stand up and leave these flats in protest when the heroin and syringes are taken out? I do not think so. The first duty of the researcher is to describe reality, in order to facilitate an understanding of it. (Lalander, 2001: 4)

Much of what I have seen and heard had required me to go longer and further than most other Swedish researchers have done, and I was worried about how the book would be received. I left out information that, in itself, was of interest, but that, had I included it, would most likely have caused the type of media debate that would have obscured the real content of the book. This reworked version, however, contains much of that information. One of the reasons for this is that one of the top dealers, most likely the number one top dealer, was arrested by the police last year and is currently serving a ten-year sentence. In connection with the investigation into his crimes, many people were called in for interview. Only a few were charged, however, which left many others quite relieved. Some of those I had interviewed were involved. I was in attendance at the trial in the autumn of 2002 and received the impression that much was cleared up, and that the people interviewed in this book are on a more secure footing than previously, particularly those who, since then, are no longer involved with narcotics. As well as including more information I have also attempted to improve the book, both generally and analytically.

Acknowledgements

The study was mostly funded by the Folkhälsoinstitutet (Institute of Public Health) for which I am extremely grateful. Thanks are due to a number of people. The staff at the open treatment clinic at the Dependency Unit of Norrköping, among them Anders Kroon, Anders Johansson and Ylva Johansson, also to the social workers at Sesam's Youth Clinic and Roger Gustavsson and Rita Hallström. I also express many thanks to my friends Lars Holst, Fia Littås and Elvin Holst who let me sleep in their apartment while I was in Norrköping and who supported me emotionally.

From the world of academics I am very grateful first and foremost to my fellow researcher and friend, Bengt Svenson, for his attention, interest and engagement without which this book would never have been written. Bengt and I also planned the project because he was doing a similar study in the bigger town of Malmö, with a thirty-year long history of heroin use. This year we will carry on with this comparative work. If Bengt had not asked me if I wanted to cooperate with him, I would probably not have entered the field of narcotics at all. I must also thank my colleague at work, Robin Room, of the University of Stockholm, SoRAD (Social Research on Alcohol and Drugs) for careful reading, valuable insight and encouragement. Thanks are also due to Jesper Andreasson, Torun Elsrud och Max Hansson and my brother Rickard Lalander. My translator Aisling O'Neill deserves thanks and much appreciation for what was often a difficult, challenging and irregular assignment. Thank you also to Thomas Johansson, Klaus Mäkelä, Pia Rosenquist and Pekka Sulkunen for support and inspirtation.

Naturally, my warmest thanks must go to the young heroin users in Norrköping, many of whom I still meet, go to dinner with, have coffee with. It is with relief and gratitude that I find that (to the best of my knowledge) none of the twenty-five has succumbed to an overdose. In fact, many of them today live a heroin-free life. I still often think about them and every time I go back to my home town Norrköping I make a point of meeting some of them.

Last, but far from least, I direct the attention to my family, where thanks are just not enough; Susanne, Emilie, Felicia and Isabelle who probably never really understood just what kind of project Daddy/Philip was engaged in, who often met me, tired, disturbed and distracted, just back from Norrköping. If it were not for them I would not have succeeded in writing this book.

Philip Lalander

Under the City's Shell

The world you live in's just the sugar-coated topping.
There's another world beneath it, the real world . . .
Quote from Blade, played by Wesley Snape
in the vampire film *Blade* from 1998.

Introduction

This book is about a special group of young people who have sought out objects
and activities that are seen as dangerous, unethical and disgusting. They have
developed a lifestyle in which drugs and criminal activities are everyday ingred-
ients and in doing so, have done exactly what their parents, school and other
representatives of modern society have warned them not to do.

They live in Norrköping, a former industrial city of 122,000 inhabitants
that has, since the early 1990s experienced both high unemployment and a
tight municipal budget. The city has been hard hit by closures and especially
well known, the closure of a factory of the giant company, Ericsson. However,
Norrköping has also had high points during the 1990s in the form of football,
basketball, annual carnivals, and cultural events as well as a complete renovation
of the old industrial area. Norrköping is a city of contrasts, between the old
industry and modern department stores, and has, since the 1970s, increasingly
shown one of the indications of a large town, in the form of a thoroughly urban
centre. The building of this centre during the 1960s to 1990s led to the old build-
ings and historical markers being demolished.

Alcoholics and drug abusers are visible in Norrköping. They gather at the New
Square, outside the off licence on Queen's Street, where the tram tracks roll past,
near Film City on the Old Town House Street or at the shopping centre in the
suburb Hageby. It is mostly a matter of mixed abuse: alcohol, pills and amphetamine. Many have swollen faces while others are thin and haggard. They are
'outsiders' and serve as a warning, as an example of what can happen if you don't
take care of your job or your studies or if you have difficulty with regular hours
and timekeeping. Police vans are often parked near these areas and mark established society's advantage over and fear of public disorder and trouble.

Even if these public alcohol and drug abusers are worth a book, they are not the main focus of this one. This book is about young people who have sought and created an almost invisible subculture. They act in places that ordinary people don't know about, and at times when most well-behaved and ordinary citizens of Norrköping are getting their beauty sleep in order to be fresh and healthy for the next working day. The book is about young 'horsers'/heroin users who live an alternative and secret life in Norrköping, even if they can move on the city's streets and in the workplaces without drawing attention to themselves in the way their colleagues-in-abuse, the alcoholics and the mixed abusers, do.

Changes in Drug History

Scene One: Autumn 1994, the popular night club Tellus, on King's Street, in Norrköping's newly renovated industrial area, on a late Saturday night. A large number of young people have gathered to have fun. They are dancing, talking and generally enjoying life. Strobe lighting and the smoke machine keep time with the techno sound blaring from the speaker system. Many of them are high on amphetamine. Others have taken ecstasy and still others are under the influence of hash. None, or only very few, have come in contact with heroin.

Scene two: Autumn 1996, a flat in central Norrköping. Around ten young men aged seventeen to twenty-two have gathered in a flat to 'base' – to smoke heroin with foil. The TV is on, and a video film is playing on the screen. They are chatting and smoking and having a pleasant time together. They feel close to each other. They look like young people usually do; well dressed, clean and tidy. Heroin is something they use at weekends.

Scene three: Autumn 2000, a flat in Norrköping. Three young men aged twenty-two to twenty-four are ringing round to different dealers trying to find some heroin. It is difficult and they have a limited number of contacts. After about ten calls they get a result; they can go and buy a little, just enough to get them by for the time being. All three have initial withdrawal symptoms and they would do almost anything for a little heroin. They are worried and stressed. When they have got their heroin they quickly look for a place where they can 'shoot up a fix'/inject heroin.

The scenes above describe the changes in Norrköping's drug history. During the 1980s and the first half of the 1990s, heroin was unusual, both in terms of use and selling. Max began using in 1993:

It was Molly and me and then there were two or three others, but they no longer live here. It was mainly only us in all of Norrköping who took heroin. It often happened that I bought in Stockholm, maybe, and I would sometimes buy for them and sometimes they would buy for us and we would take it occasionally, but it happened fairly quickly that we started taking it more often. Still, there were very few who took it then, you knew more or less who they were.

Max and Molly have the longest experience of heroin use among the active users in Norrköping. There wasn't any established 'heroin circle' including chains of dealers. On the other hand, amphetamine was easy to get. In 1995–6 the heroin circle built up: consumers, dealers and runners. It was mainly brown heroin that was introduced to new groups. The majority of the young heroin users in Norrköping were born between 1975 and 1980.

A similar change could be detected in other Swedish towns and cities, like Karlstad, Västerås, Örebro and Umeå, which prior to the 1990s had been spared from any widespread heroin use. These towns and cities have in common with each other populations of approximately 100,000, and that, previously, drug abuse was almost exclusively centred on amphetamine. In Norrköping it was initially mostly a matter of 'basing', for which brown heroin is particularly suitable. However, the majority later went over to injecting and developed the type of dependency described in the third scene. Basing became increasingly rare. What began as an experiment driven by curiosity developed, for many, into a serious dependency and an existence centred entirely on heroin.

In 1997 the media began to pay attention to the heroin wave in Norrköping. In a series of articles in the nation covering newspaper *Aftonbladet* (3–6 November 1997) Norrköping was described as a 'heroin city'. Through detailed reports the journalists described heroin from the police's, relatives' and users' perspectives. John, who was involved when 'the wave' started, has this to say about *Aftonbladet*'s article series: 'It had been around for several years before. I knew all of them who were in the paper, everyone in the article, but it took such a long time before people became desperate, before it really showed.'

The local papers called attention to what the police dubbed a 'heroin wave' and in 2000 the number of heroin users was estimated at 248 (see *Kartläggning av narkotikasituationen 2000* (*Mapping of the Drug Situation 2000*) 2001). Different agents have tried, since the middle of the 1990s, to handle the heroin problem; the police's street dealer group try to disturb the business as much as possible and also to identify drug users through urine testing. The police's detective force tries to find out who sells and which sales channels are used. Social services, the county council and volunteer organizations work at helping the young heroin users to stop using heroin.

Heroin, more than any other drug, is related to death. Fugelstad and Rajs (1998) made a compilation of the dominant drug amongst deceased drug users from Stockholm: as many as 62 per cent have heroin as their main drug. Few people in our society are unaware of heroin's relation to death. Even those who start using heroin are aware of its deadliness.

Drugs – A Threat to Modernity

> When a rule is enforced, the person who is supposed to have broken it may be seen as a special kind of person, one who cannot be trusted to live by the rules agreed on by the group. He is regarded as an outsider. (Becker 1963/1973: 1)

Norrköping's young heroin users were defined as a problem in 1997. The collective worry is partly as a result of an emotional engagement in the young peoples' future and health. It is also an effect of the city being viewed as a trouble spot, a place being threatened by something that is hard to control due to little being known about it.

The drug user is seen, in our culture, as highly problematical and that is largely because narcotics are taboo-ridden. Drug use has been society's 'enemy number one' (Christie and Bruun 1985) and the drug user has served as a picture of what happens if we do not behave ourselves. Narcotics were first defined as a problem in Sweden during the 1950s to 1970s and have, since then, had very negative associations in most people's minds. Before this period they did not have a particularly important place in people's consciousness, and to use what today are viewed as drugs was not illegal. Lindgren (1993) refers to a study by Leonard Goldberg where it is shown that as many as 200,000 Swedish people used amphetamines during the years 1942–3. They most probably did not regard themselves as serious drug addicts, as drug addicts or drug users, because a negative reference frame had not yet been established. Lindgren writes that narcotic problems began to be defined as serious problems during the 1950s. He states that narcotic abuse was viewed as a '. . . problem with particular relevance to antisocial and criminal youths' (1993: 189). The parliament decided on measures to combat the problem in 1968, measures which to a great extent are unchanged today. The picture that most people have of narcotics is as a consequence of the problematizing process that happened in Sweden during that time.

Drugs, like sexuality, are connected with desire and therefore threaten modern society. Individuals in a modern society should not, ideally, be driven by desire, but rather by rationality (Bauman 1991). They should, furthermore, put the future and not the present first. If they don't put the future first they will not regard it as plausible to cope with society's education system. But alcohol is also coupled to desire, and it may be sold. The reason certain substances are classified as narcotics and forbidden is because they are associated with something unknown and alien, whereas alcohol is something we know about and with which we are familiar.

Alcohol has been necessary for the realization of modern society. It has been used at celebratory meals to ritualize the family. It also functions as a symbol for a demodernized existence. Drink represents, to many, a necessary 'time out' from the discipline of modern society (Gusfield 1987). Narcotics on the other hand, do not have this family stamp but rather are described as evil. Alcohol consumption does not make someone an outsider, as it is not particularly problematic in relation to modern society's ideals and respectability norms. To drink alcohol is seen as normal, but to do drugs is seen as a very decisive action, as a sign of much more than is actually seen on the surface.

In the book *Modernity and Ambivalence* (1991), Bauman describes the modern state as a 'garden', and in a garden one is always interested in keeping a certain amount of order, but there are always plants and weeds which encroach, and threaten its structure, form and content. The gardeners, in the shape of different social institutions, try to fight these threats to order. Use of narcotics and dealing in them is seen as a serious threat to normality in modern society. The modern state carries on a ceaseless campaign against those who threaten its constitution and who deviate too much from the ideals considered desirable. Drugs threaten modern society, as they are not symbolic of production but rather consumption without production, and, besides, a 'black' consumption outside of the state's control.

Drug Users as Irrational Victims

Modern society's representatives tend to explain away drug use by claiming the drug user cannot think rationally. The newspapers described the first wave of heroin users in Norrköping as victims: 'Does a normal 20-year-old Swede not know that heroin is a fatal poison rather than a drug you take to feel good? Yes, they know, but they are victims of the drug barons' marketing tactics, fooled into believing that smoking heroin is not the same thing as using syringes' (*Aftonbladet* 3 November 1997, the author's translation).

The threat diminishes if society reacts as above. Reasoning which is other than legitimate is masked and made irrational and an effect of extreme forces. Many researchers (for example Bejerot 1980) talk about 'epidemics' as if drug addiction were an infectious disease. In that sense Norrköping would have suffered from the dreaded heroin virus in 1995–6. They also speak of a serious dependency, almost as if there was an all-powerful force within the individual that dictates the conditions for the individual's actions, which leads to carers placing great emphasis on removing the 'desire', through medication like Subutex and Methadone. An article about two young heroin users had the headline: 'They were caught in the grip of heroin' (*Norrköpings Tidningar*, 4 January 2001). This is a further example of how drug use is transformed into an active and thinking 'subject' and people concerned become the 'object'. The drug is symbolic of the horrible witch who keeps the dear children Hansel and Gretel as prisoners and who fattens them up in order to eat them later.

Drug users are seen as losers who live a meaningless existence full of irrational decisions and forces, and perhaps this viewpoint leads to a realization of the

Thomas theorem: if we see something as true, it becomes so (Thomas and Thomas 1928). To view drug users as irrational is a strategy used by society to combat the undesirable, that which threatens modern society (compare Foucault 1972/1992).

Many people automatically ascribe certain qualities to heroin users/drug users, that they expect heroin users in the main to have. It may be developmental problems, childhood or background problems, negligence, unreliability or a manipulative streak (compare Taylor 1987 and Lindgren 1993). People react with serious anxiety when faced with the unknown. 'How could someone who is so nice be a drug user?' or 'What kind of problems do they have?' People in general know very little about narcotics and narcotic addiction, but what they do know, because they have been socialized with a certain image of narcotics and narcotic use, is that they are frightening, threatening and monstrous.

In this sense, the drug user is seen as a stranger, double-natured, like different literary and film characters, such as Frankenstein's monster, Dr Jekyll and Mr Hyde, The Werewolf and Dracula among others. Dr Jekyll is both good and evil; Frankenstein's monster is half human, half machine; The Werewolf is both wolf and man and Dracula is a human who hates light and lives on others' blood. The drug user is both human and something else, unknown, dirty, terrifying. The drug user is both like us and not like us. Kristeva (1982) calls these dual creatures 'abjects' and means by this that which is not classifiable as belonging to any particular category. The image of the drug user should be seen as an effect of the process that has occurred during the second half of the twentieth century, where drug users have been relegated to the role of second-class citizens. The female ex-heroin user Tam Stewart (1987: 103) writes: 'Heroin addicts are society's "nouveau queers". They have replaced homosexuals and conscientious objectors as the undesirable, antisocial figures who inspire public contempt.'

Subculture and Globalization

When a group of people come together and begin to transgress different types of respectability norms and ideals, they form a 'subculture'. 'Sub' means under, and is related to power structure. They create a culture through contact with each other and as a consequence of established society's morals and respectability, where they build in different sorts of transgressions as a central part of their lifestyle. Furthermore, they construct slang, a language with words to describe the transgression and which is developed in relation to established society. The word 'subculture' means that the alternative culture is created in society and society's representatives see it as problematic and worth combating.

For the Birmingham school the subculture had a historical, materialistic basis (Hall and Jefferson 1976/1993). The expression was limited to working-class youths who by their creation of a culture strengthened a threatened working-class culture. I do not use the expression in this sense, but in the sense that other social groupings, ethnic groups, and so forth, can form subcultures. The deciding factor is how the subculture functions in relation to modern society's struggle for order.

During the 1970s Willis (1977/1993) studied a group of young working-class boys, 'the lads', who made being insolent, impertinent and obscene a part of their lifestyle. Via this lifestyle they articulated a resistance to the middle-class based school ideology they had difficulty mastering. The culture I describe transgresses boundaries to a much larger extent than Willis's 'lads', who, in comparison to those I describe and analyse, can be seen as really well behaved.

In the subculture to be described it becomes almost normal to transgress rules of respectability, and those who think in the subculture's pattern see things in a different light than established society. The subculture's members do not appear to have absorbed the morality that established society's representatives, for example parents and teachers, have tried to impress on them, but in actuality they have. The subculture develops in antithesis to established culture. Its members are carriers of both modern society's norms and the subculture's, but once in the subculture they have a tendency to act from the subculture's perspective.

It is not only the subculture that threatens society's order. No culture in today's 'globalized' world is free from the influence of other cultures. The global travels to the local via the television set and gives rise to hybridized rituals and thought patterns. Our thoughts about our lives and ourselves are not merely created in the local environment that we grow up in, but influences from outside also leave their mark (see Baudrillard 1983, Bauman 1991, Giddens 1991 and Ziehe 1993). Bauman (1991) writes in this context about 'pluralisation of authority' by which he means that media and other global agents question the modern state's authority. As protection against these external threats to society's boundaries of respectability we have censorship and age limits. However, an increasingly liberal film and music market has made it more difficult to keep such undesirable influences at bay. The cultural hegemony the state has implemented, through means such as school, is threatened and becomes harder to maintain.

This Book – A Presentation

A series of researchers (Becker 1963/1973, Agar 1977, Adler 1985, Stewart 1987, Williams 1989, Faupel 1991, Bourgois 1996, Svensson 1996 and 2000 and Jacobs 2001) have tried to give a different picture of narcotics and of narcotic users' living conditions from the images that mostly come across in the media and some of the scholarly literature, where drug users are, to a greater or lesser extent, seen as victims of forces they are not capable of dealing with themselves. This book intends to analyse the rationality that makes it possible to try, and to continue using, heroin.

My experiences of Norrköping, where I grew up, have given me a new perspective on the city, which calls into question and modifies my earlier experiences. Before I entered the subculture as an observer, I related the different parts of the city to my memories of growing up in the city. Now, when I visit Norrköping, I see it as a world of flats with an alternative and subcultural infrastructure. When I travelled to Norrköping to speak to the young heroin users I felt that I was stepping into another world with its own logic and its own rules of play. It is with this logic and these rules of play that I wish to acquaint the reader.

In total, approximately 150 interviews have been conducted, and a large number of observations with twenty-five different heroin users – eighteen men and seven women with an average age of twenty-three. Of these, the majority were active heroin users in 2000. The central question of the book is: *how can a number of young people in Norrköping use heroin and continue to do so, despite the fact that the drug is taboo-ridden and has, throughout the second half of the twentieth century, been proven to be, and continually described as, life-threatening?*

The question is addressed by an analysis of how a subculture, with its own particular logic and special rules of play, identities and rituals, develops and grows. However, the subculture can neither arise nor exist in a vacuum in relation to society in general. That which occurs within the subculture can describe how it is to live in our times.

The Layout of the Book

In Chapter 2, 'Before Heroin', I give an account of major themes in the subculture of the users before they started to use heroin. I describe their interaction with each other as a form of socialization process in which their perspective of reality changes. This is of major importance when it comes to explain why they, later on, wanted to try the 'dangerous' drug heroin. Chapter 3, 'The Secret Cave', provides further explanations about what made it plausible to try and carry on with heroin use. The 'basing' ritual is analysed as how, in the beginning of their romance with the drug, they perceived the 'heroin high'.

In Chapter 4, 'The Threats that Divide and Unite', there is analysis of the threats the subculture has to deal with. The fact that the members of the subculture become addicted provides a threat to the solidarity of the culture when it comes to keeping the activities of the subculture secret from the police. Chapter 5, 'Doing Drugs with Honour and Style', analyses the opportunities the young heroin users have to create a form of respectability once they have developed a serious addiction. Different types of honour codes are described here, and also how the heroin users try to maintain a positive picture of themselves despite encroaching physical and social deterioration.

Chapter 6, 'Who is Directing?', is about how the subculture is influenced by the world of the media. The relationship between the subculture and various films is analysed here. Chapter 7, 'The Subculture's Gender Code', analyses how gender identity is created in the subculture and what importance gender has for opportunities of hierarchical advancement in the subculture. Chapter 8, 'The Whole World is Yours', is a conclusion and a further development of earlier chapters. In the appendix, I give an account of the method I have used and discuss the study from an ethical perspective.

The interviewees' quotes have often been edited in the sense that I have left out words like 'hmm' and 'like', 'what' and 'then', among others. I have tried, however, for the sake of the text, not to change the meaning of what they have said. I have also worked hard with the translator to give the informants' quotes a subcultural rhythm without inconveniencing non-Swedish readers. Sometimes the text has been dramatized with the help of a reconstruction of an interview and observation notes. This is mainly done to give the reader the opportunity to 'live' the subculture.

−2−

Before Heroin

Basing in my Car

I am sitting in a hired car parked beside the river in Norrköping and interviewing Ben, a twenty-four-year-old heroin user. He is the second person I have interviewed. Ben looks fit, has had a session on a sun bed the previous day, and spends a lot of time bodybuilding. As I know so little about heroin use, particularly smoking heroin, I ask him to explain how it is done. He takes out a small cigarette packet and a little piece of folded paper that contains a little light brown powder and says, 'I can show you.' 'Okay', I say, whereupon he straightens out some foil that was in the cigarette packet. He shakes a little powder into one corner of it and takes out a straw made from foil. He warms the foil from underneath with a cigarette lighter and the powder begins to dissolve into a straight line. It releases a gas, which Ben captures with the foil straw and breathes in. He then lights a cigarette, takes a deep drag and holds his breath. I say nothing; I am nervous but interested in what is sometimes called 'chasing the dragon' but in Norrköping is principally called 'basing'. He says in a hoarse voice, 'And then you hold it in a while.'

After a few minutes the car is almost completely smoke-filled. Ben begins to talk about his brother, whom he wants to protect from heroin. He feels guilty, but also displays a strong sense of pleasure. He says that he will only use today and stay clean tomorrow, in order to avoid the powerful withdrawal symptoms. Before I met him, Ben had been clean for six months. The day before he met me, he had started to use again. We leave the car park after a while. Ben has to visit someone's flat. I cannot go with him.

The situation described above was nerve-racking. I usually react to dramatic situations by getting tremors in my right leg, the one I use to accelerate with when driving, which also happened this time. The drive from the car park was a little uneven. The event was, to me, extremely dramatic and filled with both potentially problematic consequences but also possibilities. It was not equally dramatic for Ben, but nonetheless it was enveloped in a series of protective measures. For example, he kept the heroin at the bottom of the cigarette packet and took it out only after checking that there were no cars in the area around us. For the young

heroin users, dramatic events, which could have serious consequences, are something of a marker, a part of their identity.

How can Ben be so cool about heroin, the killer-drug number one? I would
suggest, echoing Becker (1963/1973), that this is a consequence of learned behaviour
and also of, drawing on Willis (1977/1993), a kind of separation from established
society. Ben, and the other horsers, have a history in a subculture which made it
possible, and even rational, to try heroin later on – I will support this argument in
the following chapters. No one became a heroin user in Norrköping by accident,
nor is it sufficient to say that the drug itself pulled them into intensive drug use or
that evil pushers lured them into 'bad behaviour' (Pearson 1987, Faupel 1991,
Taylor 1993). It took a certain socialization, which led to a particular perspective
of existence including knowledge of drugs and criminality. This socialization also
provided them with a lifestyle that made it possible for the drug dealers to select
them as possible consumers or helpers in the drug trade. It also needed the perceived advantage of living the life in the subculture compared to life in school or at
home. If the subculture didn't give its members some advances compared to what
they would get without it wouldn't be interesting to participate in it, helping to
reconstruct it. They were, thus, neither forced to learn nor brainwashed; rather they
found the education of the subculture challenging, thrilling and highly instructive.
This chapter analyses this process of education, primarily the years 1990 to 1997.

Separation

'Separation' describes the process by which people separate themselves from those
people and environments that exercise control over their thoughts and actions, and
seek other persons and other environments where this captivity is not experienced
(Willis 1977/1993). For the majority of those to whom I spoke, upper secondary
school has meant a separation from modern society, in particular from school and
parents, but also from other more basic cultural values such as planning and
observance of time, obedience and belief in authority and abiding by the law.

At its extreme, it is a separation from the world and the norms of respectability,
which are central to modern society's continued existence. Many of those interviewed had already, at an early age, drawn attention to themselves through drug
use, violence and/or criminal behaviour. What happened among the group of
friends and associates was not at all reminiscent of school. Willis writes as follows:
'School is the zone of the formal. It has a clear structure; the school building,
school rules, pedagogic practice, a staff hierarchy with powers ultimately sanct-
ioned – as we have seen in a small way – by the state . . .' (1977/1993: 22). What
Willis calls the 'idea of the teaching paradigm' is also important: 'This idea
concerns teaching as a fair exchange – most basically exchange of knowledge for
respect, of guidance for control' (1977/1993: 64).

School is a socialization apparatus and can be seen as the long arm of modern society, and as such fulfilling a function: to contribute to social harmony and to see that the social ties that bind society together are maintained (Durkheim 1933/ 1984). This is school's latent function, while its manifest function is to teach (Merton 1949/1968).

School teaches how to react as a citizen. It teaches how to listen, to respect authority, to wait, to observe time and to control emotions. School is a guarantor for the continued existence of civilization. Most spontaneity and emotion is repressed in favour of an internalized self-control, something that some students accept while others resist it. School can therefore be seen as an instrument of power that, to a great extent, requires the pupils' and even the teachers' subjection to the school's and modern society's value and rule system.

The prospective heroin users' relationship to school was relatively problem-free until they reached their sixth or seventh year of school (equivalent to the last year of primary school or the first year of secondary school in Britain), when the majority of them tried to break free from the grip of school and devote their time to the types of activities of which school disapproves. The majority began to seek alternative rooms for socialization where, together with their friends and those of a like mind, they could create their own culture. Max recounts that:

I wanted to get good grades, but it was more fun to be with my mates, hang around town, do a little shoplifting, earn a little money and go out at weekends. So, I'd go down to the special class and play cards, and stuff, 'cause you did what had to be done during a lesson in ten minutes and there was a half an hour over to play cards . . . But in the beginning I only did it [went to special class] for one or two lessons, but after six months or so I managed to talk my way into being there almost all the time . . . It was computers, maths and English that I did properly, you could say, but then those were the classes I thought were fun.

Max was absent for 350 hours in his ninth year (third-year secondary) and much of what he describes is diametrically opposed to what is expected of a student in school. From established society's perspective, Max was a problem child, who did not do what school expected from him. Enrique has similar experiences:

. . . it went well in school from first to sixth, but then, when I started seventh year . . . skipping school, skipped it to meet friends, they'd ring on the mobile 'Hey we're skipping now, come on, we'll meet outside the Cinema or McDonalds, we can hang out in town, maybe lift something so we can get money for smoke', or whatever – or: 'I've a fiver' (£5) 'You've a fiver? Then we can share a lump (hashish).' 'Yeah, sure I have.' 'I'm coming, I'll be there in twenty minutes' . . . So, I just didn't give a damn about school, those kind of things.

Max, Enrique and many others share the common experience of having prior-itized the casual group of friends over the formal class and the city centre over the classroom. This would in time transform to a heroin-based subculture but in the beginning it consisted of less 'serious' events and symbols, experimenting with drugs and criminality. In the remainder of the chapter I will concentrate on some themes that I found central to a description of the activities of informal groups. These themes can also be seen as the advantages to living in the informal group in contrast to life outside the group. I also describe the consequences of living in the subculture.

Change and Adventure

The activities in the informal groups are reminiscent of that which Goffman (1967) calls 'action'. By this he means actions that are: (1) unpredictable; (2) dramatic, as they may result in problematic consequences; (3) experienced as free from guidance by others. A situation that fulfils these criteria is defined as an 'event'. To define something as action is dependent on the person who experiences the situation interpreting it as action. The opposite of action is to follow a schedule. The manifest function of a schedule is to make work and study more efficient while its latent function is to reduce the number of possibilities and reduce chance, thus creating a sense of order. I will return to these concepts, action and event, as they have been tools in helping me capture central themes of the activities in the informal groups.

When I speak to the subculture's members it is obvious that they have almost systematically been involved with and tested a series of different drugs. It seems that testing drugs has been important in their lives, in the same way that a mountain climber will test different methods of climbing. Most of them were between thirteen and fourteen years of age when they first tried marijuana. The quotation below is taken from a group discussion with three young women, around seventeen to eighteen years of age.

> *Philip*: What drugs have you used? (The questions provokes laughter all round.)
> *Martina*: If we had to count them all, we'd be here until tomorrow (more laughter).
> *Veronica*: Amphetamine, heroin, cocaine, ecstasy, hash, dope . . .
> *Linda*: Pills.
> *Veronica*: Heroin, LSD, ecstasy.
> *Linda*: Rohypnol.
> *Martina*: Almost everything.

The relatively well-known drugs that they haven't tried are Khat and GHB, probably because they aren't on the market in Norrköping and aren't very well known there. Most of those I met maintain that a strong sense of 'curiosity' was the reason most of them began experimenting with drugs. The sense of curiosity about altered perception is almost unanimous in those who later started using heroin. They seem to be extremely curious about what the immediate future holds and want it to be action-filled. John talks about his drug experiences:

> In ninth grade [third-year secondary] I smoked dope [hash] and grass. That was fun, you'd laugh and be really in orbit. Then I continued to smoke it for a good while. About a year after [fourth-year secondary] or so I tested amphetamine for the first time. It was also really okay. Then I went to a Rave and took amphetamine for the second time, then. Then it developed a little, so that I took something nearly every day and sat at home and got really talkative and sat up all night, playing cards and such. I only went out at weekends, and so there was a period when I was taking something four, five days a week. And you'd be curious to try other drugs too, 'cause everything was okay, like. So I tried LSD and then ecstasy. Ecstasy was . . . it was really fun, because it went straight to your head. It was the world's greatest happiness rush. And then I tried cocaine, and then smoking cocaine [crack].

It is interesting to note, in the preceding account, the change of tempo and of states that are so central to it. To 'be in orbit' implies that normal perception is no longer engaged, and this happens very quickly with the help of the drug, without the need for changing the environment. The surroundings trailed away because of too much amphetamine and that means that John acted as if he was insane, dedicating himself to meaningless activities (at least from the establishment's point of view) like incessant conversation, general aimlessness and card games.

The emphasis on change and altered perceptions of existence is also found in the subculture's terminology. The words 'screwed' and 'sprained' or 'twisted', as descriptive of how one is under the influence, are used by many to indicate a changed state of experience. I would like to call these expressions action terms. To sprain your ankle means that your ankle has been twisted in such a way that it no longer functions normally. The word 'sprained', as used by the subculture ought to imply much the same except that it is consciousness that is sprained, or twisted from its original state, and the same applies to twisted – both implying that the environment is experienced as different than it would otherwise be. Roger describes a hunt to become twisted or high, and to experience changes in the surroundings:

> . . . you knew it was wrong to smoke hash, that it wasn't a good idea like, that it was illegal, but it was exciting, it's like, I think you should try everything, that's the way I see it. I was curious, I am curious, but I use it in the wrong way. It's good to be curious like, if you want to know about things in life, but maybe not that way, but I want to know about things and stuff.

Roger, like many others, wanted to test everything. If they knew of one type of high, or way of getting twisted, they wanted to learn another. The words 'wired' (high) and 'speeding' (under the influence) are action-related and describe the transition from a normal state to one under the influence of drugs. The frequency of action terms shows what is important and valuable in the subculture, to speed up existence, creating action and experiences of now. It also helps to give the interactions in the group an aura of excitement.

Once one state of high has been learned, they want to explore others. Taking drugs occasionally is a way of changing perspective on reality, of not letting life get stuck in the routines we are expected to follow. Getting high demolishes this routine. If life is boring, take a drug. In their informal groups, the members live as far away as possible from routine and schedules. A schedule often has a long-term aim, while there are no such aims in the groups.

Goffman (1967: 201) writes that drugs imply the creation of possibility for action without the need for the environment to change. Hanna and Steve described an occasion when they had taken LSD and did things which they otherwise would have experienced as very strange. They went to a petrol station to buy strawberries and bought a basket of unwashed strawberries. After they had left, they realized they had lost the strawberries. They then started to search for dirty strawberries, which had to be same as the previous ones; the petrol station attendant could not understand them. Finally, they got hold of more unwashed strawberries but felt they needed a plastic bag and went into another shop to get one. Hanna had no money but the shopkeeper said she could have the bag free. But Hanna did not want to go along with this and called to Steve and another friend to come into the shop with money. They did so and put a large bundle of notes on the counter.

Effectively, nothing special happened, but they experienced this as if a whole pile of things happened. Most of us do not recall specific purchases of strawberries, simply because such occasions are an unremarkable and routine part of the flow of everyday life. If we were, however, to buy strawberries under the influence of LSD it is fairly certain that we would see the event as something that stood out in our lives; the strawberry situation would be a memorable, eventful occasion – an extraordinary experience (Andersson 1999). We could contrast the LSD experience and other drug rituals with going out to buy milk, without using drugs. Such an action would not normally generate any special sensations, things happen routinely and few unexpected events happen (cf. Berger and Luckmann 1966/1987). Mostly, we don't remember specific occasions when we were out buying milk, because the situation is part of a stream of routines where nothing special happens. On the other hand, should the shop have been robbed while we were there, we would remember it as something special, as part of an adventure. This, of course, depends on whether we see a robbery as exciting or as shocking. With the aid of drugs, release from the order of everyday life can be obtained. It becomes exciting to go to the shop to buy milk, and, as Hanna described, the buying of strawberries can become an extraordinary experience, anything can happen. Life becomes an adventure, where change is the basic state and where coincidence or chance has more importance than in society at large, where the war on chaos has made the environment relatively predictable.

The Energizers

The main purpose of life for the cat is to experience the 'kick' ... A 'kick' is any act tabooed by 'squares' that heightens and intensifies the present moment of experience and differentiates it as much as possible for the humdrum routine of daily life. (Finestone 1957: 284 quoted in Agar 1973: 4)

The incidents that the gang saw as eventful led to a reaction from the establishment's defenders, in the form of teachers, police and parents. They tried in various ways, through conversation, threats and even rewards, to bring them back to the fold, to where they'd been before the separation, a time when they'd been relatively well-behaved pupils. Hardy and Hanna expressed it like this:

We started by acting up on all the teachers to see who'd be sent out of class first, and then there were conversations, with our parents as well, to make us behave. (Hardy)

Yeah, I suppose it was seventh and eighth class [first and second year] when my parents sometimes had to come and bring me home, and on one occasion I was brought home by the police, no charge or anything, they just had to bring me home. (Hanna)

If people operate on the margins of society, in the borderland between the legitimate and the illegal, society's 'rule enforcers' (Becker 1963/1973) rush to bring them back to the norm. The problem is that the energy the rule enforcers need to extend in keeping order also becomes an affirmation for those who are transgressing order. For an outsider it becomes a question of affirmation of their power and influence – to act in such a way that established society is forced to intervene. Power is also affirmation of existence. Actions provoke response, provide affirmation and thereby proof of existence. What is done has visible consequences in the surrounding world.

Hanna remembers the first police intervention as an 'event', and as a proof that she had strayed into society's margins. A transgression of the boundaries is hardly interesting unless there is awareness that the boundary that is crossed is actually such. The outsider identity is reinforced, while knowledge of society's various boundaries is increased.

The Drifter Culture and Marijuana

Most of the people I met have a history of smoking hash. They also reflected a certain attitude that was linked to what they wanted to be: drifters with a special perspective on life. Many of the interviewees were influenced by reggae during the separation period of their lives, and this, in all likelihood, is due to the fact that as a lifestyle it portrayed such a strong contrast to modern society. Richard says: 'I've been rather influenced by reggae, by Bob Marley. I had the whole room covered in posters and had cannabis leaves hung round my neck and I've even grown weed [he laughs], that's the way it's meant to be.'

For Richard, the symbols in the form of the music, the posters and the cannabis plants form a message about who he is. He has something to identify with, something that gives his life a certain kind of structure. Others have expressed this passion for reggae, the favourites being Bob Marley, Peter Tosh and Alfa Blondie, representatives of a lifestyle that is not very reminiscent of modern society's and school's demands for rational behaviour and structuring of time.

During one of my many visits to John he had been off heroin for three months, had a job and was paying his bills. After we had talked for a while he said, 'Philip, I want to show you something.' We went over to a rather large wardrobe and he opened the doors. The inside was covered in foil and a heat lamp beamed on a healthy cannabis plant growing in a flower pot. He told me that he thought the plant was beautiful. I asked him why and he answered, 'I don't know.' He had another plant on the living room window sill, a geranium and I asked if he thought it was similarly beautiful. He answered, 'No, I don't.' The geranium has no link to his identity and to that which he believes himself to be. The cannabis plant's symbolic meaning is of much more significance than the geranium's, and is therefore beautiful. In a psychoanalytical Freudian sense, the cannabis plant can be seen as an 'object of transition', which John uses in order to manage to live a 'normal' life. He needs to surround himself with symbols that remind him of who he is.

For many, this drifter style became associated with an attitude of taking the day as it comes. A drifter doesn't let authority or schedules decide. Every day can become either an adventure or a non-event. Relaxing, taking it easy, is an important aspect of the drifter style. The style of the drifter focuses on being cool, not getting wound up about what happened earlier at school, or at home, or about what might happen in the future. In this way, the drifter's culture can help its members focus on the now, and thereby, at least temporarily, cut ties to both the past and the future. This temporary focus on the now is often achieved with the aid of drugs, as many drugs seem to have the effect of removing everything but the situation you're involved in. Roger describes how he experienced the rush from hash: 'You just hear every sound, like, that's just the way it is with hash – if you're watching television, you just see the television, if you're reading something, you just read and if you're listening to music, you just hear music.' Drugs create the possibility of shutting out the future and the past.

The drifter is the well-behaved student's antithesis, especially because school expects students to have some goals that are future-oriented. What defines school is the formalized structure, which consequently is at war with the disordered, unexpected and unpredictable. If everyone were a drifter, school would collapse. The drifter makes living in uncertainty and living in the now a lifestyle choice.

Tellus and Amphetamines

Many of the prospective heroin users continued smoking hash now and then for some years. Some still do occasionally, but they also started experimenting with other substances due to curiosity and a wish to experience more as they became increasingly bored with smoking hash. As they grew older they became more interested in pubs and discotheques. A very popular place of action was Tellus, a nightclub in the old industrial area that most of the heroin users have plenty of experience of. Until it closed in the mid 1990s, Tellus was the main centre for dancing and nightlife for young people. Today the nightclub Otten fulfils the same function. Many of the interviewees were familiar with Tellus while still underage. Hanna says: 'I started going to the club very early on. I borrowed my cousin's ID card. I started going out when I was 16 and back then I could dance all night, I thought it was great fun.'

Ben, Hanna, Roger and several others told me that they were often high when they went there, and could dance themselves into a frenzy to the beat of Goa and techno music. At least some of them were interested in dancing, while others spent more time at the bar, or working the room.

Here too, was the connection to ecstasy that many used in Tellus. It was shortly after the ecstasy boom, which, imported from England, became obvious in Gothenburg and Stockholm and was exposed in the press at the beginning of the 1990s. There was much public discussion of party drugs in general, and these discussions probably functioned as advertising for the young people in Norrköping. At Tellus amphetamines underwent a process of cultural rejuvenation in that they, together with ecstasy, became a symbol for parties, raves and boundless youth. Earlier, amphetamines had mostly been associated with the older abusers, who were in general at least ten years older than the average visitor to Tellus. Amphetamine became hip, and the place where it was made an 'in' drug was to a great extent Tellus. Roger talks about amphetamines' role as party drugs.

Roger: Amphetamine, I took it everyday, it was a party drug, totally. We went out, went to Tellus, you've maybe heard of it?

Philip: Yes I have.

Roger: Those were the days, oh wow, [with enthusiasm], the whole place took amphetamine.

Philip: Was it really like that?

Roger: Yeah, when we started, like, so did many others, it was a blast. Had a great time out there on the dance floor. There were loads of us. We could keep going forever, and then there were the parties afterwards.

Roger is exaggerating somewhat when he says 'the whole place took amphetamine', but very many did and more or less all of the people I have spoken to came into contact with amphetamine this way, that is as a party drug, and most have used, and still sometimes use cocaine and ecstasy for the same purpose: partying.

Hanna: There was a venue called Tellus and it's not there anymore but there was a circle of people (amphetamine users), who stood and danced the whole time.

Philip: Yeah, I have heard a few stories about it.

Hanna: Yeah, I bet you have, 'cause everyone else wondered, 'How can they manage to get up there and dance to every single song?' It was in that place, where they played the sort of music that is so good to dance to, like Goa . . .

Many of the prospective heroin users came from the circles of dancers described by both Roger and Hanna. The special music, Goa trance, is very much synthesized sounds, with regular fast drum machine rhythms and long-playing tracks that make it easy to be 'caught up' in the dance. *Destination Goa* is the most popular record produced in the genre. The tracks' names allude to transcendentalism and transgression, for example, *Talking Souls, Hallucinogen – Talking Pussy, E Rection, Out Here We Are Stoned* and *Adrenaline Drum*. The titles describe an existence a long way away from the Western world's demand for rationality. Other titles describe ecstasy, dreamlike states and extraordinary experiences. Transgression hangs in the air intensified by smoke machines and strobe lights and creates a feeling of euphoria and immediacy. With drugs in the system and the effects of music, time stands still and subjective concentration ceases. The environment allows transgression, and many of the prospective heroin users took advantage of this to break free of their feelings of imprisonment. The feeling was intense, and they wanted to go back there again.

The prospective 'horse' users were no longer satisfied with alcohol and cannabis, now they have tried alternatives that were more in harmony with their ambitions of staying up all night – dancing and feeling free and successful – actions that would stretch out in time.

Criminality and Violence

> By the time they have had their first encounter with heroin, most addicts have also had some criminal experience. (Faupel 1991: 54)

Some of the prospective heroin users were really involved in crime as part of a lifestyle. Early in their careers it could be shop-lifting, stealing cigarettes from warehouses or breaking into summer houses. Drug use, violence and criminal behaviour have something in common. They are activities considered illegal by society. Action arises from the tension between rules and rule breaking. As previously mentioned, there is accessible energy in the margins. Steve told me that for a while, between seventeen and eighteen years of age, he earned quite a lot of money in a regular job. Despite this, he spent his weekends breaking and entering. I asked him why:

> For the money's sake, and also because it was exciting to do something illegal. If I were to, say, break in to the house here beside us, and knew that it was going to be soon I'd think: 'Yeah, fuck it, soon, in five or ten minutes we'll do it!' The adrenalin starts to flow and you feel . . . it's a real kick while at the same time you're scared, you know. While you're actually doing it it's really difficult you know, but even so . . . and then afterwards when you've pulled it off it's just, if it's gone well, it's just 'whoosh' [he breathes out]. It is a lovely feeling.

Strictly speaking, it's not a crime for no reason – the reason is action. The risk of being caught and the awareness of crossing a line generates a kick, the pulse and adrenalin both rise. The crime, occurring as it does on the border of society, can be seen as action with varied changes of tempo that become a journey of experiences. Before the crime, the criminal has discovered the possibility of committing it. The thief has, probably, passed the house a couple of times and checked it out. He has also, probably, studied the house owners to see what routines they follow. Then there's a waiting period, for the right time to 'go to' or as it is sometimes expressed 'to make a break.' They break in, in a way learned from their mentors, mostly with a companion. The whole enterprise feels very much like teamwork; the participants are nervous but also very much together. They do what they are going to with high pulse rates, and then leave with their loot, the tangible evidence that they have done the deed. When the thieves are back in safety a sense of calm comes over them, made possible by the fact that have just engaged in a seriously high-tempo and pressurized event. It is reminiscent of the calm after a storm; the contrast is pleasurable. Roger describes something similar with regard to robbery:

Philip: What is it about robbery that's exciting then?

Roger: To take it and get away with it, you know, counting the money is fun afterwards. Sometimes your heart starts to beat really fast you know. If you go in and get a register with say, five hundred to six hundred pounds then it's a little nerve-racking, and then afterwards . . . 'Whoosh' [he breathes out]. It's really great!

Willis writes about shoplifting: 'A remarkable sense of freedom – except that it is private knowledge – comes from having challenged convention and being rewarded for it' (1977/1993: 95). It is also about experiencing contrast between two different types of tempo, one fast and pressurized, the other calm and stress-free. Take it – and get away with it. Doing something that you completely decide for yourself and that is done without others' approval implies a break with the power of routine.

Richard relates that the only reason he committed crime was for the excitement, to live as an outsider. He had a rather large sum of inherited money but despite this, usually under the influence of amphetamine, hash or pills, he would commit crimes:

We went up to OBS, in Ingelsta (a large shopping centre on the outskirts of Norrköping) and took a great big drill machine and couldn't get it completely into the backpack, so it stuck out. Then my mate, that I smoked hash with and had started smoking heroin with, said: 'Ah . . . We can't get out', but I said 'Check this out, you'll see', so I went straight past the checkout that was full with people and she stops and shouts 'Hey you, what have you got there?' and I said 'Never you mind' and then I began to run and loads of people after me. There were many times like these, silly things that really didn't mean anything more than that we had fun. We could run up and kick a police car's mirror to pieces, just so as they'd . . .

Excitement is central and fun, that's more or less the way they saw it. Some would say that it was the drugs that made Richard commit the crimes. However, the way I see it, the drugs made it easier for him to do what he wanted, rather than actually initiating his criminal activity. Drugs in this case have no independent existence beyond the subject who undergoes the actions. Those who received amphetamine as medication during the 1940s hardly went out and committed crimes. For Richard and his friends it is more about a lifestyle focused on trans-gressions, of being infatuated with action, and only finding this action on the borders of society.

Criminal activity provides excitement and so, too, does violence. Most of the interviewees, particularly the males, but even a couple of the females, spent some of their time as teenagers engaged in some sort of martial arts: kick boxing, Thai boxing, Tae Kwon Do, or boxing. Many of them had also engaged in the more usual and less socially aggressive sports, like football and handball, but as they became more socialized by the subculture, other sports became more interesting. The sports they chose are the ones that often appear in media debates on violence and youth problems.

In other words, they engage in sports that established society spends energy counteracting – half-legitimate sports, which contradict the modern spirit of pacifism. Enrique and his gang had their own premises where they practised on stolen combat sports equipment in order to become hard and to be able to take a beating when necessary. They practised being tough in order to roam the streets safely at night, to gain respect and to feel strong. They would later have use for these skills when they began selling drugs together. The skills could be exploited if a customer was late with a payment or if competition with other dealers developed. Their motivation was in all likelihood not as farsighted as this, but rather, as with both the drug use and criminal activity, about experiencing action. Below are a couple of instances of action based on violence.

The Fast Reward System

> Drug traffickers rejected society's normative constraints which mandated a life style of deferred gratification, careful planning, and sensible spending. Instead they embraced the pursuit of self-indulgence . . . the dealing crowd was strongly driven by the pleasures they derived from their way of life . . . only those people who found the reward system enticing enough to merit assuming the risks were persuaded to strive for greater involvement in this world. (Adler 1985: 83)

The quote above is from Adler's very exciting ethnographic study of smugglers and dealers in California. As one of the basic motives for becoming a trafficker she mentions money and, with them, a means to provide a hedonistic lifestyle. This way of life can also be seen as one of the motives for becoming involved in the criminal subculture. Ordinary school is expected to produce conscientious individuals, who deem it possible to 'behave themselves' and who accept the deferred reward system in the form of lengthy periods of study, grades, further study, and at last perhaps a job and thereby money. The informal groups offer fast money, drugs, sexual experiences and, last but not least, exciting events via both criminal activities and drug use. Much of what is valued in the subculture can be bought with money. Enrique says this: 'I got a tenner [£10], maybe twenty from my parents when I was going out, by the end of the weekend I had maybe a hundred in my pocket . . .'

With money in his pocket Enrique felt free, powerful and presumably grown up. Money became a way to demonstrate both to himself and to his immediate surroundings that the subculture's 'fast reward system' far surpassed that of the school's deferred one. What is received in return for being good at school? Perhaps a good grade, the teachers' respect and parental approval. What is received in return for being good at selling hashish or shoplifting? Money and desirable material objects, naturally, and with them a sense of freedom and adulthood. Willis writes that money becomes a medium through which 'the adolescent can deal with adults nearly on their own terms' (Willis 1977/1993: 93) and contributes to strengthening the gang's self-confidence. In comparison to those of the same age, such adolescents feel adult and competent. They handle large sums of money, something that ought not to be possible for secondary school students, but that, on the contrary, the prospective heroin users are well able to do. Money is both a symbol of freedom, strength and independence and also an important element in the realization of short-term plans. It enables them to be present 'where the action is', in the pubs or the clubs, and to buy drugs to further sharpen their existence.

Consumption is worshipped in capitalist society, but there are rules as to how to consume. One of those rules is that the consumer must earn money through work or other legal means in order to be able to exchange that money for goods. Many of the prospective heroin users chose a quicker and more exciting route to being good consumers. They systematically stole or developed relationships with people from whom they could buy cheaply. Much of what they consumed symbolized the good life, at least, from a hedonistic point of view: drugs, fine clothes, gambling, alcohol and dancing. Money is used both as a symbol and as a means to obtain a hedonistic lifestyle.

The money was quickly acquired and could be quickly exchanged for experience-enhancing substances/drugs. The tempo in the subculture is different from that, for example, of school. School's time divisions are lessons, weeks and terms. Studies are pursued and grades given at the end of term; knowledge and patience are exchanged for approval in the form of a grade, or disapproval in the form of a bad grade. There is a long-term aspect in this reward system, which for some is also a punishment system. Grades in themselves are not particularly valuable, but something that may be used later, when looking for work or entering higher education. The grades' application is therefore transferred from the present to a distanced future. In this sense, the school's reward system is markedly different from that of the subculture. In the subculture, quick money is made, quick break-ins occur and long-term planning is seldom undertaken. The subculture takes a 'short-term perspective logic' (focusing on the present) that creates a feeling of uncertainty, an antithesis to all types of long-term planning, which characterize modern man's struggle against uncertainty.

The Social Dimensions

Drug use may help to create strong social bonds between the users mainly because in modern society drug use signals independence from the establishment's control.

Doing something that goes against society's regulations is a demonstration of power over society, and to do it together strengthens the social bonds in the group. Living, imaginatively, at a far remove from the norm develops a strong sense of exclusivity. This has the effect of distinguishing 'us' from 'them', which means the group makes itself unique. During an interview with Adam the following was said:

Philip: Can drugs give the feeling of being a part of something?

Adam: Yeah, a strong sense of belonging, while at the same time it isn't true, often you only have friends just as long as you've money and drugs, but it feels strong anyway, kind of that it's us and them.

Philip: And who are 'them'?

Adam: They can be lots of people; they can be ordinary people, people who do different drugs, party drugs. It's like there's different gangs. You might think like, those who do party drugs and stuff are just hobbyists . . . and they don't know anything . . . and things like that.

The description of the defining of boundaries is clearly seen here. Drug use makes the group exclusive and indicates experience of life. During the first few years of drug use the informants used, almost exclusively, as a collective. Roger relates:

It's a companionship thing. When I started smoking hash there wasn't anything else to do all day, so we just went and smoked hash, I smoked with him [his best friend] and we had a load of other mates as well, who were with us. And so we went and bought hash and all smoked it together, had great fun, talked, went round town, and things . . . Went to people's homes. There was great sense of companionship, but that disappeared years ago.

The quote outlines, in fairly nostalgic tones, how hash strengthened the social bonds between the friends who met up. This was partly due to using hash in a ritualistic manner, sharing the pipe or the joint. Through the use of hash, contact with people who are only known superficially is deepened. They know that they are doing something forbidden, and this feeling unites them.

That hash can be a symbol of 'togetherness' became quickly clear to me when on one occasion I was asked if I wished to participate. I understood it was a friendly overture and, in a way, felt myself honoured. I declined, but this incident shows clearly the symbolic aspect; to smoke together has the function of strengthening social bonds, in the same way that people in established society ask each other to dinner. Taking hash has the effect of loosening self-control, and displaying more of one's true self than is usual, while at the same time being a more secretive activity than something legal, like say drinking beer or lemonade. Hash and other drugs are ways of getting to know each other – promoting a more naked state, an exposure of self. It can be compared to that which occurs in saunas where the absence of clothing means that the participants react not from social positions or expectations but meet as equals. Collective drug use can mean that social interaction is experienced as equal and lacking in hierarchy.

The exclusive nature of hash in comparison to, say, alcohol makes it the perfect drug for initiating new contacts. This applies both to those who sell it and to those who only use:

> In the beginning it was the companionship and friends and such, but later I found I was good at grafting [selling drugs] and it was then that other users began to notice and they started hanging out with me, and to expect freebies and the like . . . so doors are opened if you're good at dealing. (Max)

Philip: Where did you do your smoking?
Roger: Around. In school, and then in town. We were often with the Chileans. It was us, and then there was another gang, there were many gangs really, there often is. We were with everyone, mostly with the Chileans, but also with others, we knew everyone. If I went into town I could meet anyone at all and if I had a little hash I'd chat them up a bit, and then we'd go. There were many of us.

For Roger, hash stands out as a symbol for almost unlimited company. In this sense, meetings are made possible between people who don't share a past and who don't necessarily need to know each other particularly well. Through hash they show that they are 'on the right side', that they belong to the subculture, that they are drifters, that is, cool guys (or sometimes girls) who don't get excited unnecessarily and who don't allow their life to run on a treadmill steered by organized power structures. Similar findings is described by Faupel: 'Any square who observes street junkie interaction soon learns that two junkies who have not previously met and who are of different regions, races, or ages can converse over a wide range of topics in a manner not understandable to an outsider. Such a fact is a manifestation of a shared culture' (1991: 20).

It's to a large extent the language and the mutual interest in and knowledge about common things that make these forms of associations possible. In Norrköping hash use can be likened to a membership card to the drifters' social association, an open sesame! It can be compared with alcohol, which doesn't provide the same exclusivity, even if it often fulfils the same function. If you meet someone you don't know carrying an off-license bag, and you also have one, it is unlikely that you'd go up to the person and say 'let's go to my place and drink together.' If we look at external attributes as signs of who we are, then an off-license bag is not particularly revealing as most adult Swedes drink alcohol. There are not, however, so many who smoke hash, which, besides, is illegal and therefore a much more revealing attribute of identity. Hash is, in this sense, to use Goffman's expression, a pronounced 'tie sign' (Goffman 1961/1971), much more pronounced than alcohol, as the group that uses it is both smaller and, to say the least, breaking the law.

To use hash is not just seen as drug use, but also as an attitude to life in general. The hash-using drifter has not only chosen to smoke hash, but also to take the day as it comes and not to submit to any formal structure. To smoke hash symbolizes freedom, particularly when it is seen by many as a 'truant drug', a drug that is used by individuals when, on their own initiative, without permission from teachers, they skip school; as such it is also related to freedom from the establishment. At the same time as being gradually excluded from the society of the better behaved, more and more like-minded people are encountered, drifters who do not follow the straight and narrow. This leads to developing strong and intimate ties with others who are like-minded. Roger, on the subject of his best friend:

> We're best friends. When we started smoking hash we pooled our money. It wasn't how much money have *I*? Instead, we said, 'How much have *we*?' So we put some aside for hash, some for food and so on. He's my best friend. We have had such great times together; *we've tried everything together*.

Roger and his friend became like relatives, blood brothers who shared everything, no matter what happened, and he misses this friend, with whom he has done so much, but who is now in treatment. The part of the quote expressed in italics 'we've tried everything together' describes what bound together the members of the informal groups: testing and the adventure inherent in it. In this way, the group produces its own history of action that can be built up quickly, as it deals with events; situations that are dramatic for the characters involved, such as break-ins, and testing drugs. Building a common history on boring routine situations does not provide the same sense of exclusivity and secrecy. According to the rationale presented in this section, drug use clearly fulfils three functions:

- To create boundaries against the surrounding world in order to strengthen the bonds and ties the informal group needs. This is ultimately about creating a belief that the group's bonds are unique and that the group members are loyal to one another.
- To deepen social contacts, in that the drug promotes feelings of equality and makes signals of status and prestige unnecessary, and it doesn't take much time to create a history of action.
- To find new friends and quickly create social ties to these friends through a feeling of community and belonging and shared experience which the drug use promotes.

The Mentors

The individual members can see participation in the informal groups as a form of reinforcement and acceptance where the feeling of strong common bonds goes hand in hand with a sense of being skilled and competent. Many made contact with experienced dealers, through buying drugs, as well as in other ways. To be accepted and reinforced by these mentors from the subculture required no school grades or certificates, just a strong interest in learning and a well-proven sense of loyalty. Contact with experienced people was central in many of the informants' stories. Steve says that many of his friends thought that he was older than he actually was. He acquired a false identification card so that he could frequent places with an older clientele, like the popular nightclub, *Tellus*. This made it possible for him to almost entirely associate with older people. This would increasingly become the group that socialized him. Hanna also talks about associating with older people: 'I've always hung around with people who are older than me, I have done that since I was little . . . at least two years older. My parents were sometimes suspicious, but I don't think they really noticed anything in particular . . .'

Older friends symbolize, first and foremost, an eventful life. To hang around with people that are classed by others as suspect or even dangerous can give the feeling of mastering existence and also become an affirmation of existing at the margins of society – the mentors are icons of outsider-ship. The subculture, in this sense, offers an alternative adult existence. One of the symbolic aspects of childhood and youth is immaturity, being seen as incompetent and insufficiently mature to make rational decisions. It takes a long time to attain the age of majority if the establishment's ways are followed. Associating with older people in this case was almost proof that he was becoming adult. In comparison to other classmates, to use Willis's expression, 'conformists', this alternative adulthood was very clear. Willis writes: 'There is no doubt that this ability to "make out" in the "real world" . . . and to deal with adults nearly on their own terms strengthens "the lads'" self-confidence and their feeling, at this point anyway, that they "know better" than school' (Willis 1977/1993: 25–26).

These older mentors have been male, both for the men and women in the study. In the world where 'things happen' these alternative teachers are more attractive than those who subscribe to the ideology of school and the establishment. Most of the interviewees developed closer relationships with these mentors than they did to their official teachers. Steve learnt to sell drugs at an early stage. By keeping his eyes and ears open and paying attention he became a very good student. So good, in fact, that when he later began to sell both heroin and amphetamines he was never once convicted. He built himself what in business terms would be called a career.

He was willing to learn, not history or algebra, but breaking and entering, profit calculating, deliveries, and so forth. Teaching in the underworld is like an apprenticeship, where practical aims are achieved by, and learnt through action: learning by doing. By participating, the necessary skills and rules are acquired. As a result, many youngsters experience the underworld's teaching methods as attractive. Max relates why he preferred to hang around with older people:

> I don't really know. It works better if you know what I mean. I think it had a lot to do with being responsible for myself, an older head on younger shoulders. I thought others in school were really immature. They were fine in their way, but I found it difficult to identify with them. Older people have always accepted me. Nobody thought I was a brat or anything, I was mentally older . . . that's why, I think.

It is obvious above that Max felt reinforced in company with his mentors. The dealers are often self-made social psychologists, who know the importance of treating others with a certain amount of respect, confirming the other as a person of value. Steve told me, after he himself started dealing, that it's very important to make assistants, for example, the runners, and the clients, and the buyers feel good. One of the 'fat cats', who Steve got a lot of his heroin from, bought Christmas presents for Steve in order to show appreciation to his collaborator.

I've been told that one of the top dealers was like a father figure to some of the small-scale dealers. In the trial in which he was convicted he made a point of stating that he hadn't merely been an evil person selling drugs, but that he also helped people with problems, giving them advice and sometimes financial support. This is a perfect strategy to build loyalty and motivate, as his collaborators' existences are reaffirmed by him as worthy of respect. On one occasion when I met Roger he was extremely pleased because he had met a dealer who had treated him well. 'He offered me a gram for £80, I was invited to his home, and he even gave me food.' What Roger saw was not an evil dealer profiting from him, but a nice person who was interested in helping him, and perhaps the dealer saw his actions as a form of generosity. I realized later that the person Roger had spoken about was the top dealer described above.

Drawing on Scheff (1997), it could be said that people are constantly in search of top dealer affirmation and acceptance and this is done in everyday interaction. If they do not receive this acceptance or feel pride in their situation they find other situations in which they do, and they will want to repeat situations that are affirming. Aspelin (1999) draws on Scheff in a study on interaction in classrooms. According to Aspelin, the pupils' psychological attendance is dependent on the type of social and psychological situation in the classroom. The more the pupils are affirmed as valuable people, the more interesting school becomes for them, and the more they want to learn. The subculture's mentors are skilled at this type of motivating.

The Consequences of Alternative Schooling

> ... joining these social networks required a commitment to the drug world's norms, values and lifestyle, and limited the degree of involvement individuals subsequently had with nondeviant groups. (Adler 1985: 122)

Many of the informants describe how the distance between themselves and their well-behaved friends developed. This was a two-way process involving both a loss of interest in the conformists except as definers by exclusion of the group's strength and exclusivity, and their exclusion from the group of conformists due to their engagement in forbidden and illegal activity.

Enrique describes how his gang tried hash at a party and had an attack of the giggles, and just lay on a bed laughing, as the others at the party perceived it, at nothing at all. Many describe this 'laughing at nothing at all' as an important point in using hash. The others at the party let the gang know that they didn't want any 'bloody drugs' at the party, to which the gang responded 'We don't want to be at your boring party anyway. Come on, let's go.' What happened here is yet another element in the separation between the gang and the establishment. In Douglas's (1966/1991) words the better-behaved wished to keep the party 'clean', and from their viewpoint drugs were something 'unclean', while at the same time they did not regard alcohol as something unclean despite its association with violent behaviour and vomit.

The gangs became increasingly marginalized in relation to other youths and adults while at the same time 'the common others', following the norms of established society, were increasingly referred to as 'losers', as those who do not know what life is about. I have also been told that when a pair in a larger group began to intensify their drug use they left the larger group, or would be pushed out by it, as 'too frequent' drug use threatened the group's identity. Many groups used drugs to manifest the group's identity but some defended themselves from a perceived overuse of drugs. However, those who used drugs with higher frequency found, to a large extent, new friends who were practising the same habits. To be an addict is, after all, not something that is valued by most, and if someone or a few in the group intensify their drug use then the group's sense of identity is threatened.

What has been described so far is a separation process whereby the young prospective heroin users start distancing themselves from school, parents and better-behaved friends to become part of the subculture that they help to create. During this process contact with established society's representatives diminish, and the socialization they undergo is increasingly through contact with the like-minded, who teach each other about crime, drug use, drug selling and other illegal activities.

Learning to Transgress

> Membership of the informal group sensitises the individual to the unseen informal dimension of life in general. Whole hinterlands open up of what lies behind the official definition of things . . . The group also supplies those contacts, which allow the individual to build up alternative maps of social reality. (Willis 1977/1993)

The consequence of separation and interaction in the informal groups and keeping contacts with the mentors is that a specific perspective on reality is created. The group's members put their heads together and agree on how to see life in general. Here they can, with each other's and the mentors' support, construct a mental map of the world where behaviour that is seen by others as contemptible becomes reasonable and legitimate and where the abnormal becomes normal. It is about the production of strong belief (Bourdieu 1979/1992). This belief is confirmed beyond doubt when it is communicated by the group, and when it is united to the actions which the group engage in which are in accord with the group's logic. It is the same as within the scientific community when scientists agree that their perspective is the best and most suitable and where actions within the community contribute to strengthening this perspective (Kuhn 1970). The group consolidates, legitimizes and naturalizes this perspective on existence as the only true one.

The perspective of reality can, using Bourdieu's (1979/1992) structuralistic theories, be called 'habitus', which means a kind of filter, a 'structuring structure', through which people interpret reality. Habitus is created from the meetings with significant others, also including media, in a process of socialization. I claim that the separation processes have changed the perspective of reality for the young heroin users and have thereby made certain acts possible and even rational, viewed from the logic of the subcultural habitus. Closely related to habitus is taste, which, according to Bourdieu, may be seen as consequences of how habitus is constructed. The taste for specific types of red wine is, for example, not a consequence of nature or an individual trait of the actor. Rather, it can be seen as a consequence of a certain habitus, which, in its turn, is a consequence of learning. The sensations of the wine are experienced because of socially constructed knowledge about wine and what the person relates the wine to, for example, uniqueness, success, fine culture and so forth.

The young, potential heroin users, have developed a subcultural habitus during separation, through social interaction, which means they have a common perception of existence that differs sharply from how the 'better-behaved' see it. They have learned to transgress. In this sense it is also reasonable to assert that they have developed a common taste for drugs and a certain type of criminal activity. In the subculture there is a taste for the forbidden and secret, for boundaries to transgress and also for experiencing fast tempo and the 'now': It is of major importance to show that you have lived a life full of experiences. This search for experience can also be seen in other cultures. According to Elsrud (2001) it is important for backpackers to show signs of experience in order to indicate, through action and speech, that they have not followed the easy track, but rather a difficult and risky one. The focus on experience is internalized in the backpackers' minds through reading magazines and books and through meeting and talking to other persons on the trails.

The subculture of prospective heroin users has similarities to backpacker culture, but it is another kind of experience, not built on travel destinations or guided by 'Lonely Planet' guides or other travel literature, but construed from being in the margins of society. Both in backpacker cultures and in the subculture of prospective heroin users, experience may be seen, using another of Bourdieu's (1979/1992) concepts, as a symbolic capital, that is, a form of resource leading to an improved position in the social group or category the beholder belongs to (see also Thornton 1996). To be experienced in the subculture implies having tested drugs: there is a subcultural habitus that, for the members of the subculture, motivates drug testing, and this motivation is to a great extent learned in the group through contacts with mentors and through watching movies as described in Chapter 6. As the members of the subculture want experiences to give their lives meaning, they do not wait for them to come to them any more than a wildlife photographer waits for his subject to enter the viewfinder. They search for possibilities for action, through drugs and other adventures. They also create it, by creating action and by using dramatic terms.

In football-supporter culture the knowledge of the players, strategies and rules may help to intensify and deepen the experience of a match. Watching a football match with this perspective makes it seem as if everything outside the arena, including the future and the past, is shut out. A lot of Swedes have difficulty watching American football because they have not been socialized in a culture that has given them the knowledge necessary to understand the game, they have not played it as children and it therefore has no meaning for them. Knowing about it helps you commit, as it becomes a meaningful activity. The same applies in the subculture – you learn from friends and mentors how to do things, how to smoke a joint or what kind of weed is preferable, how to dry it, and so forth. This knowledge is an important part of habitus, giving drug use a meaning related to the users' identity, to the identity of the drifter and to a world beyond the ordinary.

The knowledge is, as previously mentioned, not learned in an abstract or theoretical way but through learning by doing, in which the student practically experiences the education through his or her body. It is a school of testing in which the grades you have from ordinary school do not matter; you do not need them to be good at the alphabet of the subculture. This school is, thus, open to anybody willing to try. There is always room for another drug user. The subculture is doing what the formal school pretends to be better at – enabling the students to search for knowledge through active choices. This is what they do in the subculture and its members believe that 'this is our choice, we have no authorities'.

Another important consequence of the creation of the habitus of the subculture and, thus, a form of lifestyle including knowledge, preferences, language and style, is that it becomes easy for the actors to sort out the like-minded from the straight or conformists. The hash examples showed that quite clearly. This will, later on, be an important aspect in explaining why they were chosen as possible consumers and helpers in the heroin trade and not someone else. The socialization in the informal groups and the contacts with the mentors equipped them with necessary signs and a drifter attitude that a straight person would have difficulties interpreting but an insider in the culture would detect immediately.

The Medical Mind

Living in the subculture made certain substances a kind of solution to different types of everyday problems. I would say that a medical mind was inserted in habitus. On one occasion I was spending an evening with John and Peter. This was in 2001 and both of them had, with the help of Subutex and other forms of support, kicked their heroin habit. John was sad because his girlfriend had just broken up with him and Peter felt lonely and was longing, quite desperately for a girl by his side. I came to Peter's apartment at about eleven o'clock and we were about to head for Otten, the successor to Tellus when it comes to nightlife. When I entered the kitchen, they were preparing themselves for going out. They had two bottles of Vodka on the table and a few cans of the energy drink Battery. Peter offered me a beer, a Lapin Kulta. He said he bought them especially for me as he himself doesn't drink beer. 'It doesn't do so much with your head.' We talked and Peter had, with John as an advisor, bought new clothes, not his style but quite modern, 1970s-type jeans and a close-fitting T-shirt. John, who was more up to date in his way of dressing, said: 'This looks good, with these on you'll get the chicks, no problems', but Peter answered, 'I look like a fucking gay in them.' We assured him that it's quite normal to feel awkward when you change style, but that he would get used to them.

After chatting for a while, Peter pulled out a CD case, and a little white powder. He laid down two lines, one for himself and one for John. They each snorted their line. I asked them why they had to take cocaine, when they risked both their driving licences and losing their social workers' trust and Peter answered that he wouldn't dare talk to girls without it, that he always takes cocaine when he's going to a nightclub while John answered that he needed cheering up. During the evening, Peter had a certain amount of success with a girl that he had liked for a long time. The cocaine was not enough to cheer John up.

They have learned all of the above in 'drug school' and much more. The drug user has a head start on those who know nothing about drugs and who do not accept their legitimacy. If a problem arises, you can always take a drug, while other young people have to make do with alcohol. Different drugs have different functions and different areas of use. You learn this, how to 'twist' your consciousness while holding a balance, if you subscribe to the drug school's ABC. By entering into the subculture, step by step, the young people develop specialist skills in drug use. The drugs themselves become more and more a fixed part of their consciousness. They learn that drugs mean an altered state of experience, and drugs in this way become a means of getting ahead in life, a way of tackling different situations. Drug skills and drug use become fixed as part of a strategy for situations in everyday life. They become part of an emergency solution that can rescue them from almost any problem: tiredness – amphetamines/cocaine; sadness – almost all drugs; anxiety – almost all drugs; in this process of socialization they develop what could be called a 'medical mind'. It is also clearly an effect of the fast reward system. Ben, Max, Peter and their friends wanted their bodies to look fit. In order to achieve that, they started training at a local gym. However, they did not have time to wait patiently for their muscles to grow, but took anabolic steroids to speed up the process. It was never a question of whether they should take them; more a matter of what sort of anabolic steroids they should use. Other horsers were interested in vitamins and some had taken Viagra to improve their sex lives.

The medical mind is a reference to the kind of mental logic used by people who believe that medication can cure any problem – if you need to lose weight, take a pill, if you have a headache, take an aspirin, and so on. Why wait when you can obtain almost immediate effect?

A Subjective Culture

The benefits of participating in the alternative schooling are numerous: togetherness, experiences of the now and of adventure, a feeling of increased control of life and a way of creating an identity based on outsidership and experience. These short-term rewards make it plausible and rational, from their phenomenological understanding of the world, to increase their motivation for learning.

From a sociological point of view their fascination with drugs, violence and criminal activity should be seen as attempts to transgress the boundaries that established society has set. Simmel writes about man's situation in a modern rationalized world: 'This is how problematic situations arise, typical for the modern man: the feeling of being surrounded by a series of cultural elements which are not meaningless but also, basically not meaningful for him; together these elements have a strangling effect . . .' (Simmel 1918/1981: 204 – author's translation).

The quotation above describes the fundamental drive behind every form of subculture and counter-culture, through which the members can, with the means on offer, create a 'subjective culture' that can be identified with and that the individuals experience as their own choice. Drugs, criminal activity and violence have good qualities in that they are not recommended by modern society. This makes them suitable elements in a subculture. What is common to these elements is that they fulfil Goffman's criteria for action, and action only occurs when there is energy in the form of risk, subversion and, not least, transgression of boundaries.

By transgressing, a feeling of living in a reality other than that represented by society is created. Attaining that other reality is facilitated through criminal activity, violence and drugs. To conclude, a quote from Bauman describes what this chapter has dealt with: '*Transcendence* is what, everything having been said and done, culture is about. Culture is about expanding temporal and spatial boundaries of being, with a view to dismantling them altogether' (Bauman 1992: 5).

–3–

The Secret Cave

It's a lovely drug, it's just a pity it's so poisonous.

Ben

My First Collective Basing Session

A few weeks after I had Ben smoking heroin in my rental car he invited me to a 'basing session'. He had tried to reach me several times by leaving text messages on my phone that I hadn't seen. He had also tried to get in touch with me through a social worker who knows me. Later he told me that he had met a policeman from the drug squad and they had talked about my project. The policeman suggested to Ben that my project would be impossible because I wouldn't get any useful information from the heroin users. Ben told me that after hearing this from the policeman he wanted to help me as far as possible, to show the policeman that he was wrong. When he calls I come to the conclusion that he is using heroin. He sounds a little hoarse, high, a little bit distant. I can hear his friends in the background, they are probably basing together. I tell him that I can meet him about seven o'clock because I have an interview earlier, at six o'clock. He says OK, but he doesn't give me an address or any hint as to where; instead he will call me later.

He calls me again and asks me to buy *The Yellow Paper* (a paper dedicated to small ads), because a friend of his is thinking about buying a car. They want to look through the paper to search for a car that evening. I cannot get the paper. I try at a few places and give up, thinking it is best not to be too late; they may get nervous. The interview takes more time than I thought. I drive to a supermarket that Ben told me about, and call him on my mobile. Without a mobile phone my job would be a lot more difficult. He answers and comes to get me. He is dressed in a tracksuit, open at the neck so that you can see his chest; his well bronzed and well trained muscles and the thick gold chain around his neck. He tells me that the gold chain cost around £1,500 and that he redeemed it from the pawn shop the week before. I tell him that I couldn't get the paper and he says: 'No problem, I think I know a place, we can go there.' So we do; we chat a little. He comments on my haircut. The last time I met him I looked a little shabby because I was tired and hadn't had a haircut or a shave for a while. 'You look much better now', he says.

I don't think he is very high at the moment, he responds well without hesitations. After a while he says to me that he wants me to drive to a certain area of town. It is a place where I lived as a child. I know Norrköping like the back on my hand. I stop and stay in the car as he jumps out.

He is gone for a few minutes, comes back and we drive to find *The Yellow Paper*. I definitely feel nervous waiting in the car while he's making a buy, since it's the first time for me. I tell him as he comes back that if they are into dealing or other suspect activity I don't want him to tell me. It is better not to know. He says OK but makes a point of telling me what he has said to the other guys, waiting in the flat, about me, that I'm OK and that I do keep my promise about not telling anybody in authority of what I see. I tell him how important this is to my research. He repeats how important it is several times that evening. Maybe I made him nervous by telling him not to say anything about dealer activities.

We manage to get *The Yellow Paper* in a tobacconist's and drive to the flat. When we get to the flat, I am apprehensive. There are three other guys present, all just over twenty years of age. They are sitting on a sofa. One of them is a tall muscular guy wearing a baseball cap. He doesn't say very much. I interpret it as his scepticism about my presence. Another guy, whom I interview later on, looks more like a drifter, relaxed and informal in dress, constantly with a smile on his face. He tells me a lot and seems to think it's pleasant that I am there. He doesn't live in Norrköping anymore, but studies at the university in another town. He only uses horse when he's in Norrköping and every time he goes back to the town he now lives, he has to go through withdrawal symptoms. The tall guy, they tell me, just uses about every fourth week. He is what Zinberg (1984) would have called a 'recreational user', letting heroin use be a highlight in his life, still taking care of his job and social relations. According to Ben he's the only one he knows that has managed to keep it like that, for four years. I ask him if I can interview him, but he answers me with a short, but powerful 'No! I don't want that.' And I don't push him further. The third guy, a rather short guy whom I later interview, doesn't use at all. We were in his apartment, though. When I talk to him a few days later he says that he doesn't believe that smoking heroin is all that serious. However, he also says that he doesn't really like to have them smoking in his flat.

The TV is on, showing 'Jeopardy', but at a low volume, nobody cares what is being said. The flat is an ordinary studio, a living room, a partitioned sleeping area and a small kitchen. There is a marijuana plant on the window sill; it's a present from the relaxed guy to the tall guy. There is also a blanket wrapped around it so it won't get too cold. In the kitchen there is foil on the table and a few bags and some other stuff. In the bathroom there is a picture of a bodybuilder with an enormous penis and a text saying something about the combination of doping and Viagra. There is much talk about bodies, mostly from the tall guy who mentions that he has seen a porn film with a woman who had extremely hairy legs. Porn films are a regular topic of discussion. In the kitchen they discuss Ben's addiction to heroin and make jokes about what he would do for a bag. Ben laughs with them when they say that he would give a 'blowjob' to get some horse. Most of the time I sit in the living room interviewing the relaxed guy. However, I also spend time in the kitchen and watch them basing. They talk a lot while doing it, with hoarse voices, making jokes. Ben tells me, in a serious voice, that these guys are some of his oldest friends. He and the tall guy read *The Yellow Paper* trying to find bargains, commenting about the ads. When they smoke the high doesn't seem like the nod, their heads don't fall forward to touch their knees, rather they smoke, talk, walk around, smoke again.

On the living room table there is Coca-Cola, which obviously goes well with heroin, and sweets. Ben has a bag of lollipops that he shares. I get the impression that this is to some extent like an ordinary get-together evening where people meet up, drink a little, and chat. They are old friends who have good contact with each other. I don't feel any threat in the air, it feels good, almost natural, to sit there. Ben asks me if I want some Coke. I reply by asking what kind of coke he is talking about. He laughs a little and tells me that he was out a few days ago and that he took some 'coke'. After a few hours I decide to leave. Nothing spectacular happened and I was tired. Just before this observation I had done three interviews combined with observations. My head was full of thoughts and at this stage in my research I was sometimes quite shaky, having problems sleeping. I said goodbye to them and they continued their smoking.

Preparing the Substance

The situation with Ben describes an event that used to be fairly typical among Norrköping's young heroin users: to sit in flats and smoke heroin. This part of the book is the most ethnographic. I have been present during a fairly large number of occasions where heroin has been used. Mostly it was when 'basing' but I have also been present when people injected. During the most intensive year of my field studies, in 2000, most of the smokers started to inject. This chapter refers to the social and cultural processes that made it possible for the young heroin users to take into their systems what is, in Douglas's words, the 'impure' substance, heroin. The body, in Douglas's (1966/1991) description, is a 'fortress' that is 'under siege' from the forbidden, taboo-ridden and illegal. Matter and objects that cannot properly be classified or that are classified as bad, as a sign of individual decline, defeat or social degeneracy, must in different ways be cleansed or, to use Douglas's term, be prepared and thereby made suitable to for intake, primarily through the body's entrance to the outside, the mouth. Douglas writes: 'Before being admitted to the body some clear symbolic break is needed to express food's separation from necessary but impure contacts. The cooking process, entrusted to pure hands, provides this ritual break. Some such break we would expect to find whenever the production of food is in the hands of the relatively impure' (1966/1991: 127).

The quotation refers to taking substances into the body, which, when ingested, are associated with impurity. Cooking, according to Douglas, is a form of ritual cleansing. However, some things cannot be eaten even after preparation, as they are altogether too strongly threatening. What is threatening is decided by what a particular culture sees as threatening. The substance's symbolic associations are not fixed, but can change in such a way that one seen previously as associated with degeneracy or defeat can acquire a more positive character. The social and cultural process that gives a substance this new association I call 'sociocultural preparation'.

The ingestion of objects into the body can be seen as a ritual. Gusfield (1987), for example, writes about weekend drinking in industrialized societies as marking the transition from regularized time (work) to leisure time. In order to make the leisure time plausible to believe in, symbolic substances are required that merge with the individual in the same moment they are ingested. Those substances not only say something about the individual, but also about the group, and the group's arena. In 'rites of passages' (see for example Turner 1967) the substances used often have ambiguous associations, and being placed, as they are, on society's margins are also energy-laden. Alcohol is one such common substance in Western society, symbolizing togetherness and degeneracy, intoxication and the dissolution of structural meaning (Lalander 1997).

Before beginning this sociocultural exploration, certain factors that were necessary for the exposure of these young people to heroin should be highlighted. One factor is that someone, or some people, decided to market the substance in Norrköping; another is that potential consumers were already available in a network the sellers could reach. The subculture described in the former chapter is one such network, including a big number of groups connected to drug dealers, and heroin dealers mainly use already established contacts to increase availability and spread the sale of heroin. Since 1995, anyone participating in the subculture's action environment will sooner or later come in contact with heroin. The potential consumers are relatively well experienced in drug use and a number have sold both hash and amphetamines. They stand out as the most likely consumers and dealers, equipped with a certain habitus created through alternative socialization and, thus, a specific style. The first heroin was distributed to a number of people who had connections to different groups of potential users – pub goers and drifters, who frequented various action environments and were, therefore, accustomed to and relatively unafraid of drugs and criminal behaviour.

In other words, dealers and potential consumers at a lower level were available. This is only one aspect, but an important one, of the social and cultural characteristics necessary for heroin dealing to succeed. Those in the subculture's action spaces have developed a taste for action and action substances. They have also, among other talents, developed considerable skills in both drug use and criminal behaviour and activity.

In the following section I develop the analysis of how it became possible to sell and consume so much heroin in Norrköping from 1995 onward. I begin by looking at the product's symbolic nature, prior to the sociocultural preparation, in order to study the transformation process the substance undergoes in order to become desirable. I also give an account of the experiences of the heroin 'high' and the ritual of 'basing', because those aspects are of vital importance in explaining why they continued to use heroin.

The Drug of Death and Social Failure

A few of those I spoke to refused the first time they were offered heroin. John describes how he and his friends reacted when it was first offered:

> They were my best friends; we hung together all the time. There were five of us who stuck together, hail or shine, we did everything together. One friend came up and we were hanging out in a flat at that time and he had some horse with him and said: 'If you want to try it, it's really cool', but we refused. We said, 'Fuck, no!' (He laughs), but then he came back again another time and then you just had to try it, like, and it was so good. So then you kept it up. And soon you were taking it every day.

I asked him why he and his friends refused the first time and he replied: 'Ah, I don't know, I suppose it was things you heard. Heroin, it sounds so serious, like, it has a more dangerous ring to it than amphetamine or cocaine, so I suppose that was what we thought about.' For John, and many others, heroin was linked to overdoses and death (even if it also was, being a drug, linked to action and to proof of experience).

I have spoken to some people who were involved in Norrköping's drug scene in the 1970s and 1980s, and they consider heroin, more than any other drug, a symbol of degeneracy and destruction. Olsson and Lenke (2002: 73) write about heavy drug users in Sweden: 'There are clear indications that (intravenous) amphetamine users have regarded heroin use as something strange and dangerous'. Heroin was the one drug where you could bet on getting hooked. Many therefore avoided heroin and contented themselves with amphetamines, hash, pills and alcohol. To them, the word heroin denotes something threatening. To be hooked on heroin is to have failed in creating a life for oneself. It is the opposite of autonomy and freedom, so desired as part of the separation process, and definitely not anything the Western industrialized person wishes for himself. I call this symbolical association, 'the threat of destruction'.

Heroin, even to the most liberal mind, is seen as the heaviest of drugs and the number one 'killer' drug. Its place is closest to the border and to subjective dissolution, and this, more than anything else, is what causes angst to modern mankind. John's words 'it has a dangerous ring to it' are another way of expressing that it has the clang of death. Bauman describes death as follows: 'So death – an unadorned death, death in all its stark, uncompromised bluntness, a death that would induce consciousness to stop – is the ultimate absurdity, while being at the same time the ultimate truth! Death reveals that truth and absurdity are one . . .' (Bauman 1992: 14–15).

Death, like other unsolvable riddles, reminds us of the littleness of mankind and the uncertainty of existence. It shakes our ontological security – our 'sense of continuity and order in events' (Giddens 1991: 243) – and exposes the fragility in what we otherwise take for granted. We therefore avoid it, and all that relates to it is kept in places where it can be avoided. According to Bauman, death represents a serious threat to modern society. The modern aims at explaining and rationalizing existence, but death cannot be explained and therefore we pretend it does not exist. This can also be a part of the perceived threat the heroin user represents – that those concerned are linked to death and thereby, from modern society's perspective, impurity.

That heroin is linked to death is very likely an important aspect of understanding the often very negative attitudes people have towards this drug. Death is taboo and that which is linked to it acquires an evil reputation. In most people's minds, heroin users are associated with prostitution, death and misery. This is so even among the young heroin users themselves in Norrköping, although it is not as strongly felt as among the well-behaved, as it is a part of the drug paradigm and thereby also associated with positive meanings.

Cheating Destruction and Ignoring Death

In order to sell heroin in big numbers and with huge profits the image of the good, heroin, must be socioculturally prepared in some way. If a seller wants to sell a good it's a disadvantage if people who have used it walk around in misery giving it negative associations. Norrköping should be viewed as a new heroin town, which means that the down-and-out drug addicts were amphetamine users and not heroin users. This explanation is also in line with Parkers et al.'s (1998) analysis of the new heroin cities in England during the 1990s. The heroin users in Norrköping who were around in 1995/96 looked young and fresh, and those who were recruited later still look that way today. There was no concrete evidence in their immediate surroundings that basing would lead to death, social misery and maladjustment. The situation described above made it a lot easier to create the demand for heroin.

Another very important aspect of this process of making heroin possible to consume has to do with the technique of ingestion. Pearson writes about 'chasing the dragon': '. . . it was a recognition that proved to be crucial, in that it removed a formidable cultural barrier against self-injection, which undoubtedly allowed the heroin habit to spread more widely than would otherwise have been possible' (1987: 2). Smoking heroin, which, in the beginning, was the dominant technique, did not tally with the earlier views of serious drug abuse. Smoking heroin was not as problematic as injecting. In this way, heroin was de-dramatized and made more like hash or amphetamines. This is vital to understanding the 'cleansing' process heroin underwent in Norrköping, and most likely in other Swedish towns. Peter, on basing:

> No, yeah, well I don't know. I wasn't thinking along those lines at all, that it was dangerous. More like exciting, maybe. And so anyhow, I never injected, I just smoked. It was an important point, I think. You think it's less dangerous to smoke. Of course, it is harder to overdose, but the dependency is the same.

From the quote it's apparent that basing makes it possible to use heroin with reduced overdose risks, and in that way, heroin, which is loaded with associations of death and anxiety, is made less threatening. Basing makes transgression with a certain amount of control possible, and the symbolic associations with death disappear.

By basing, the threat of destruction could also be handled. As an activity it was hardly reminiscent of the down-and-out junkies shown on television. On the contrary, it could even be regarded as exciting and cool. Heroin was given alternative symbolic associations because the way in which it was used had changed. However, the positive excitement aspect of heroin was kept. It was still something dangerous and thereby exclusive, but no longer necessarily coupled to a 'loser' identity. Basing can be seen as doing the worst there is, but also not quite the worst. After all, it's not injecting. Basing, in this way, offered a means of carrying on with the most extreme of activities while at the same time keeping at bay any picture of being down and out. This became obvious in a discussion with Hanna:

> You think when you smoke you're not an addict. Like they said when I sat in the back of the cop car. I was going in for questioning, when they came and got me, and I sat in the backseat and they rang up and said that we were coming in and that it was a girl: 'Yes I have an addict with me in the back', he said, 'a female one', and just hearing someone saying addict . . . He thought smoking hash was serious because he asked 'Are you on something?' and I thought there's no point in trying to deny it because they'll see I'm on something, but I'm not going to say opiates, I won't, they can find out for themselves and maybe it won't come up in the results, they can be wrong, you can get lucky [she laughs]. But I just said 'I've only smoked hash' and even so he said addict, and I think 'addict', and I see someone who's dirty and awful and like completely wrecked.

The technique of basing hides the association with serious addiction and social downfall. It becomes possible to maintain an identity of relative success. The special technique and its symbolic associations also hastened the recruitment process because it did not seem as serious to take the drug through basing as it would have been to inject for the first time. To initiate a 'virgin', to push a needle into someone's vein for the first time, is more tangible than helping someone to smoke heroin.

Another aspect of the process of preparation, which to some extent is related to the technique of ingestion, has to do with how they looked and how they interpreted others' perspective on them. It is, according to Goffman (1959/1974), important for people to hold up a 'façade' that portrays that one is moderately successful in life. Heroin use is a sign that can destroy that portrait, but constructing the outward façade in a particular way and letting other symbols dominate upholds the illusion that one isn't degenerate. Most of the young heroin users were well dressed, had nice mobile telephones and some had thick gold chains. Many had money in their pockets, provided through crime, often more than their contemporary, more 'well-behaved' schoolfellows. They did not therefore find it particularly credible that they would become failed drug addicts.

Another aspect, related to the one above, deserves mention, and that is that friends, both verbally and by example, guaranteed that heroin was a good thing to consume (see also Pearson 1987). The person who first offers heroin is often a friend, or maybe the person from whom amphetamine or hash is bought. It is often someone with whom one has a good relationship, someone who is in some sense trustworthy, someone you like and trust. The person offering does not look like a 'drug addict', in fact, it may be someone who works, takes care of his or her studies, but every now and then smokes a little heroin. As Faupel writes: 'Most young users were first turned on by close friends who were themselves just beginning to experiment with drugs' (1991: 52). The provider seems far removed from someone 'hooked' and thereby imparts a particular image of heroin to the consumer. The image looks like this: 'Heroin is very exciting, but not fatal and not inextricably linked to social and individual downfall.' Those who offer the heroin do not see themselves as addicts and neither do they believe that those they are selling to have to become hooked on the heroin; this way they can also salve their own consciences. They do not see themselves as supplying a fatal drug, but rather as providing the means for a strong and positive experience, as helpers. In this way, their identity is cleansed from society's criticism. The provision of the drug by friends reduces its death threat. The trust in their friends means that the would-be users cannot seriously believe that their friends mean to kill them, instead, that they mean well – providing heroin becomes almost a matter of generosity (see also Sutter 1969 and Faupel 1991).

One last aspect is that the heroin users, before they had started with heroin, had experimented with a series of other drugs without becoming hooked. When I had spoken to twenty-five of the interviewees, all of whom later became addicted to heroin, it was clear that when they started using, it was not with the intention of becoming addicted. Rather it was a matter of experimenting with heroin, and an ever more frequent use of heroin in combination with their curiosity for transgression and search for action. 'Curiosity' is a word almost all of them use when trying to describe why they started experimenting (see also Brown et al. 1971 and Faupel 1991). Friends had told them that it was an indescribable kick, and kicks have to be explored. After all, you don't get hooked on something just by testing it a couple of times – so they believed.

What is described above is the preparation that made it possible to try heroin for the first time and then a few more times in order to really know the effect. However, had they not enjoyed the experience then, in all likelihood, they would have stopped using heroin after the first few times. That was not the case for those I interviewed. The heroin experience was so strong that they allowed it to spread into their everyday lives. The following section is about what they achieved by consuming heroin, and what it was, in both the drug use and the rituals surrounding it, that made it necessary to continue using it.

To Be Born 'Normal'

> When the heroin's in my blood
> And the blood is in my head
> I thank God I'm not aware
> I thank God that I just don't care.
> ('Heroin' by Velvet Underground, 1967)

My intention in this section is not just to describe the effects of heroin but also how they interpret them and formulate the intoxication in words. The talk of the drug and the belief in this talk is of major importance to associate the good with positive effects. Most of the heroin users to whom I spoke have difficulty putting the heroin experience into words. John describes how he experienced heroin in the beginning of his romance with the drug:

> So you tested it and were very high, ran and puked the whole time. Still, you feel so good, so that you think it's nice to puke [he laughs]. It's not that drunken puking that hurts, but more like it just comes up all at once. You get really low, mellow, so that you just sit and nod the whole time. You feel really fucking [he laughs] great, quite simply. Except it isn't like hash, not that way, 'cause then you're high in another way, this way you're more alert, the other way you're so dizzy and you can hardly keep in the giggles, and that. But this way you're more like a normal person, you just feel so very high and sit like this with your head on the table.

Notice that he says that you are more like a 'normal person', even though he did throw up (see also Pearson 1987). Others describe the experience as not being particularly pleasant until the third to the fifth time. Maybe the heroin experience isn't so special, yet that it is means that the majority choose to continue. The thought 'this isn't particularly special, but even so, I had a really strong feeling of wellbeing' (see also Stewart 1987) can even further de-dramatize heroin. Heroin has been demonized by the mass media, but the encounter with it is not as dramatic as they had thought. The credibility of the picture constructed by the media is further undermined. You think, 'this wasn't particularly remarkable, so it can't be particularly dangerous, either'. When you have done something that you have a large amount of respect for and notice that it is neither that dangerous nor astounding, a new interpretation is created and the heroin is de-dramatized. This is more or less what the young users thought: 'This wasn't so remarkable, I am in full control, and I can try it again.' It may also be that if they didn't think it was particularly spectacular the first time that they have to try again to see if it is this time.

In order to distinguish heroin use from other drug experiences we should concentrate on its description as more 'normal' than other drugs. LSD sometimes gives rise to hallucinations, amphetamine and cocaine make one feel alert and extremely active, hash changes how reality is experienced, it makes you dizzy and if you are out and about with hash in your system you can be almost guaranteed that it will be noticed by others. But what happens when you take heroin? It seems to be harder to explain this. Some say that it's nothing special, but even so there must be something special with the sense of calm that is part of, and comes with, the rush. Heroin provides a sense of wellbeing that is reinforced when it contrasts so strongly with the action substances that are used to accentuate the experience of challenging boundaries. Other drug experiences are coupled with action, but with heroin that is unnecessary, you feel good enough as it is. When you use heroin, the boundaries become uninteresting, on the basis that if you are high, you get on so well in society, and that you get on so well is based on the fact that society, in this case, has no influence on your wellbeing. The boundaries disappear, making you feel normal.

Another effect of the high when using heroin is that you can control your thoughts and emotions, often expressed as a form of wellbeing. Steve emphasized the peace that comes with heroin:

> . . . if you've had a fight with someone or if you're really upset, or really angry or sad or anything, then the feelings just disappear. You can suppress them. It's not that they disappear completely, if you want to you can call back up again. If, for example, I feel bad about something, I can take . . . I can just put them away like in a file, but I can also take them out again and argue and feel sad as well, but I can also put them away when

I want. You can control your feelings in a way that is almost dangerous, because then
when you come down again, everything comes back at once.

It sounds like the perfect drug and therefore life-threatening; a drug that can deal
with existential anxiety and release the user from tension and stress from social
obligations. Prior to this Steve had experienced Norrköping's underworld as
stressful and difficult, but with the heroin he managed to put his business in order
and experienced existence as more simple.

This wellbeing, that you had maybe 100 things to think about, but you could relax, the
thoughts didn't spin round in your head so fast . . . it was almost something that you
needed in order to keep track of things, like a helping hand in the beginning. Then it was
easier to keep going with what you were doing, and control it, the criminal things that
we were doing. It was nearly like it helped put things in the right place, so that you
remembered things, when you should be doing something, so that not everything was
so trying, so that things were more organized.

Steve's existence in the subculture had become problematic as he spent much
of his time dealing and in that sense his life had become more like ordinary
people's lives with stress and obligations. However, with heroin he managed to
solve his problems quickly and efficiently.

Also related to emotional control was that they perceived that difficult things,
like talking about themselves, became easy, and they could, without frustration,
guilt or shame, share their life stories with one another. This also indicates that
boundaries became uninteresting – you no longer care what others think. Being
alive is so pleasant that society no longer needs to be challenged. The stoned heroin
user does not have to measure up to different types of demand he or she otherwise
would have to, like being masculine/feminine. The heroin user becomes self-
satisfied. Richard says:

So, we lay and spoke about feelings and things that we or I had never spoken about
before, like those things that guys don't talk about, no inhibitions about anything and
even so you felt fairly normal. Not like when you're drunk and sit and slur, but we could
sit there and chat about feelings. The letters I've written to Maria, and other girls as well,
I didn't think I could write like that, they're really [stops and searches for words] great,
if I say so myself.

The frustration and ambivalence that Richard otherwise experienced was blown
away, which made it possible for him to talk about emotions. He didn't need to act
and create 'now' experiences through criminal activity and violence. He could find
a way of expressing sides of him that otherwise were repressed and beyond the
definitions of what one may speak to others about. Richard no longer needed to be

'hard'. He could break away from the strictly regulated homosociality and become close to other people.

Heroin answered a need for many, enabling them to talk about their feelings with a friend. The relation between man and the substance can be compared to a therapeutic situation. If strong confidence in the therapist is created, then patients can speak relatively openly about their feelings and experiences. The therapist becomes loaded with positive symbolical associations. Heroin delivered Richard and when he speaks about heroin today, it is almost as if he is speaking of a love affair. There is a similarity here in that a love affair can be like a delivery from the routine and being bottled up, and it is also similar to the situation where patients fall in love with their therapists, or students with their teacher. The teacher and therapist symbolize a rebirth enabling the patient or student to see their life from a new perspective that opens up new possibilities. Heroin can also attain this type of significance and this is likely the reason why so many describe their relationship to heroin as like a love affair (Svensson 1996 and 2000).

The harmony and sense of wellbeing is, for many, so strong that once having experienced it, it is very difficult to forget. As Smith and Gay (1972) put it in their book-title, it's so good, don't even try it once. There is a risk that other experiences pale in comparison, and that the rest of one's life can be spent chasing similar experiences. Many later look back, with longing, to their earliest experiences, but rebirth via heroin happens only in the beginning, and then it is the contrast to the life before heroin that makes the experience complete.

The Ritual

The early experiences of heroin cannot be fully explained without paying attention to how it was framed with symbols and rituals. As Jackson-Jacobs puts it in his study of crack-smoking university students, the rituals are of major importance, even when it comes to analysing the effects (Jackson-Jacobs 2001). It is probably the combination of experiencing the physical effects of heroin and the effects that come from participating in a collective ritual that makes the experience so strong.

The heroin experience was best shared with a few friends, and without interference from disturbing influences. Furthermore, most are not particularly interested in sex, as the heroin experience in itself is sufficient. Many are no longer interested in chasing men or women in the bars, although the bars themselves can still be important for making social contact. Sometimes, other drugs are used when going out to pubs, like amphetamine, cocaine or ecstasy.

Heroin was, however, mostly a drug used in flats, a flat drug, and some even use the word 'flat sitting', which underlines the centrality of the flat in the heroin-users' world. The group is isolated from the prevalent nightlife, which in turn means a further separation from 'normal society'. John describes this process when we discuss from a time line:

> Here [around 1992–4] it was more like we took hash and grass, we were out doing things, playing football and the like. We were very active then, and when you took amphetamine or coke or ecstasy [1994–5] or something, then you went to a disco and just stood and danced all the time, if you know what I mean. And then, after, you maybe smoked a little hash and went out and sunbathed and such, took it easy. Then when you got into heroin [autumn 1995], it was just sitting around in flats all the time. Even in the summer, you can't smoke heroin outside because it's windy, so then you end up staying in all the time except when you go out to buy heroin.

The subculture was changing, and out of the hash-and-party culture a heroin-based flat culture grew up. Those who became hooked on heroin changed their movement patterns in town, and were seen less often in public (see Faupel 1991). The centrality of the flat was not only because of the effects of heroin and that preparation required a calm, draught-free environment, but also because their drug use was more and more criminal in nature, and it became important to stay out of sight of the police. A few continued to go out even after increasing heroin use, but not as often and seldom with their earlier enthusiasm – they had found something more important to think about: wellbeing. In the following text we enter the 'flat world' to try and understand 'flat sitting'.

'Flat Sitting'

> Yeah, yeah, I can swear to you that a really cosy evening for any heroin user is to sit in a nice house with a television and a sofa and everyone has enough heroin so that they're content, tinfoil, and those who inject have their tools, I mean everyone shares, and then maybe some sweets and a few films. That's a really, really cosy evening. Every heroin user would agree with this even if they might leave out a few things, just as long as they had the heroin, the sofa and the television, but that's a really great evening while other people think that it's a glass of wine and some cheese and biscuits and pleasant company . . . It is so cosy, you could say, it is fantastic to sit and talk and watch films and be that close to each other. There are different discussions and all that sort of thing. You sit and fall asleep and sometimes wake each other. That's how it is . . . (Ben)

Even heroin users in other parts of the world would probably agree in what Ben describes about the cosiness of heroin use. The word cosy is otherwise used by ordinary citizens when describing an intimate moment with someone, a moment when two people are close. We also speak about 'a cosy evening' with the family, when we are together and have different types of props and symbols that signify togetherness, for example, candles, crisps and the television. The cosy evening is one without demands, and is in sharp contrast to working hours, on the job or in school and can therefore been seen as a time-off activity, where the participants are relaxed. The word cosy signals informality, and if someone says that they are going to dress cosily, that means that he or she is going to dress in casual and comfortable clothes, like cosy leggings and an old baggy sweatshirt. These events are played out back stage where the participants can leave off the masks they otherwise wear, in order to give themselves over to easy sociability (Goffman 1959/1974). The demands society places on us to work and perform are abolished during such a time.

A little heroin is placed on foil. The powder is heated with a cigarette lighter and the heroin begins to run and emit a gas that is inhaled by the user with the help of a straw made from foil. A trace of the liquid heroin is left on the foil as shown below. Initially, it can be difficult, for example, the heroin can be overheated and go to waste, but the technique is subsequently learnt. A part of the ritual is to inhale cigarette smoke quickly after the heroin vapour. The intention is to dilate the blood vessels and to keep the heroin vapour down.

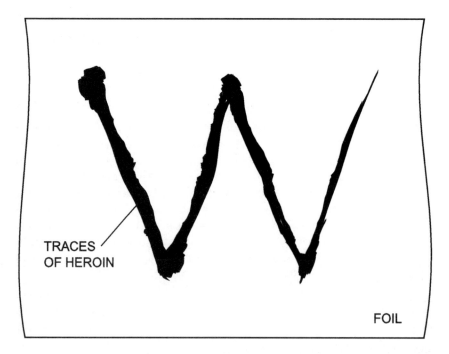

Figure 3.1 The traces of heroin. The drawing shows, roughly, what the trace of heroin looks like. The foil is folded so that the heroin can flow.

Heroin only becomes a ritual if it is given significance. In the next section I describe the frame of the ritual, in the form of preparation and the relationship to the outside, that is the world outside the ritual and against whose borders the ritual defines itself.

Preparatory Work

Many of the users describe how they collect money beforehand. Ivan talked about 'tenners' (£10), that everyone in the group put a 'tenner' in the pot and then they bought heroin with it. Ivan is now addicted to injecting heroin, but when he talks about this phase, he laughs, as if remembering something pleasant. The collecting of the money is an event that strengthens the social bond. Similar events occurred even in connection with drugs like hash and amphetamines.

Playing with the foil, that is, getting the foil ready for basing, is an important part of the ritual. Before they started smoking they might have been sitting at a table, either in the living room (or combined bedroom and living room) or in the kitchen. They prepared the foil and divided the heroin. This produces the sound of rustling foil, familiar to the heroin users, and sound is an important ingredient in many rituals. Doing things together strengthens bonds, even if those involved don't have a common history. It can be compared to doing military service, where weapon cleaning and boot polishing can strengthen social ties, or sewing circles where women meet to sew together and where they talk to each other while cutting and pinning cloth. The activity surrounding the foil gives rise to a feeling of similarity and for many it becomes almost a sport to do it as well as is possible. Peter told me that he used to dream about the foil. Now Peter is clean, but when we talk about the foil he grows nervous. He tells me that he started to feel an urge for heroin as we began talking about the foil. Peter had by this stage been off heroin for a year, but the foil as a central symbol activated a series of memories of the ritual itself.

The foil activity often started before the heroin had arrived in the flat. In these situations it was like children waiting for Santa Claus. Hardy relates: 'It was a particular process, so it was. When you sat somewhere and waited, and when someone came in, you sat beforehand and began to get your foil ready and waited. It was just like being a little kid on Christmas Eve, so it was.' A prison inmate told me that before a heroin delivery, everyone was in high spirits, they knew it was coming soon and they behaved in a way during the waiting period that is hard to describe to anyone who has not tried heroin. He, too, compared it to waiting for Christmas. When Santa Claus came, everyone was satisfied, but if he didn't, the prisoners sat in their cells, depressed and feeling duped.

The anticipation, waiting for heroin and the different types of preparation are important elements in the ritual, in a way similar to the preparation a family makes for a cosy Friday evening, when those who have been separated by work, school or day care look forward to it, and in different ways prepare themselves through buying different types of wares symbolic of togetherness, like crisps, alcohol and lemonade. Part of the flat, mostly the living room, has also often been designed in such a way that the 'cosiness' can occur; the sofa, the armchairs and the table where the wares can be placed. The waiting and the preparation energize the ritual, and the symbolic wares make it more reasonable to believe in what the ritual conveys.

Basing and Framing

When the heroin arrives the common actions commence, the dividing of the heroin and placing it on the foils in order – soon, soon, soon – to inhale the vapour and chase the dragon with a foil straw. For many of the users it was a case of sharing the foil and taking every second 'line' or 'row'. In this way the foil was sent around among the participants in a way similar to the hash pipes wandering among the collective. This is not dissimilar to the activity of round buying in a pub – the collective's members are forged together and a common experience is created.

After some 'trickles', 'rows' or 'lines', they become high or in their own terminology 'beautiful'. The word is probably the one most frequently used by the Norrköping heroin users. I remember myself, when I was younger, how people used to say they were 'beautiful', which could mean drunk. 'Grann', the Swedish word, actually means beautiful or attractive. The word as used probably means beautiful aimed at a state of mind, but not in the original sense, but more that one is 'gone', hazy or muddled in mind. It is similar to how the words 'twisted' or 'sprained' indicate that something is happening with comprehension.

Television is a central element in almost all stories about the collective smoking heroin, or basing. In many groups the heroin experience was prepared for by buying sweets, lemonade and, not least, heroin. In most cases, video films were also hired. The formula: TV + sofa + sweets + lemonade, provides associations of a normal TV evening, and a normal person would recognize himself even if the lemonade for the adults was exchanged for alcohol or tea. Of course, adding heroin to the formula would change the associations to something else. However, in various ways it seems that the model for the ritual is derived from the Western weekend culture, which, since the 1950s, includes a more and more frequent incidence of TV-watching, and where television, which was initially a status symbol (of modernity and progress) for those who wished to display that they were modern and wealthy has become a symbol for the masses, a symbol of intimacy and family existence. The heroin users are not different from others in this sense; they like to get cosy together.

The cosy evenings with heroin, just like cosy evenings in general, are described by most of the users as calm and harmonious occasions. The emphasis is not on contributing anything, but rather on merely being. The television watching is mostly about receiving and that is also in keeping with the drug's characteristics. With the help of the drug they relax and with the television on they do not need to react to any great extent.

The Secret Cave

On a number of occasions I was invited to the basing sessions. As I described in the introduction to this chapter, I was never given an address, but rather had to meet someone who was going to be there and he showed me later how to get there and also became my 'gatekeeper' on these occasions. On the way there we might sometimes stop at shops and video rental outlets to buy the props necessary to 'set the scene' for the cosy ritual. They often asked me to stop in the vicinity of some flat, left the car and came back after five or ten minutes. The activity was surrounded by secrecy – it was an activity beyond the established culture's boundaries of respectability, and as such had to be protected from the outside, and above all the rule enforcers' sight (in this case the police).

Sometimes one of the participants in the ritual would listen in the stairwell for the sound of possible police. If the doorbell rang, they were extremely cautious. John says: 'Yes, that caution is there all the time – to always lock the door when we come in and when the doorbell rings, to always check the peephole. That feeling of caution is always there.' The experience of enclosure is probably all the greater because of the secrecy, a feeling that the events that happen within the flat's walls are very far from what happens in society in general. Initially many of the drug users had ordinary jobs or studied, and in this sense lived a somewhat Dr Jekyll and Mr Hyde-type existence. The split increases the pleasure and the sense of secrecy that is integral to the flat experience. The contrast between working life and the flat life could be staggering. Most of those who spoke of the initial stages of heroin use mention this secrecy as an important aspect. The classical sociologist Simmel writes: 'The secret offers, so to speak, the possibility of a second world alongside the manifest world . . .' (1950: 330).

The flat with the friends was almost like a cave, which symbolizes the exit from society and the entrance to another social situation and reality, where together they could create the illusion of a problem-free existence and where they could become closer to each other.

The Dangerous, Safe Heroin

This chapter has discussed how brown heroin became a success on the market, making some people very wealthy while others became addicted. This was made possible because of a sociocultural preparation taking place in different informal groups. The process through which heroin was prepared for use is summarized in Figure 3.2.

However, even if the death threat paled somewhat, enough that some dared approach heroin, it did not completely disappear, and if it had, the drug would have lost some of its energy or magic. Death gives rise to serious angst for modern man, who is continually seeking explanations and who, when they cannot be found, experiences serious existential angst.

Death is taboo, while at the same time it is fascinating. In rock music symbols such as the skull and crossbones and black, the colour of death, are frequently used, and within sports there are competitions that are seen as extra interesting just because they are connected to death and thereby excitement. Formula one motor racing is one such competition, where death is an ever-present possibility and the mass media throng to cover the eternal battle against death. Climbing Mount Everest derives its popularity and charge/energy from the fact that it is about death and conquering death. In this sense, these activities have an extra charge precisely because they are associated with death. Maybe it is because these activities, which occur in the margins of society, involve defeating death. They so clearly dramatize the boundary between structure and chaos, and the boundary between life and death is the most dramatic that there is. Death is modern society's antithesis and, because of that, it is fascinating. As Bauman writes:

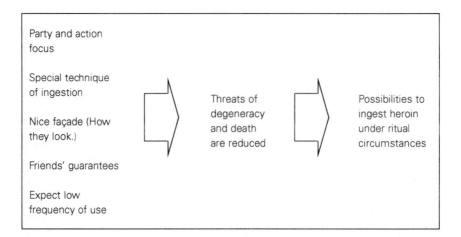

Figure 3.2 Reducing the threat of heroin.

Death is the absolute *other* of being, an *unimaginable* other, hovering beyond the reach of communication; whenever being speaks of that other, it finds itself speaking, through a negative metaphor, of itself . . . death is not like other 'others' – those others which the ego is free to fill with meaning, and in this meaning-bestowing act to constitute and to subordinate. (Bauman 1992: 2)

Other 'others' can be persons or phenomena that act in ways different from those we are used to, and that through their existence wake our feelings of ambivalence. However, we can sort them in pigeonholes, subordinate them, or, quite simply, sweep them under the carpet, and pretend they don't exist. Death, however, cannot be merely ignored and neither can we answer the question of what death is. It becomes, therefore, the strongest symbol of non-structure or chaos and can be said to be outside society in that it is impossible to understand. It also becomes an aspect of the most absolute border we can imagine; the border between life and death, where life and death represent each other's absolute opposites.

Situations that occur near these absolute borders, or where there is the feeling of approaching one of those borders, become especially dramatic – more so than those described in the previous chapter. It is similar to gambling, but with very high stakes. We are approaching Russian roulette, even if we're not quite there. In Russian roulette the starting odds are usually death 1: continued life 5. With heroin the play isn't with these high stakes; it is enough to know that death is somewhere in the neighbourhood, and the game receives its character and stands out against all other activities. Objects connected to death provide a charge.

However, those who partake in the formula one circuits or who climb Mount Everest are, of course, not kamikaze pilots offering their lives to a higher cause. In formula one racing, there are numerous safety precautions, as well as any number of technical innovations designed to increase safety. For the young heroin users it was a matter of group danger, and they were equipped with rituals and expectations. They had, furthermore, in most cases of first usage, a mentor with them. Trying heroin was mainly about creating an extraordinary experience, but even so the experience was described as more 'normal' than other drug experiences. It was also a kind of rebirth where they could talk about themselves in a way they had never previously done. The tough and jargon-based hard attitude changes in a second to intimacy and closeness. It is my opinion that the drug made it possible for them to see themselves in an analytical fashion, where their social aspect was removed from themselves as subjects. In this sense they could see their past as if on film and they could therefore talk about it without having to take full responsibility in relating it to themselves.

However, the experience can only be completely understood by examining the ritual. This was, to a great extent, a copy of the post-modern Western home, where the family has become a small media-consuming unit, whose members experience togetherness when they are all looking in the same direction, that is, at the television. This togetherness produces a time out from daily life in general. The time out is characterized more and more by symbols of this different (but ordinary) social order. Crisp packets, lemonade, and alcohol are increasingly the symbols that contribute to reconstructing the interpretation of the situation as a cosy moment. It was much the same among the young heroin users, except that they switched the alcohol for heroin and thereby attained an exclusivity and secrecy that is difficult to reach through alcohol. The cosy moment was a secret moment where the participants were bound together by doing something illegal together and which they also saw as contributing to a link with death. Existence was like being in a cave in society to which no others had access, only those who were a part of the collective. The heroin ritual became a way to create a harmonious family and in that sense the illusion of a society without opposition, where every person can act without living up to different types of roles and expectations. The heroin ritual also has an element of rebirth from societal ties and the creation of strong bonds of togetherness, which would later be sorely tested.

I finished the previous chapter by quoting Bauman on culture pertaining to transcendence but also the destruction and widening of boundaries. Bauman writes, just prior to that quotation, that Durkheim's 'anomic suicide' occurs when culture stops being tempting and seductive. The anomic suicide pertains to the consequences of a society that cannot give its members satisfactory lives, it is a consequence of existential analysis that concludes negatively. Instead of committing suicide a culture is created that has its own boundaries, its own symbolism, its own time concepts, etc. Many choose to live in the present in order to not think about society at all. Action, as described in the former chapter, is a way of creating an environment where one doesn't need to feel imprisoned and disciplined. One of the points of this chapter is that the heroin experience and ritual make it possible to believe that it is pleasant to live in society, when the connection between subject and society ceases to matter. Society has no longer any power, then man is free. Suicide is completely uninteresting to anyone high on heroin.

-4-

The Threats That Divide and Unite

Heroin, it's my life, it's my wife

'Heroin' by Velvet Underground, 1967

John and the Injection

I'm to fetch John in town, and then we're going home to his place. He lives on the outskirts of Norrköping. When I speak to him by phone, a few hours before our planned meeting, I can hear that he's using again. I thought that he'd been clean for a good while, but that isn't the case and by now I have learned to interpret and discover the signs that disclose whether someone is 'on' or 'off'. Among other things, I hear that he is more tense than usual, and that means that he's back on the 'chase' again. I meet him and he jumps into the car. We exchange greetings. I have an errand at the off-licence, but John stays in the car.

I have met him many times and trust him, but when I come back there are two young men in their twenties in the car. I hesitate about getting in and signal John to ask if it's okay if I get into the car. He waves me in and I shake hands with the guys in the backseat. They are dressed the way young people usually are, jeans and short jackets, no obvious style markers like reggae signs or turned-back baseball caps, but they are pale, paler than normal for the time of year (autumn), and that is a sign that they spend time indoors or have late night habits. They greet me politely but are otherwise rather quiet, particularly the taller of the two. It is a little uncomfortable for me, having two strangers in the backseat. I understand, however, from the conversation, that they are old friends of John.

They ask me to drive them to the southern part of Norrköping. We set off, they talk a little, and I drive. We come to a parking spot where I am asked to stop. One of the guys, the taller one, hops out of the car and we wait for perhaps five minutes until he comes back and gets back in again. Before he gets out, John says 'Don't tell who you came with.' When he comes back, they ask me to drive to Eneby, an area on the outskirts of Norrköping. I drive there and we drop off the two guys, who now seem to be in a hurry. John and I head back to his flat, for coffee and to do the interview.

When we get out of the car, John is in a hurry. He walks quickly towards the flat. I have forgotten my phone in the car and tell him I have to go back and fetch it. He says 'Okay, but you can find your way to the flat, right?' He is really in a hurry. When I arrive at the flat a few minutes later all his equipment is laid out beside the cooker. A spoon, tartaric acid (citric acid and ascorbic acid can also be used), heroin, a filter, a syringe, kitchen paper, a cuff and scissors; everything needed for a fix is there. A few minutes later, John is ready, has a small amount of blood in the syringe, and, relatively slowly, begins to inject the brown substance. To an outside observer the heroin doesn't seem to have much of an effect and I realize that he has not taken a particularly large dose, perhaps out of consideration for me. He becomes calm and the interview can begin. I have to make the coffee for us, even though we are in his apartment. Ever since I picked him up, John has been completely intent on the heroin.

John is one of Norrköping's first heroin users. Since 1995 he has been using heroin, on and off. In the past year, he has made several serious attempts to stop. John is, like most of the others I have interviewed, very pleasant to talk to. They are mostly calm and soft spoken, which can have to do with them being on something, but also with the specific drifter's attitude; to take it easy and not get worked up. John's flat, like many of the other users', is in good condition (there, are of course, exceptions). It looks more or less like a student flat; it displays a form of compact living, what's necessary is there: sofa, table, music centre, and so forth. He is, at the moment, working and paying his bills. Few around him know what he is actually doing – only me and his friends who use. The situation with John describes an event that is fairly typical among Norrköping's young heroin users who have intensified their heroin habits.

Group and Grid

In this chapter I analyse how the culture is affected by two facts: (1) more of the subculture's members are increasing their heroin use; (2) the control of heroin use and distribution is seen as a big problem in Norrköping, and established society's attempts to control the subculture are intensifying.[1] It is a threat, from both within and without.

The threat from within is about a commodity becoming so exclusive and so attractive that the demand for it, in relation to its exclusivity, calls the social bonds created in the culture into question. Solidarity and the internal order can become a problem. Douglas (1970) considers that every culture needs an 'internal order', that the participants in the culture follow rules that mean they can trust each other and their system. She calls this internal order a 'grid', which determines how the participants within the subculture are expected to interact with each other, the norms that regulate relationships and hierarchy within the system. When the grid is weakened, the participants may follow their own norms and impulses when interacting with other members of the subculture. When heroin becomes extremely exclusive, this grid is threatened as the need for the substance induces selfishness. What was described in the previous two chapters as almost a social game or pastime (albeit for high stakes) is transformed and becomes an individual serious business, which threatens the group's intersubjective transcendence. The culture created with the help of drugs with the purpose of enlarging its freedom and experiencing the charge created by transgressing boundaries has become less pleasant to live in.

The threat from outside is primarily about established society's representatives, the police who use all possible means to prevent the ingestion and sale of illegal substances. Society's rule enforcers attempt to uncover the subculture's activities and, thus, influence the shaping of the culture and the ritual activities engaged in by the subculture. According to Douglas (1970), every culture is composed of a 'group', with boundaries, formed against outside threats. As the subculture is highly illegitimate, it is also separated from society and the boundaries are pronounced in comparison to other groups' boundaries. For the young heroin users it is a matter of plain-clothes police, rule enforcers dressed like 'ordinary' people, who dedicate themselves to apprehending those who partake in the subculture. The heroin users' group is therefore concerned with how to handle the threat from outside. The most serious threat is the drug squad, who try to force the heroin users' boundaries from without and who attempt to gain 'inopportune intrusion' to the back regions of the subculture. Goffman defines this as the situation where a member of the public (in this case a rule enforcer) goes behind the scene in order to: '. . . catch those present *flagrante delicto*. Though no one's intention, the persons present in the region may find that they have patently been witnessed in activity that is quite incompatible with the impression that they are, for wider social reasons, under obligation to maintain to the intruder' (1959/1974: 204). The second part of this chapter deals with how the culture is formed in answer to this threat of inopportune intrusion.

The Heroin Mind

The basing could initially occupy many hours, and later several days, and in the beginning occurred mostly at the weekend. However, this concentration on the weekend was, for those who became hooked on heroin, a transitory stage. As the young people became more dependent, their use of heroin spread out in step, from Friday/Saturday usage, to one encompassing all the days of the week. Most became quickly aware that heroin was not a party drug. Party drugs were amphetamine, ecstasy and cocaine, and by using them as party drugs the consumer was also partly protected from developing a too-prevalent drug usage. Heroin, on the other hand, does not have that inbuilt protection. After a while, the young people gave up going out when they were high, so that it lost whatever aura it had had as a party drug. Heroin became for many an everyday drug that, in contrast to amphetamine, ecstasy and cocaine, should preferably be used in the flat more or less any time of the day or week. The drug use was, thereby, freed from the constraints of specific times and places and more and more of the users' activities began to centre round the obtaining and intake of heroin.

The accounts of progression from weekend use to daily use are many and it often seemed to be a question of having a little heroin left over from the weekend and wanting to feel 'beautiful' even on Sunday and Monday. If we compare the heroin experience to a rebirth, in which the subject is 'freed' from society, then this increased use becomes understandable. The majority of those who begin to use heroin do not think that they are on the road to addiction; they mostly see Monday usage as an exception, rather than the rule. They are not completely lacking in respect for the drug. They know they can become addicted, but they live for quite some time in the belief that they are not 'hooked' on heroin.

They gradually approach a state of intensive misuse, or addiction, from an earlier state of using experimentally, recreationally and in a relatively controlled manner. Moreover, they are initially less tolerant to the drug, which means they get by on a very low daily dose. A bag for between approximately £20 and £25 might last for two days, which implies a cost of about £65 a week. A night of heroin is initially cheaper than a night at the pub and, of course, in the beginning at least, more exciting and secretive.

When the need increases the heroin user's way of perceiving the world changes. It becomes reasonable to talk about the 'heroin mind'. Increasingly, existence centres on heroin and the different ways of providing economically for it. They become addicts in the full sense of the word. Their daily life becomes dominated by thoughts of heroin, highs and lows, and obtaining it. The quotation that prefaces this chapter was used by one of the young users and when it comes to the second part, 'it's my wife', it is very apt, but only for those who never (or almost never) stop thinking about their wives. The first part is truer, 'it's my life.'

Time perspectives, for those who are heavily dependent on heroin and who live at the bag level, are short and focused on one thing; heroin. To 'live at bag level' means never earning much money and having a very short-term drug plan. Furthermore, the bag user is dependent on the dealers and must maintain a good relationship with them (cf. Faupel 1991). The dealers at street level represent a step up in the hierarchy. Enrique, a dealer and a user, describes his customers who live at the bag level and who therefore need to come to an agreement with their dealer:

I never need to go round and pawn things or do break-ins in order to have heroin. There were some customers who could come with a stereo or a mobile or a camera or maybe a leather jacket and say, 'Can I pawn this until tomorrow?', or sometimes they came with a welfare cheque, when they'd got some help from social services, but they couldn't cash it for two days or something, so they'd leave the cheque instead, and I'd think 'Yeah well, he'll have the money, then.' So they'd leave the cheque for . . . say they were to get £200, well maybe they'd pawn it for 100, 'you get 100 worth of horse', then when they'd come to get the cheque you followed them to cash it and that way got your money directly.

Those who come to Enrique live at 'bag level' and every day is about getting the resources to buy heroin. Enrique, on the other hand, has continuous access and does not need to ring dealers, go shoplifting or steal from friends. There is often a tension-filled relationship between these two positions, of dealer and bag-buyer, characterized by mutual dependency, but, nevertheless, the bag-buyers must subordinate themselves, though only to a certain point, which I deal with later.

Only that aspect of the world that, in one way or another, relates to heroin is of interest to the bag-buyer and the heroin-using dealer. For the bag-buyer the hunt for heroin is more desperately expressed, as those concerned, in contrast to the dealer, are often out of heroin and are in forced withdrawal. Friends are interesting if they have something to do with heroin and objects are interesting if they can be traded for heroin. This is an aspect of the 'heroin mind'. A user on his way through town sees things other than those seen by, say, a non-using secondary school student. The heroin users see the drug squad/police where others wouldn't notice them, drug abusers that others wouldn't notice, public toilets (where heroin can be taken) and opportunities for theft (for example by studying shops' alarm systems). Many users see goods in shops as if marked in bag prices, suggesting that heroin has become the real hard currency in the subculture. When a user is going away for a while he or she doesn't just need to pack a suitcase; a drug plan is also needed. It is the same situation when the heroin user is going to associate with people who are not involved with heroin for longer periods of time, like, for example, during the holidays.

One guy described life at street level like this: 'The only thing that means anything is getting a hit.' After anything from a couple of weeks to a year or two, many of the users start needing fairly large doses. Most experience that they no longer get any great effect from using the drug; they no longer use it to become 'beautiful' and they just take it to stay 'well', or 'normal'. Some use a gram a day, others a half gram. When the dosage increases it becomes all the more difficult to support themselves in a way that is in accordance with the subculture's moral code.

The Subculture's Economy

Much of the young users' existence is about getting the means that can be bartered for the subculture's brown gold. As heroin is so expensive and as the users develop a strong need for it, 'grafting' becomes an important aspect of the young heroin users' daily life. Max says: 'Grafting is getting money in some way. Everybody grafts in his or her own way. Some steal, some do other things. But grafting is above all making it go round, so that you can get drugs without having to con someone.'

The word 'graft' (Swedish – *drifta*) is a rather old slang expression from the criminal world and means getting money for use on drugs. A hard grafter is someone who is good at providing for himself. Many of the expressions used come from an earlier generation of drug addicts. Grafting refers to what in an economic system is called production, whereas the drug use could be called consumption. As drugs are illegal, they are also expensive. The dealers add on what could be called a risk charge. If the subculture is to survive then it is necessary that at least as much is produced as is consumed, or the economy will not function. To graft is the subculture's answer to work, and can be described in terms of several different aspects.

1. Sale of drugs. A certain number of users have good contacts further up the sales hierarchy, which means that they can buy smaller amounts on 'tick' or approval. This means that they might, for example, buy 10 g on credit at £80 per gram and then divide it into 0.2 g bags, which they sell at £40 per bag. So they make, if you don't count costs and wastage, £120 per gram. They can, therefore, calculate how much they need to sell and how much they can use themselves. However, not everyone can sell, or there would be no buyers. Those who squeal/inform the police, or who in any other way have abused a trust, by, for example, using up drugs that were meant for sale, have lessened their chances of being trusted. For those, there are several other alternatives. Most of the users I spoke to, however, have experience of peddling. This way of grafting will be further explored later in this chapter and even in the next, as it is a central aspect of the subculture.

2. 'Running' for others. If someone has the kind of contacts with dealers that other, less well-initiated users, lack, then those concerned can 'run' for them, that is, collect the drugs for them and get some for themselves in payment. For newly recruited users, it can at times be hard to get hold of heroin, as they have not yet established themselves as reliable customers, and there is often a worry that a new client could 'squeal' to the police. 'Newbies'/beginners, are, in the meantime, at risk of being duped, as the runner may give less money to the dealer than he charges the beginners. The runner might also tamper with the bags, so that 0.2 g

become 0.15 g, or alternatively, cut the heroin. Beginners are dependent on the runner, as they have not yet developed their own dealer contacts.

3. Stealing, shoplifting, fencing. Some users steal clothes or other goods that command a value. Sometimes they try to sell the goods for money, or otherwise they may do jobs on order from the dealer. If the dealer wants a stereo he can, together with the customer, pick out the one he wants. Crispin, a small-scale dealer, explains how it is done: 'They go to someone who has the stuff and say, "Four pairs of Levis, you can have them for £10 a pair, can I have a bag for four pairs?" They maybe already knew what size you took, so they stole four pairs in your size and came here with them.' The price is always a lot lower than that of the shop.

If we see the subculture as an economic system, then only grafting as described in point 3, theft, brings in resources from the outside – it generates capital, while dealers and runners take from the resources already within the system. Naturally, even legal sources of finance are used: wages, social security payments, inheritances and loans, among others. Thefts and legally obtained resources accordingly finance the subculture, and are of major importance because the culture cannot finance itself.

The bag-buyers are the subculture's working class; their work does not generate much profit for them, but rather for those who are at the top of the sales hierarchy. They work hard, but without a monthly shift roster, job description, health insurance or union representation. Every day they need to earn enough to pay for the daily dose, and also preferably the next morning's consumption as well. Their life structure involves good days with enough amounts of heroin, and bad days, with a shortage.

Those who sell on a small scale are the subculture's small businessmen; they take deliveries from those higher up and then supply the bag-buyers. The majority involved in buying and selling on know that this isn't easy living, as every occasion involves a test – the books have to balance and preferably show profit.

Economizing

Veronica is twenty-three and looks more worn than others I have met. The stereotypical picture of the worn-out addict is not far off. I only managed to meet her twice before contact was broken. She resembles Faupel's description of a street junkie:

> . . . low availability and diminished life structure most closely approximates the stereotyped image that most people have of heroin addicts: that of down-and-out junkies who

are desperate for drugs they do not have the means to obtain. The street-junkie career phase also most closely resembles the image of the pathetically unkempt addict, unable to maintain even the most rudimentary hygienic standard. (1991: 111)

Veronica's life is chaotic when I meet her. I interview her in her room, in her parents' house. She is restless during the interview and I understand why, after a while. She is beginning to withdraw and has very little heroin left. I ask her if we can keep going until four o'clock and she says 'Eh, yes . . . but.' I then ask how often she needs to take heroin and she tells me that she must visit her grandmother at four and 'how am I going to manage to get in a smoke in between?' (She laughs.) She asks if she can smoke during the interview and I do not prevent her. When she smokes the heroin I notice that the foil pipe is straightened out, and then that smoked with a new foil pipe. This is repeated three times. Actually, most users do 'smoke the pipe' as well, but to do it so often is a sign of lean resources. Her parents do not know that she uses heroin. The reason she smokes heroin is that her veins are in such bad condition that she can no longer inject. As we are getting into the car, I notice she has two plastic bags with electronic equipment in them. It later turned out that she has stolen them from her parents' place of business, something she was later officially accused of. Her parents also threatened to accuse me formally as an accomplice, for transporting the goods.

Smoking the pipe is an 'economizing strategy'. If tea were as valuable it would be like using the same teabag several times. To 'smoke the pipe' is a way of decreasing outlay. There are several different measures, which the users teach each other. Another economy measure is to save the filters that heroin is drawn through before injecting it. Heroin that can be reused collects in these filters. It's like saving old tea bags. Another measure is to take rohypnol before taking heroin. This is believed to increase the effect; that is, one feels 'beautiful' without having to use so much heroin. Yet another method is to stop smoking or basing, and to inject the heroin instead. This, initially at least, means that not so much heroin need be used; it is a more efficient use of the resource. The effect is more tangible, and happens faster, so it is not merely a method of economizing, but also a consequence of the subculture's logic – to seek out new transgressive experiences.

The subculture is a supply-based system, and, like other such systems, does not always manage economically. The bag-buyers have a very tight budget, which becomes especially difficult, as their lives are dependent on whether they can find extra resources when their need for heroin has become so strong. Under these circumstances, a type of activity that threatens the subculture's norms and the bonds between its members can develop. The activities to be described in the following passage are not labelled grafting, which underlines their status as definitely dishonourable activities.

Social Cracks and Lack of Trust

> It happens a lot that people stick together – two who help each other and smoke together, carry on together, hang out. And that kind of thing always ends up with not being friends in some way. So, I'm more of a loner, I move round a bit, because I don't want any special friend or clique that I smoke with; it always ends with trouble. (Ben)

The quote above describes a tendency in the subculture – how the individual, after a while, becomes more and more solitary. This aloneness can mostly be attributed to the relationship between the subculture's economy and the development of heroin mind. The bag-buyers' income is not always sufficient, which means they abandon the informal rule system (the grid) that otherwise regulates relationships within the subculture. This type of breakdown in trust develops in the subculture when heroin becomes so scarce, and the need for it is so strong, that individual members of the subculture find it hard to keep the culture's norms. Social cracks occur, as a consequence of a breakdown in trust. Peter and I discussed freeloading:

> *Peter*: I've always hung with those who have, it's always been that way.
> *Philip*: Yes . . .
> *Peter*: Because, in order to someway . . . yeah [breaks off] . . . well, borrow, then.
> *Philip*: Do you think you could change who you hang around with, if you noticed they didn't have anything left?
> *Peter*: Then they're not in my world. They don't exist anymore.
> *Philip*: So you can change who your friends are?
> *Peter*: Yeah, sure.
> *Philip*: But you're pleasant until they run out?
> *Peter*: Yes of course I'm the salt of the earth . . . yeah, of course.

It is not directly apparent from the outset that the freeloader is out after heroin, as he (or she) pretends to really like the other person, but in reality, it is a matter of a 'game', which is about 'milking' the other person's resources. When they dry up, a new possible supplier is sought out. Freeloading or sponging does not contribute to the subculture's means of support and the sponger is viewed as a 'stingy bastard', a parasite. The subculture's relationship to the sponger is similar to modern society's emphasis on good behaviour; doing the right thing, having a job, not burdening the system. Going round exploiting others' generosity does not contribute. However, a few of those I have interviewed have made just this a speciality, and this calls into question the idea of trust between the subculture's members. It is honourable to play a role in front of the police or social services in order to avoid house searches or to save other members. To con 'one of their own', however, is a breach of norms, and is associated with low status within the subculture.

'Dirty tricks.' Stealing from friends is even less well thought of than sponging. It can happen that someone is asked by friends to fetch heroin, but that the person puts a little aside for his or her own use. It may also be less subtle: someone simply takes money or heroin from some friend. Most are aware that this happens, and that they may even be duped by someone close to them.

> Heroin changes people's personality so much, so some can play dirty just for pure profit. You might ask someone 'Can you go and buy for me?' 'Yeah, sure', and he takes some out, just to make on it, even though you were going to treat him, like. Those kinds of things, they lead to you losing contact, you get so pissed off with them. I think it's really lousy behaviour. (John)

Another way of being 'dirty' is simply not to pay the dealer. Hanna, a using dealer, told me that it has become 'more usual' that people simply 'misbehave': 'Those others from that group, they really carry on, they do. They are a really lousy bunch. They promise on their honour, like on their mother's graves, that they'll pay the next day, and then they just don't give a shit about it.'

Squealing and snitching. Hanna, like other street dealers, thinks that the sub-culture is becoming disruptive, that people are not bothering to pay, 'are squealing about this and that', and 'snitching' on each other. When the group splits, former friends may start 'talking shit' about each other, which makes the split all the more tangible. As they have used lots of drugs together, they have also been close and have a lot of information on each other.

They do not completely think it through, that it's the need for heroin that makes people under pressure abandon the subculture's norms, but rather blame it on the individual who is seen as unable to behave properly. To be hooked on heroin is, therefore, not a mitigating factor. It is more like, as one dealer, Steve, said to me, 'If you can't do the time, don't do the crime.' A tough logic rules, where few feel sorry for someone who in whatever way has not behaved himself. If someone gets 'beaten up' after having 'filched' what they were meant to sell, there are few tears shed.

As the need for heroin is so strong, and as not everyone is equally good at grafting, envy occurs, which can jeopardize earlier friendships. A guy who sold heroin told me that he no longer had much contact with his older friends because they were envious, and, in that sense, dangerous to have anything much to do with. The envious can 'squeal' to others, and sometimes even to the police.

To live in a world where people associate with each other, not primarily because they like each other, but in order to take advantage, and where one is continually at risk of being duped or 'ratted out', is presumably mentally difficult. The user is not liked for who he or she is, but rather for his or her resources. This makes the heroin user's world difficult to live in. To be drawn into this game, in order to survive, must also be difficult to take – to become a person that one doesn't want to be. The world is not, however, always experienced as full of betrayal; they often meet people they can become close to. But in comparison to the initial, or early stages, it is much more like this than otherwise.

Heroin develops from a collective project into an individual one (Svensson 1996 and 2000). This process is reinforced by the fact that the heroin ritual described in the previous chapter loses much of its social base. The foil could be shared, but most of the syringes are not, because of HIV and hepatitis risks. Others do not wish to share, because there is a risk that there will thereby be less for them. Life becomes less pleasant and the social bonds are threatened, but because they are so deeply into it, so engaged in grafting, it is not at all certain that they recognize just how unpleasant the life actually is. When they have lived in the subculture for a number of years, many feel that no matter how treacherous it is, this is where their friends are. Those who have left the subculture can see the treachery and the social cracks much more clearly than those who are still part-icipating. When they are involved, they often lack the necessary distance to analyse the social bonds.

The dealers experience the breakdown in trust very clearly. In this sense, the subculture is like 'ordinary society', where the older generation complain about the younger generation's ideas and manners and believe that morality is in danger (cf. Cohen 1976/1992). Those who infringe against the given order threaten the culture and in order to handle these threats, reprisals are created which can be used when the transgression is serious. In ordinary society, prisons and other closed insti-tutions and establishments perform this function. In the subculture you may be beaten up, not allowed to buy anymore, or be labelled a 'rat', a 'tightwad' or a 'snitch', who cannot be trusted. The subculture has its own rule enforcers to protect what passes as normality within it. The character of the crime and that of the punisher and the probability of retribution determine the punishment.

Imprisoned in the Flat

I am about to give Max a lift from one flat to another. One flat is on the north side of town, the other on the west. The distance between the two is roughly two kilometres, a reasonable stretch to walk. However, as I have a car, Max deems it suitable that I drive him. He even seems to think it would be safer. Before Max leaves the flat he listens for sound in the stairwell, and checks the peephole. He then decides to leave the flat. However, before he goes out into the street he looks to the left quickly and then to the right. We walk briskly to my car, which is parked some twenty metres from the entrance. When I have started the car and am about to drive out from the parking place, another car slows to a crawl, and two men look into our car. I say spontaneously, as I have by this stage taken on some of the heroin users' way of thinking, 'That was the drug squad!' 'Yes, it was, eh?' says Max, and both he and I become nervous. The presumed drug squad car drives off and Max [and I] breathe out. He then asks me not to drive out on to the main road immediately but to circle the block; I follow his directions. Afterwards, we drive through Norrköping's centre towards the other flat. He wants to be let out a little before we get there so that he can walk in through the yard. This way, he thinks he will be all right if the drug squad is waiting by the entrance.

I met Max many times, and when he was most occupied with dealing he would want me to drive him to the town centre, perhaps to buy a hamburger or to meet someone, when he could easily have walked there in under five minutes. He has since then stopped both dealing in and using heroin, and we can now meet and go round town, talking about everything under the sun, without him looking nervously over his shoulder the whole time.

The example above illustrates an important aspect of the subculture; the misanthropic character and the different types of strategies used in order to avoid capture by the police. Walking down the city streets is unproblematic for most of us who do not belong to the subculture. We can go out and shop, eat lunch, meet friends, go to art exhibitions and so on. When we are in town, we have for the most part a basic sense of trust, that nothing terrible will happen us, that we won't be attacked and that it won't start raining roof tiles on our heads.

Participants in the subculture have another view of the town. Being seen on the street means risking being taken by the drug squad for some, and for others that they may be seen by someone they've 'messed with' with in some way or another. They may also be scared of meeting someone like, for example, a social worker or a relative if they are high. Their own flat is the only halfway safe place in their environment, and the expression, 'my home is my castle' is apt especially for the young users who are involved in supplying and selling heroin or other drugs. The streets, on the other hand, are enemy territory where the drug squad lies in wait.

In this section, the alertness the subculture shows towards threats from without is described and analysed. Specifically the focus is on aspects of the subculture that are a direct consequence of the heroin users being followed by the rule enforcers, who are mostly dressed like ordinary people, drive ordinary cars and even appear on bicycles. Modern society tries through laws, prisons and institutions to deal with the problem of prohibited boundary transgressions by placing the members of the subculture in areas where they cannot transgress any boundaries. Roger, for instance, told me that four of his best friends are either in prison or have been placed in compulsory care. The majority of those to whom I spoke have experience of the police and have been arrested, and some of them have been held in custody. These experiences have contributed to building up the subculture as a protection from the outside. There are three main aspects to this protection, which I will give an account of.

1. Knowledge of the primary threat, that is, the police.
2. Strategies for preventing the police from gaining the upper hand. These include the formulation of a special language and the use of mobile phones as means of communication.
3. Desirable character traits. In order to deal with the rule enforcers the subculture members need to develop and live up to a certain type of character in order to keep their secrets secret. The persons who develop these competences will succeed in the subculture with a more or less permanent supply.

Information on the Drug Squad

Steve, a dealer and a stable addict, told me that he sometimes experiences his existence in the subculture as a game of chess between him and the drug squad. Another informant compared ordinary people to extras, with the subculture's members and modern society's rule enforcers as the actors. In sport, at least at the elite level, it is usual to learn about the opponents' tactics and develop strategies for one's own team's advantage. In order to avoid being unnecessarily caught the users need to know a fair bit about the police and the law, which becomes especially important when the police who are after them are plain clothed. Roger has the following to say:

> They drive Volvos a lot; they have the most ordinary cars around, ordinary family cars so that they can blend in well. I know most of the registration numbers. I can rattle off, maybe eight, nine, ten reg numbers, when I see the plates – I don't now, but before I used to check the registration on every single car. [He laughs.] Paranoia!

The heroin users use this knowledge to continually scan the surroundings, to see if there are any signs of danger. This is very clearly underlined in the following quote from Steve:

> And you have to check the whole time; 'What kind of car is that?' and you have to check out what kind of people you're meeting. Even if you don't have anything [drugs] on you, you have to know if they're keeping tabs on you right then, wherever you're going. If I go down to the kiosk, for example, it would be like that I look round, look at what cars are in the car park, because you recognize them, even if it's the drug squad's cars, you know the registrations, and then you check them. You can go towards the kiosk, check to see if there are any cars in places where there aren't usually, look at the parking places to see if there are any special cars there, you look around the whole time. It becomes a habit, to . . . all the time, that you . . . Yeah, you worry all the time, even if you haven't anything on you, it's like you're thinking about it the whole time.

I was out walking several times with Steve and could thereby notice how he checked his surroundings. Steve is a rung below the top level, and delivers to flats, and, thus, is in direct contact with the customers. To detect danger in time can mean that he manages to get rid of the heroin he has with him. However, Swedish law also states that it is illegal to have heroin in your system. Therefore, heroin users are also illegal in themselves and can be arrested on the streets whenever they are seen. This is extra problematic for Steve, as he also sells, and if he is caught and tested positive for heroin, a house search almost automatically ensues. Another useful skill in the subculture is knowledge of the difference between serious and milder narcotic crimes, and different possible penalties. It is also important to know what methods the police use and what technical equipment they have for listening in, and so forth. This type of knowledge can be used to form strategies. Steve says:

> They [the police] can sit and listen to what we are talking about right now, through the telephone. They can activate it. If we sit here and talk and the battery is in, they have the kind of things that can activate the loudspeaker in the phone, even though we aren't speaking on it, only they activate the speaker in the phone. And they can even sit up there with a directional microphone aimed at the window, and through the vibrations in the glass they can hear what we are talking about. They are allowed to use bugs now, so that's something you have to think about, and then if you live in a flat, they can use heating pipes, or water pipes from other flats, anything that comes in from another flat. They can sit in the flat above and place sensors and through the pipes know what we are talking about, so it's really GSM phones that are best.

He could then name a series of different mobile phones and talk about their good and bad points. Mobile phones are of great interest as they are so unbelievably useful for the criminal subculture. Naturally, they are of extra importance to those who deal, and who are thereby of extra importance to the police.

Strategies

When it comes to strategies I have been able to interpret three different types: (1) emergency strategies; (2) avoidance strategies; (3) preventative strategies. Emergency strategies deal with situations involving a confrontation with the drug squad, and actions designed to avoid being deprived of freedom. John, a freewheeler, tells me below about one such occasion:

> I had two friends up in the flat, and me and a friend had been and bought from someone, because we were going out to the country, and so we went down the stairs without turning on the lights and when we got to the bottom of the steps there were three cops under the stairs and they rushed out and took us then. But I had my deal in my mouth *and I swallowed it.* And I had a straw too and they got me on that and then they did a house search. And one of the guys had four baggies or something lying on the kitchen table, but they missed them. [He laughs.] And then they rushed in and there's two of

them lying sleeping and then *the girl says* [to the police] *that she wants to get dressed and they can't look.* So she did it in the kitchen and *she just took a newspaper and put it over the powder that was lying there.* And they didn't find it. They didn't check under the paper, or anything.

I have highlighted with italics what I see to be emergency strategies. It means having such a level of preparedness that if you are taken in by the police, the desired effect is to reduce the penalty in order be back out on the street again quickly, and so that you don't end up withdrawing in custody or detention, as one experienced user and dealer told me. It is also usual to throw away the heroin you have, or flush it down the toilet.

'Avoidance strategies' are about acting in such a way as to avoid direct confrontation with the drug squad. If someone has heard that they are investigating a case of possession, then there are good reasons for being careful, and for not moving around unnecessarily. The users can do things in such a roundabout way so that the rule enforcers don't get a chance to stop them. They are often careful when they leave a flat and look out through the window beforehand to see if there are any suspicious cars below. It has sometimes happened that a user has been forced to stay in a flat for a long time because they have seen a police car nearby, or because they have had a call from someone who was thinking of coming up, but who turned round because he or she had seen a suspected 'drug squad' presence on the way.

Other examples of this type of strategy are taking advantage of the peephole, which means it is possible to see outside before you open the door. The police have no right to enter a flat without particular reasons and the subculture's participants are very much aware of this, so aware that many have made it a routine to be careful on leaving the flat.

'Indirect (preventive) strategies' can in turn be divided into readiness, privacy, masking, informal alarm systems, and relationship strategies. This type of strategy is obviously the most important but also the most complicated. This is about acting in such a way as not to risk being caught in the future, and so that if caught, you will only be charged for a fraction (preferably nothing at all) of what you have done (see also Adler 1985: 111). In other words, it is about living in such a way that you minimize future risk. It is especially important for those who deal, as they risk most.

'Readiness strategies.' It is very important to keep up to date on what is going on. If there is a clean-up of a situation going on, then it is extra important to keep informed and to know if one's own dealer or customers are involved and to act in such a way that the risks are minimized, in the event of, say, a house search. If the police do search, then binding evidence ought not to be found in the flat. Many of those who are held in custody in connection with a clean-up of a heroin situation are users, and may go into withdrawal if they cannot get heroin. This gives the police the upper hand during an examination, and they can also ask for names, 'off the record' – that the names named will not be part of the official report. Under such circumstances it is possible for the user to be released quickly and deal with the problem of withdrawal with the help of more heroin. This is a very important reason for keeping up to date. The places where drugs are sold are important as information centres, as this is where the dealer meets customers and can hear about what is happening in town. I have even met dealers who sometimes meet each other and socialize in order to talk about dealing. It is a good opportunity for people in the same boat to exchange experiences without having to risk someone informing on them. On these occasions they also get to express what they think of their customers without their presence. Dealers, for example Steve, Max and Hanna, can on these occasions also discuss how to plan future strategies. Of course it's important that they have a history of experiences together that makes them trust each other almost completely.

Keeping minimum quantities of illegal drugs in the flat is also a commonly used readiness strategy. It is better to keep the major part in a secret place, in the woods or somewhere else where no one else could possibly find them. (See also the introduction to Chapter 7.) One dealer kept them in his basement area, but the police put a spy camera in place and detected this, and several people were arrested and given prison sentences. Those who are higher up the hierarchy take advantage of the runners to fetch and divide up the heroin, and in this way avoid certain risks. Enrique told me that he and his dealer friends used the runner system to avoid keeping so much in their flats: 'Then, when we began selling so much, we got those runners, that you gave maybe two grams to, to sell, so you didn't have to keep so much at home. But we never had the whole lot in the flat. You hid it somewhere else and had small lots at home.'

'Privacy strategies.' There are two types of possible public who need to be kept out. The first are the police and the second are the customers. In order to shut out the police, secure communications equipment is used. 'Comviq Kontant' (a no-subscription, cash card mobile phone system) is of great worth because it is seen as being more secure, in that you do not have to subscribe and provide an address. In order to buy a card, you do not need to give any personal information. You can also use stolen mobile phones and put in a start-up package. The mobile also has the advantage that those who live with their parents can do their business without having to use the family phone and thereby risking discovery of what they are doing.

Every customer can be seen as a potential snitch, owing to heroin's illegality, and an important principle to keep in mind in order to survive is to keep the size of the customer base down. (See also Adler 1985: 114.) Hanna told me she had only five customers, mainly for the reason given above. Many customers mean a lot of coming and going, which can, among other things, make the neighbours suspicious. The principle is that a too large customer base is a risk, which increases the drug squad's possibility of entering into the backstages of the subculture. Enrique says: 'I had eleven customers, max, we all had. We set a limit, we agreed that it was a maximum of twelve customers we could have or otherwise it got dangerous, so I had just eleven regular customers, they maybe helped out others, but they never gave out my number.'

Described above is a 'system of trust' and it is important that there are as few links as possible between the different levels in the dealer's hierarchy, as every link is a potential risk. In order to survive in the subculture it is important that people don't 'blab' too much – spread information about where they get their heroin. It becomes extra important as those who buy their heroin at street level often play detective and try to figure out where the heroin comes from. Their interest is not strange, given that they pay a very high price for it, and that it is extremely important to them.

'Masking strategies'. Not even GSM telephones are completely secure, which means that speech is coded, so that if the drug squad are listening, they cannot get binding evidence for use in a prosecution. The language used on the mobiles is thereby a direct consequence of heroin's illegal nature. Steve describes how it might happen.

> No one rings and says like this 'Yeah, Hi, it's John, I want three grams of amphetamine,' because you can go down for that in court. You can say, 'How's it going?' 'Things are great.' 'Yeah, Can you help me?' 'Yeah, yeah I think I probably can.' I mean if you say something like that, and then maybe say 'We can . . .' or 'Yeah, we can drop by' or the opposite, or you can say like, 'Yeah, we'll meet up', I mean, it's nothing that would stand up in court, even if it's ok for surveillance purposes, I mean, they follow you, like, and take photographs, when you meet people and that kind of thing.

Steve knows from previous experience of the drug squad not to say anything that could be evidence at a trial or anything else that would help them in their surveillance. I have myself heard plenty of phone calls and I have never heard heroin mentioned or any places named or any weights given. Even if the police listening could possibly draw the conclusion that the conversation was about drug dealing, it is not enough to use in a court of law. The word 'help' is frequently used in the culture and if someone who didn't know anything about drug dealing should hear such a conversation they would probably believe it was about help in moving home, or getting a lift somewhere, which is the point with the coded language. The police, however, know what it's about, it's just that it's meaningless, and from their point of view, counterproductive, to arrest someone when you haven't the evidence that a crime has been committed. Tape recordings of sentences with words and phrases like 'help' and 'I'll try' and 'can I come?' and such like are not enough.

In masking situations, it is all about behaving as if the rule enforcers were present, even if they are nowhere in sight. The subculture has evolved a communications system where constant attention is given to possible inopportune intrusion, to behaving as is if an unwanted audience understands what is going on backstage (Goffman 1959/1974).

Another type of indirect or preventative strategy is the 'alarm system', which, despite shortcomings, is prevalent in the subculture. Hanna describes:

> There'd been a robbery in the grocery shop that's just beneath his flat [a dealer]. There was a police car right outside the entrance, and some guy, who was going to go up to get a bag, who rang and said, 'Nah, I'm not coming now, 'cause they're like, right outside'.

Mobile phones make possible spontaneous, fast and flexible internal communication between the subculture's participants. Place is no longer of major importance. If the mobile phones did not exist many would have difficulty in communicating with each other at all, as their tight budgets often mean their ordinary phones are cut off. Dealing is made much smoother, as the dealer doesn't have to be in the one place in order to take orders and decide on deliveries.

'Relationship strategies'. It is important to take care of relationships in the subculture in such a way that information on what you're doing does not spread out and that no one under police interrogation finds it feasible to 'snitch'. The relationship between a dealer and a customer is particularly sensitive, expressed as follows in a quote from the street dealer Hanna: 'I'm like both a god and some kind of devil at the same time. They're really pleased when they get it, but if it happens that I can't help them, then there really is a whole pile of shit talked.'

The 'snitch risk' means that the customer has a certain amount of power over the dealer, even if the majority are so completely in accord with the system that they would not inform, and of course the customer is dependent on the dealer for the daily dose. The possibility still exists, however, that someone in a moment of weakness will squeal and that means that the dealer cannot behave too nastily toward the customer. The dealer is placed in a difficult position if, for instance, a customer wants keep a slate or buy on credit. If the dealer says 'no' in too severe a fashion, the customer's anger could be turned on him. In these cases, it is better to point to the golden rule, 'money first, then the heroin', or to help them think out a repayment plan. Dealers try, in general, to maintain good relationships with regular customers.

Crispin did some dealing for a while in order to earn extra money. He worked 'legitimately' during the day, and as soon as he came home from work he started with his other business. He turned on the mobile, and the lines were open until two o'clock in the morning. As soon as he turned on the phone, it started to ring – he was a busy man, who had what others needed. Even if he turned off the phone at two o'clock in the morning, he let his regular customers throw stones at his window, or shout, even later at night. He had highly developed social bonds with his customers, which meant he abandoned the sales principle. However, this is dangerous and can draw attention from the surroundings. The perfect relationship, in order to avoid exposure to risk, ought to be 'not too intimate', but 'not too distant' either. If the contact is too intimate it can make the contrast between the friendship and the occasion where someone cannot pay, or be helped, too strong and the social bonds are threatened.

Envy of the dealer is also, from the dealer's viewpoint, a potential risk. To visit someone who has plenty of heroin, when one has so little oneself on a daily basis, is a struggle and makes it hard to feel any solidarity with the 'fat cats'. It is therefore vital that the dealer does not in anyway brag about his resources. There are examples of dealers who have bragged and blabbed in such a way that the police and prosecutors have been able to collect enough witness-based evidence to convict them in court.

The threat from modern society's rule enforcers makes such strategies necessary. Those who best manage to live up to these standards show evidence of what can be called 'strong character', and this is what the next section deals with.

A Special Character

These capacities (or lack of them) for standing correct and steady in the face of sudden pressures are crucial . . . I will refer to these maintenance properties as an aspect of the individual's character. Evidence of incapacity to behave effectively and correctly under the stress of fatefulness is a sign of *weak* character . . . Evidence of marked capacity to maintain full self-control . . . is a sign of *strong* character. (Goffman 1967: 217)

I have often heard that you must be good at the game in order to succeed in the subculture, while at the same time having enough self-control in stressful situations. You have to be rational even in critical moments and situations. Ultimately, it is about acting in such a way that the rule enforcers are not afforded a glimpse into the subculture. John told me about an occasion when the drug squad stopped him and they didn't even bother to try to get information from him on the subculture's secrets. He said that they knew that he wouldn't say anything and therefore they didn't really try. He thought it was because they knew he had been in the game for a long time and it wasn't much of an idea to try. A meeting with the police reinforces the character seen as desirable in the subculture; to be able to keep sufficient control despite the obvious risks in the sphere of action.

The strong character is about what Goffman (1959/1974) calls 'impression control', the capability to act in such a way as to give clarity to the role and play it well, while at the same time maintaining such distance to the role that it is possible to play it flexibly. Those who are deemed to have a weak character may get a 'screw-up label'. A person with this type of character may, for example, be so nervous during a robbery that he drops his weapon, or, in connection with a heroin transaction, fluffs either the delivery or the payment. The epithet 'screw up' is an expression meaning something gone wrong, and people who have been labelled this way are usually those whose self-control is not sufficient for them to be considered trustworthy. They are incapable of maintaining control over the role they have, for the time being, been allocated. The strategies described above are to a great extent about keeping a cool head in critical situations and not making matters worse by flaring up or becoming too hysterical, and – which is very important – keeping cool enough to be flexible in the face of unforeseen events. This way of staying in character resembles what Adler writes about smugglers: '. . . dealers' and smugglers' reputations were based on their previous dealing-related behavior within the community. These factors could have a profound effect in determining individuals' success or failure, since they reflected on both their competence and their connections' (1985: 98).

In the subculture it is not merely about showing this kind of façade under pressure, but also when meeting other members of the subculture. Being a dealer requires displaying a strong character. It is about meeting people and showing these people that you are to be trusted: that you don't 'blab' and, above all, if you should be caught, that you don't provide the police with any information. It is also about showing that you can account for yourself and, in this fashion, act like those in ordinary society. If you do not pay your bills and have bad debts, then you will not be considered creditworthy. A trust-based capital is accrued, which means being regarded as one who is good to do business with, who stands up for life in the subculture, with a strong character and who is also a worthy player of the game. Those who occupy dealership positions in the system and who dominate the 'grafting' have had teachers. I asked the dealer Sam how he had managed to get such a good position in the dealing hierarchy:

> It was because I began so early on, did a little crime and then, well, this person asked if I wouldn't prefer to deal instead of getting stuck on break-ins and such, he's relatively big in Norrköping, even though he doesn't have so much to do with heroin, it was mostly amphetamine, and he was a guy who, if you reckon there are maybe three who sell a lot, he was one of them. So, when I started dealing I got to know other people, and when you behave well. It's one thing if you deal a little and then go to pieces, but if you look after business and it goes well, then you meet other people and get to know new people and get asked to parties and meet guys from Stockholm and other people and you get to know them as well. It's not as if you can meet them and talk to them for fifteen minutes and then later just suddenly call them up. It takes time to establish contact. You can't just ring because you've met them once; they'll either tell you to go to hell, or otherwise you'll get beaten up.

Sam showed the more established criminals that he had what is called a strong character, which meant that he was deemed a good prospect by the criminal world. He says that 'he behaves himself' and means by this that he managed to live up to the norms that are expected of him by the gatekeepers of the underworld. Ultimately it is about being sufficiently calm/cool that the calm can be used to counteract various types of risk. Strategies and techniques are learnt while at the same time contacts are made. It is necessary to act in such a way that one isn't adversely labelled, as Vinny (someone who left the subculture) was. Sam tells us about him:

> He's a few years younger than me, and he never thought before he said something, so people up there didn't like him, they like, used him, and he didn't catch on. He didn't really know how to behave . . . when you're among criminals you need to be cautious the whole time, it's not that all criminals are crooked or will try to rip you off, but some are, and some are good. You have to learn how to be, and then, if someone is nasty to you, maybe it's not for the best to get directly into a shouting match, but maybe it's better to keep the occasion in mind and then have it as a trump card in a later situation.

This is a description in a roundabout way of what a strong character is. The criminal has to have what Goffman calls 'role distance' and, thereby, be capable of flexibility (1959/1974). Persons with strong characters are able to read a situation, quickly and efficiently, and decide how to react to it. They have to be careful, but not paranoid, passively watchful, which means paying attention to what others are saying. They shouldn't flare up and lose their temper, as this is not compatible with the desired characteristics. Finally, they should be able to suppress their need for immediate reprisal, and instead wait until what has happened can be used to their advantage. Ultimately, it is about 'getting into character' at the same time as holding a distance from the role. If successful, they will be seen as persons of strong characters.

Sam also told me that he didn't believe Vinny was part of the subculture because he wanted to be, but rather because he was unhappy. I interpreted that as meaning Vinny, like many others, couldn't hide his inner anxiety and unhappiness, which means that he had problems keeping a hold on his reactions. Later, he became so emotionally involved in his role that he couldn't maintain distance from it in the desired way. As Vinny didn't have the capacity to keep this dramaturgic control, he also became a potential snitch. His inability to disguise his inner discomfort might have made it relatively easy for the police, under interrogation conditions, to get names and other information from him. The 'weak character' is a potential opportunity for the police to encroach into the subculture. Those with 'strong character' and a highly developed loyalty to the subculture's rule system say nothing.

In Chapter 2 I used the expression 'capital of experience' to describe the importance of having experienced dramatic situations – action. Using the same way of reasoning it becomes plausible, as the subculture is increasingly criminal, to use the concept of 'character capital' in order to capture a central quality to gain a good reputation. Drawing on the informants' stories, character capital is of importance in gaining social capital: social relations with people in important positions in the culture (Bourdieu 1979/1992). The amount of capital decides how their life structure is. With a high amount you can be a stable addict (Faupel 1991) with a more or less permanent supply of heroin, but with a low amount you have to live with uncertainty when it comes to drug supply.

The Snitch

A strong character is necessary for drug dealing as well as for other types of criminal activity, but, most of all, in pressurized encounters with the police, who try by all lawful means to combat the subculture by inducing the participants to give up their colleagues and friends.

The snitch brings the boundaries between one group and another into question, as he or she is neither a group member nor one of the opposition. The police are, according to the users, easy to understand in that they do what is expected of them. The snitch, on the other hand, is acting against those he has socialized and laughed with. Spies have generally and historically been seen as traitors, and Judas Iscariot is perhaps the most notorious of them all. Judas sold Jesus for thirty pieces of silver. A snitch sells his or her friends, in order to free himself or herself, to avoid punishment, or maybe because he has realized that the subculture's game is nothing to support. If someone has snitched, there are seldom mitigating circumstances, and punishing a snitch is not seen as a horrible act, but rather as making the point, a reminder that a serious breach of the rules has occurred. The snitch has helped the establishment infiltrate the subculture and is therefore a threat to the boundaries that the subculture has set up and that the outside world, in the shape of the police, is continually trying to force.

In Swedish the word for snitch, 'golbög', is made up of two parts; 'gol', the sound a cock crowing makes, which is a root metaphor from the animal kingdom, in this case a cock that crows uninterrupted without any sense of strong character. The word 'bög' is slang for homosexual, and homosexual men cross the boundary of what is permissible, and in that sense become androgynous, and androgyny is one of the things that most seriously call into question our order of classification. The snitch is neither part of the subculture nor of established society and, in this sense, the word 'golbög' is a very apt description. The snitch threatens the subculture's boundaries.

Sara had her flat raided; the police, however, found nothing, She wondered how it could have happened, and discussed with others who might have been in custody in the days prior to the raid. They found out that Peter, an old friend that Sara had done business with, had been in custody for two days about a week before the raid. No one else she had done business with had been detained. She and her allies put two and two together and came to the conclusion that Peter had most likely gone into withdrawal, and when the police put pressure on him for names, he had provided hers. This was her conclusion, but she wasn't completely sure, and she realized that if she was going 'to do something' to him, she needed better evidence. Below are some extracts that show how she thought:

> . . . now there is someone who couldn't keep his mouth shut, and I've begun to suspect who it is, because there's one guy who has been in custody and it fits with the time they [the police] found out about it. But I'd prefer to have proof before I accuse him, because it's difficult to go out around accusing the innocent . . . I think I have to prepare myself for the worst, so that I'm not seriously disappointed, but Peter, well, we've been better friends, yeah, I suppose I could have worked it out if I'd thought logically, because he is a bit nasty, a little selfish, more than others anyway. Everyone gets like that on heroin. I don't really know what to do in this situation, because the worst you can do to someone is to rat them out. It's getting like no one cares about ratting you out in this town, it's become so common, if it was anywhere else he would have been kneecapped.

Sara harbours a suspicion that it is a weakening of the social bonds that has made it possible for Peter to squeal. She believes that his dependency on heroin has weakened his character, but this lack of character is interpreted as selfishness, a lack of the solidarity necessary for the subculture's stand against the rule enforcers. The drug dependency makes it harder to maintain a strong character, which is necessary in order to stay calm during an encounter with the police.

An Overdose Dealt with Strategically

The drug squad are a serious threat to the subculture, which has consequences when it comes to how the heroin users deal with overdoses.[1] The majority would not ring for an ambulance if a friend took an overdose, for the simple reason that the ambulance crew would also contact the police who would then raid the flat. No one wants the drug squad in their flat, particularly not if the flat is, hitherto, unknown and the police have not yet discovered it, and also if drugs, scales and stolen goods are being kept there. In the example below, Dave takes an overdose and his girlfriend Hanna works out for herself what she is going to do.

Hanna and Dave are in Dave's flat. They have just smoked hash, sat and conversed and taken a couple of rohypnol. She has more experience of and a higher tolerance of heroin than Dave, which means she needs fairly large doses in order to be 'well'. Dave, on the other hand, needs maybe a quarter of Hanna's dose. Hanna lays out a little heroin for him with acid and water and warms it, to then draw it up from the spoon through a filter. Dave takes the syringe and Hanna says 'be careful, take half first' so he only 'shoots up' half, whereupon she 'shoots up' her 'fix' and, almost straight away, begins to feel the effect of wellbeing spreading through her; the heroin is 'working' well. Dave wants to feel as good as she does, on the border between consciousness and unconsciousness, and injects the rest. He tells Hanna 'I can't see anything' but she thinks he means that it is dark so she puts a lamp in front of him. Hanna is high, so she hasn't really noticed yet how serious the situation is. Dave's head is in contact with his knees and he seems stuck in that position. Hanna tells him to sit up and he does, for a while. She doesn't really know what's going on because she thinks that if you take an overdose you collapse at once and this doesn't look like that. Dave looks at Hanna with a faraway gaze and then she sees that he is completely blue in the face, which means lack of oxygen. She knows, by now, that he has overdosed and that it is a matter of life or death. At the same time, the blue, absent face, disgusts her. She said to me: 'He was blue, it was so disgusting, with purple blue lips and everything. He looked dead.'

She thinks, 'what am I going to do?' and begins to try to do heart and lung massage on him. The bed is too soft, so she has to drag him down onto the floor. She hits him in the face, which has the effect of turning him even more blue in the face. She pours water on him and screams, 'wake up!', but gets no reaction. He says nothing, and isn't showing much sign of life. By now she starts reluctantly thinking that she ought to call an ambulance. She doesn't want someone's death on her conscience. She rings and the following exchange occurs:

Hanna:	It's my boyfriend, he seems to be unconscious, I can't wake him up.
Emergency	
centre (EC):	What's the address?
Hanna:	Ah, I don't know.
EC:	Okay, run out and check it then.
Hanna:	But I can't leave him, are you stupid or what?

Hanna is under great pressure and almost panic-stricken, despite being high. The conversation continues and Hanna says, 'wait a minute' and goes over to her boyfriend and tries to resuscitate him. She also runs down and checks the address she's at so that she can give it to them. They ask what is wrong with him and she answers: 'he's taken too much of something, but I don't know what.' She is aware now that a heroin overdose would mean police involvement. The conversation stops and, shortly afterwards, Dave wakes, which makes Hanna calls the emergency services again and say that they don't need to come. But they reply: 'but we want to come and look at him' and Hanna says, 'That's not a good idea, because he's getting dressed now, it was probably just me being a little daft.' What happens next is unclear, but Hanna and a friend, Mike, whom she had rung when Dave showed signs of lack of oxygen (it is not clear whether she rang him or the emergency services first), take Dave out and walk him round for hours so that he doesn't 'come apart' again.

One thing has been left out of the story above, but it comes up when Hanna and I continue the conversation. Even in the midst of her panic she kept thinking like someone participating in the heroin-based subculture. At the same time as trying to revive Dave she gathered up various types of evidence – the gear, hash, heroin, rohypnol – and stuffed it in a crack in the mortar under the bathtub, which had been tiled in. When Mike arrives he is given the task of hiding these things outside. It was a big risk to give out the address to the hospital.

The story is a reconstruction but almost certainly very close to that which occurred on a summer night in 2000, and is not an unusual type of event in the subculture. A few summers ago, two young people from Norrköping were found outside a block of flats in Stockholm. They were both dead from an overdose and the flat owner did not want any police involvement. The story about Hanna and Dave describes the reasoning, which is one effect of heroin's serious illegality and which makes it unsuitable to use the resources provided by society for saving lives, as the establishment's institutions are all joined with each other in the war against disorder, in this case, heroin. The users can seldom go to the police for help in the same way other citizens can, as contact with the police would mean discovery. Agar writes '. . . the implicit assumption that police are available to intervene in cases of breakdowns in interpersonal relationships is also not true for the addict. If someone steals from him or cheats in business transactions, he must correct the situation alone, or at most with one or two trusted others' (1973: 125). Those who live in the subculture have to trust to the alternative laws within the subculture, laws that are necessary if the subculture's fragile normality is to be maintained.

The Secret that Strengthens

From the need of heroin, and as a consequence of participation in the subculture, a special perspective on existence is developed: the 'heroin mind'. This should be seen as a part of the lenses the individuals use when they make sense of the world – as a part of habitus (Bourdieu 1979/1992). As this frame of experience is developed, and not everyone can graft in a way accepted by the subculture as honourable; some start to use unacceptable methods of supporting themselves and thereby transgress against the grid that is meant to regulate interaction in the subculture. These crimes give rise to conflict within the culture and weaken social bonds. Conflict is especially serious in a culture that is threatened from without by the rule enforcers of society, who, in different ways, try to destroy the subculture.

In order to counteract the threat, the heroin users learn the drug squad's strategies. They appropriate such knowledge as can be used to detect dangers, while at the same time building up a series of their own strategies to handle these dangers. The knowledge is shared between the subculture's members. The strategies contribute to defending the culture from the representatives of modern society's attempts to gain information about the subculture. Skilled use of these strategies indicates a strong character. The most serious threats to the subculture, after the police, are 'weak characters', who are negatively labelled as 'tight bastards', 'big mouths', 'cunts', 'rats', and worst of all, 'snitches'. The strong character is capable of acting with strong self-control in stressful situations. This includes being able to control movements as well as feelings, and the ability to distance oneself from the role being played and, depending on how the situation develops, being able to change how the role is played. Meeting the representatives of the law is a big test for those dependent on heroin, and the outcome can almost be seen as definite proof of character. Heroin is both an opportunity and a threat to character. If a person succeeds during an interrogation without giving up anyone else, they are appreciated as someone with a strong character. By staying calm under the drug's influence, it can be easier to 'keep a cool head'. However, having to come close to withdrawal means that the desire for heroin increases. When this happens it is possible that those concerned 'snitch' or 'blab', anything to get heroin into their body. It is easiest for those with a continuous heroin supply to show a strong character even though they have embodied the heroin mind.

The model of the strong character develops because of the subculture's position as highly illegal, as well as because of the type of activities the subculture's members have to go through, for example meeting the police, stealing and/or selling drugs. This is an effect of the alternative socialization that has occurred within the subculture, where the young heroin users have learned to participate in an action environment and have thus learned to 'keep a cool head'. To survive in risk-filled environments demands completely different skills from those needed to live in a safe environment. The strong character is like the model of the 'drifter' in that it describes a person who does not get worked up unnecessarily – someone who displays good self-control. The drifter's character is marked, in this sense, by the signs of self-control, which functions as a protection against threat from without, although not so obviously as in the case of the strong character. The subculture's character has developed more backbone, has straightened up, very much because of the threat from police, and – not least – the threat from within, which is created because of the increasing need for money to support the drug habit and because many of the participants are in poor economic shape. The drifter has grown up and become a strong character, which is the main sign of adulthood in the criminal world. The drifter's character is more associated with 'games' than the strong character; he is more of a professional career man, who works in a dangerous environment and is expected to handle stressful situations. Both the drifter and the strong character are action characters and as such are closely related. The threats to the subculture have made a strong character to be the most important symbolical capital, creating possibilities for climbing in the hierarchy.

As social relationships are threatened and subject to conflict, a lack of respect for others and, thereby, a weakening of trust occurs, although this does not necessarily mean the culture cannot hold. It is sufficient that the drug users share certain assumptions on how they are to act, which in its turn creates an identity that others like them can share. To know that others also use drugs is not really enough to create this identification, more is needed, but the threat from without strengthens the notion of a group. Douglas writes: 'when the community is attacked from outside at least the external danger fosters solidarity within it' (1966/1991: 140).

To an extent, they have a common enemy and to that extent they develop common strategies and share knowledge, strategies that can be seen as rituals and a common role model/character to emulate. Much of the strategic work is done according to rituals, especially when it is of a verbal nature. Douglas (1970/2000) refers to Bernstein's use of the terms restricted and elaborated codes, the first applying to messages where very little of the actual meaning is given in the message and the second applying to the opposite – that the majority of the message can be read. The language of dealing is to a great extent built on restricted codes and can therefore contribute to strengthening the group member's feelings of belonging to the same group and culture. Wuthnow et al. (1987: 104) write about Douglas's language theory: 'When a restricted code is utilized group sentiments are automatically reaffirmed, for when one speaks in code others must utilize their baggage of shared assumptions to understand what has been said. Restricted codes are so brief that without some prior knowledge it is impossible to decode what has been said.'

The culture's stamp of secrecy means that most of their activities involve a ritualizing of the collective. The activities involve, without the actors mentioning it, a form of definition of what the subculture is and how one should behave in it. Goffman (1959/1974: 142) writes: '. . . there are what might be called "inside secrets". These are ones whose possession marks an individual as being a member of a group and helps the group feel separate and different from those individuals who are not "in the know". Inside secrets give objective intellectual content to subjectively felt social distance.' The acts and the language are marked by secrecy and this quality is very important for the subculture's ability to survive despite very strong individual needs.

Every secret act reminds the members of the collective and what kind of social system they share. Other, less illegal collectives, do not need this secrecy, as the threats are not so conspicuous. The word 'snitch', for example, is used a lot and it is a most important word, marking the boundary between those on the inside and those on the outside. Every time the word is used, it ritualizes the moral regulation that keeps the group somewhat stable. Every time a snitch is punished, the cracks in the boundary are more tightly sealed. Drawing on Merton (1949/1968), using secrecy strategies and secret codes of communication has a manifest function – to cover criminal activity. However, the latent function is equally important: to recreate the solidarity of the culture despite internal problems.

Note

1. The majority hardly calculates on taking an overdose. Many see it as stupidity to take an overdose – that someone who overdoses hasn't learned how to dose properly. The following three reasons for overdose, according to the young users, can be given: those who overdose (1) are unaware of their own tolerance (like those who have been off heroin for a while, or haven't yet learnt to dose properly) (2) have obtained extra pure heroin – the overdose can be the result of a change in dealer, where the new dealer is more generous with the heroin and doesn't cut it as much, or (3) a longing so strong to gain a state between dreaming and reality that so much heroin is injected, that the high is guaranteed. The third point is one of dissolving boundaries.

–5–

Doing Drugs with Honour and Style

The Meeting with Roger

I am waiting for Roger outside Norrköping's public library. The last time I met him, he was in trouble. His mother had threatened to throw him out of the house. I met him and his mother in their house on the outskirts of Norrköping, and things between them were, to put it mildly, tense. Hip-hop music and the American gangster films have influenced Roger. He is twenty-one, but looks younger. When I last met him, he asked me to guess how old he was, and I said, 'Eighteen, maybe.' He answered, 'I thought you would say that. Everyone thinks I look younger than I am.'

He is a little late, and as I wait, I get the feeling that someone is watching me. I've been in the field for roughly three months and I often get slightly paranoid. Sometimes, when I phone someone in the subculture, I hear crackles on the line, and start to worry about being bugged. It is no doubt a consequence of what I have experienced. I see it as a sign that I am beginning to adopt their perspective on existence. After a while, Roger turns up, dressed as usual in baseball cap, baggy jeans, fancy trainers and a short jacket. I see at once that he is high. His pupils have contracted and the colour of his eyes is much more noticeable than usual. He gives me a 'cool' greeting, a type of high five. I have learned by being with him that sometimes talking is not that important, he seems to like being silent at times. He tells me that he was kicked out of home yesterday, and expresses contempt for his mother: 'she's never loved me, she doesn't know what love is.' I suggest that we go to Oxelbergen, a place on the eastern outskirts of Norrköping, but he would rather go to Lindö, about five miles east of the town where the wealthier people live, a high-status area with a rather large marina. I believe the reason for his decision is that he does not want to meet any police or social workers, as that might mean a urine test and make it difficult for him to keep his work placement, which he has told me he enjoys. It could also cause problems for him, when it comes to renting his own flat, something else he has talked about.

We drive to Lindö, chatting all the while. He asks how the research is going. I tell him I have travelled 500 kilometres that morning from Malmö in the south of Sweden to Norrköping and that I could only do about thirty kilometres per hour because of the snow. He expresses a fascinated interest in how there could be so much snow down there, and none in Norrköping and hands me a box of gummy bears. The last time we met we discovered we have the same taste for sweets. We laugh about it. He has also told me earlier that he enjoys shoplifting, so I imagine that the sweets are stolen. He also tells me that he is so hard up that earlier that day he returned a cable his mother had previously bought to a TV shop. He got thirty crowns back. Nevertheless he has managed to get heroin. He tells me that he bought a gram and sold three bags, and can therefore use two bags, and still has £20 left over.

We park by a café in Lindö marina. I begin to interview and he often wants to stop to smoke, cigarettes that is. During a break, while he is smoking, I forget to turn off the tape recorder (I tell him later and ask if I should record over it, he says it does not matter). Then he shows me his kit, a small leather case, not unlike a glasses case, where he keeps two syringes, filters, citric acid, among other things. He even has a small container with water, of which he says 'This is the exact amount for a fix . . . mostly you just go into a bathroom, there's water and even toilet paper, but if there wasn't any water to be got . . .' I say to him: 'You have what you could call a little survival kit, then?' He answers: 'Yes [laughing], most do . . . those friends today, they're brothers, they have ones this big, everyone has such big kits, this one is tiny.' He sounds proud when he shows me how all the pieces of his kit are neatly placed and packed. I had already realized earlier that he had most probably injected the heroin, because during the interview he had problems staying awake. I worry that he might want to take a hit in the car. He asks if I have ever seen anyone take a hit and I say: 'Yes. Several times.' I answer in this fashion, because right now, I cannot bear to watch and because the question could be construed as an opening for him to show me. A fix in my car could lead to an overdose, and he has earlier described for me, almost poetically, an occasion where he once took a hit at eight in the evening, blacked out and didn't wake until two in the morning, with almost no idea where he was. He does not take a hit, perhaps noticing by my reaction that I hoped he wouldn't.

We drive back to town. He wants to be dropped off outside a pool hall, a place where his friends meet. He says he is going to stay with his probation officer who has a mobile home outside Norrköping, and that the mobile home even has cable television. I feel a certain melancholy as I leave him at Norrköping's pool hall. Sad, because I see he is stuck in a form of denial. He says he does not have a problem with drugs, that he can stop at any time, while at the same time he is as high as a kite. He says he wants to live, while drastically challenging death. He speaks fondly of Thai smack, and, almost without feeling, describes how it killed seven people last summer, as if this somehow reinforces the quality of the smack. There is something sad about him, the disappointments in life that have brought him to this tragic pass. I tried to get in touch with him several times after this with no success. A year-and-a-half later I found out through Hanna that he was in jail, sentenced for drug-related crime. The Swedish version of the book was finished by then, and I sent him a copy.

Threatening Self-Images

Roger, Max, Molly, Steve, Sam, Hanna, Enrique, Crispin, John, Ben, Peter and others developed a serious addiction to heroin. For Roger it was a matter of sometimes taking the fix in a public toilet and not knowing where to sleep next night, drifting around in search for friends and, because of a well-developed heroin mind, in search of resources to buy heroin. According to interpretations from the larger society, Roger is a miserable person in need of help, but he himself and other heroin users may interpret his situation differently. In this chapter I analyse how the 'horsers' can develop a form of respectability in the subculture. As in the previous chapter, it is about handling the threat from within and from outside, however, the threat considered here is not primarily to the social bonds, but to the members' identities. The realization of being seriously dependent on heroin gives rise to feelings of shame, and injecting heroin is extra problematic in that it too closely resembles the stereotype they try to keep themselves from becoming. As I described in Chapter 3, one of the conditions that made it reasonable to try heroin in the first place was that it was smoked.

The shame of drug abuse is created by established society, which perceives the drug addict as a social failure and a creature of low status. There is, however, no condemnation of drug use in the subculture. Narcotics have the same position there as alcohol does in established society, but an even less problematic one, as the subculture does not have regulatory authorities that try and regulate sales. From the perspective of the subculture, however, it is not trouble-free to be hooked on drugs, and this is mainly because those who are seriously dependent are not considered trustworthy or autonomous. When the majority are hooked, however, this is not necessarily so great a problem. This is supported by the fact that a few years back it was much more serious to be an injecting heroin user than it is today, as the majority who smoked heroin in 1996–7 have turned to injecting. Even if many are injecting, it is still not quite problem-free. Steve talks about how he experiences his injecting:

> There are many who don't even know that I've ever used a syringe. I have always tried to keep it secret. There's a few more who know now, because people have told each other. But before, I've told them not to say anything to others. People see me in a good way, that I'm all right, and I don't want them getting another picture of me because I use a syringe, because I'm still the same person, still take care of myself anyway . . . I still think the same way and still help, still am nice in the same way . . . Like, I'm not nasty the way some people can be. Say that you come and leave a gold chain here and for

example pawn it, and say 'Can I borrow £150 for this?' 'Yeah, when do you get your money?' 'I can get some by Friday.' 'Okay, but I have to have the money by five o'clock', I might say. And then you ring at six or seven or maybe on Saturday and I say, 'No, sorry, I've sold it.' I'm not like that, I've never been. I'll wait a week, two weeks, maybe a month or two months, and I won't sell it, they'll get it back. And I never take interest, even if someone owes me money. Even if it's 200 or 500 or 1,000, I have never taken interest on the money and have always tried to take the best way possible. And I don't want to destroy that by letting them find out suddenly that I inject. So I have tried to keep it secret from almost everyone. There's just a small group who know about it.

Steve is worried that the picture of him will change; that others will re-evaluate him as a person – that they will think his character has weakened – that he will be seen as a failure. The shame many experience with regard to being hooked is, thus, an effect of both the establishment's prejudices and the difficulty in living up to the subculture's demands for strong character. Being hooked is a black mark, as it means dependence, lack of freedom and, not least, a flawed, weak, character.

Most of those I have interviewed have developed a serious abuse problem, and the majority have also started injecting heroin. This means that, at least insofar as serious abuse via injecting goes, they are nearing the stereotype of drug addiction, which is, in general, seen as of low worth by society.

A series of signs indicate the decay of the subculture's members, morally, bodily and in their ability to perform. Initially they based on the weekends, went to the pub and had fun as a group. After a time, many are high every day of the week, many are injecting, and many more are withdrawing, either at home or in detoxification units in hospital. Heroin has gravitated from being something that seriously spiced up the weekend to something that has become a daily project. The users are confronted with the down side of abuse. The foil is exchanged for a syringe and many take it alone, in toilets, or where they can, without any youth culture framing in the form of films or music. Their daily activities begin to resemble those indicative of serious abuse. The stereotype becomes reality. Their realization that they are hooked becomes all the more tangible, which makes it harder for them to maintain the illusion of freedom. This ought to produce a negative self-image among the young heroin users, but it is not that simple. In this chapter I will show that there are a series of possible ways the subculture's members can interpret these situations, which differ from the interpretations by the establishment. These make it possible for participation in the subculture to be less than entirely shameful and give rise to occasions that increase self-respect. The subculture's members can even sometimes feel proud, exalted and successful, on the basis of the subculture's particular logic.

The young heroin users try to 'clean' their identities from the accusation that heroin users are degenerate from three different aspects: (1) that they are morally degenerate, especially the dealers, who lack morality and are 'scabs' who don't work and who live off others; (2) that they are physically and mentally degenerate; (3) that they are losers and at the bottom of society's hierarchy. Most of those to whom I have spoken do not recognize this stereotypical picture of themselves. They have seen people by the Sergels Torg (a square in the centre of Stockholm, known for the high frequency of addicts) who conform to these criteria, but they refuse to see themselves like that. In the remainder of the chapter, I try to show how the young heroin users in different ways handle this stereotype, which is a threat to their self-images.

A Subculture's Morality

One way of increasing the worth of an identity is to live up to the code of honour extant within the subculture. If we think back to the section on grafting (Chapter 4), dirty tricks and sponging are low-status methods of grafting. In the subculture, as in other social systems, there is a desire for a certain amount of regulation. This can mean that, from the bag buyer's perspective, you get 'decent bags' – ones that contain almost 0.2 g of relatively pure heroin and, from the dealer's perspective, that people pay their debts and keep quiet about things that do not need to be spread round. Rules are needed so that participants in the subculture can trust the system. If you live up to these rules, you receive reinforcement from the subculture. The existence of rules can, from a functionalistic perspective, be interpreted as an aspect of survival, to prevent internal conflicts and anarchistic tendencies – to keep the culture together and to make survival and preparation against threats posed from the outside possible. The rules, in addition, serve the purpose of making it possible for the participants in the subculture to feel that they are half-way decent people.

One of the rules is that stealing from home is not a legitimate activity. This rule protects the families of the members from the consequences of the subculture. Even if someone has stolen from home it is nothing they boast about; it is low-status activity in the culture, although this type of stealing doesn't threaten the culture's social bonds to the same extent as say, dirty tricks, like buying heroin for someone else and keeping back some for yourself. The rule is there so that the subculture's members can feel that there is a form of honour in the subculture, that they are not morally degenerate, and, in this sense, it is a matter of a rule that underlines for the members that they have not, despite their serious use of narcotics, fallen all that low. There is another sense in which stealing from home is seen as 'low', and that is that it is proof of desperation, which is the opposite of an attribute of strong character. Stealing from home is the opposite of a 'decent break-in' to, say, a truck depot. If you steal from home on a regular basis and this becomes known, it is likely that you will be placed low down in the subculture's hierarchy and designated a desperate 'rat' that has no honour, and will use any means to survive. Some of the interviewees admit to having used most of the dirty tricks, but at least they haven't stolen from home. A minority have admitted to it, while the majority have admitted to selling heroin without being the least bit ashamed.

On one occasion I was in a flat where collective basing was going on (I described this scene in the introduction to Chapter 3). I sat and talked to a guy, Dan, who was only there visiting, but who had lived in Norrköping previously, and who had been hooked on heroin since 1996. We started talking about how he had been introduced to heroin circles and he said it was his friend, Ben, who had offered first. Ben was actually there, beside us in the room, and had heard what was said, and despite the fact that he was high came over to us and said, 'yes, that's true, and I regret it like hell.' In the meantime, Dan said, 'if you hadn't fixed me up, I would have fixed it anyway' and Ben seemed somewhat relieved. This example illustrates what in heroin circles is called a 'virgin', an old drug user's term.

Virgin is the first use of the drug. To do a virgin is something that happens, but nothing that people brag about (see also Taylor 1993: 43). On the contrary, many are ashamed of it. The rule, not to 'do a virgin' is the subculture's criticism of itself, but, with regard to smoking heroin, is not considered as big a crime as helping to do the first injection. Those who introduce others to heroin often say: 'if I hadn't done it, somebody else would have', or, 'they'd have found a way and if they'd tried it by themselves it could have been dangerous.' There are ways, therefore, of avoiding this rule of the subculture. If someone is seriously dependent and has no immediate access to heroin, then it is probable that if they got heroin in return for fixing a virgin, they would do it. Being hooked makes it harder to live by the subculture's code of honour. For those who manage, and never fix a virgin, however, it has the effect of increasing their worth, like saying: 'I may be a drug addict, but at least I've got some morals.'

The virgin rule is more problematic for the dealers, as in their daily occupation they risk selling to people with very little experience of drugs. Some of them say that they only sell to those who are already hooked on the drug. Below I'm interviewing Ben:

Ben: I used to sell amphetamine, but only to those I knew were serious addicts.
Philip: Exactly . . .
Ben: Then if they helped someone new, well, I can't help that. But I never sold to anyone, myself.

It's a question of defending himself from the responsibility for having spread heroin to recruits, as that is shameful. By maintaining that he only sells to addicts, Ben washes his hands of the affair, keeping his self-identity clean. These types of justification were particularly common when they interacted with me, as I am not one of them. In interaction with authorities, they would, most probably, keep completely silent about selling, while when meeting those of their dealing colleagues they can trust, they can talk freely, without ambivalence. There are, thus, a series of rules that the users are expected to live up to. However, these are not absolute and they can be got round.

Blaming the Other

The subculture's organization and hierarchy also make it possible for the individual members to pass the moral failures on to other parties, to blame the system and suchlike. Blaming someone else, of course, doesn't just occur in the subculture. Employees blame their bosses, and 'ordinary' people blame immigrants or politicians. It is a matter of projections where the responsibility is laid on others, and the individual goes free. In the subculture it is usual to blame those at the top of the drug hierarchy, who sell despite not using themselves. Steve has the following to say:

> I think it is terrible of them to sell heroin just for the sake of the money. There are quite a few here in town that do it. It really is driving people, well maybe not driving them to death, but even if it's not directly, in the long term it is. I think that it is terribly wrong. It's one thing, I mean I'm not saying it's better, but if they're doing it to get by, because they have to take it themselves, and if they sell to those who already take it.

Steve has made maybe £50,000 during the past few years, but even so he does not feel any great responsibility for what has happened in Norrköping. The blame is laid on those who almost never get mixed up with the subculture's members except through distribution of heroin and contacts with runners. The 'top brass' in the sales hierarchy mostly don't use heroin themselves and this is seen as the most despicable aspect of a dealer, at the same time as it ought to be a dream for many dealers further down the chain, to be able to live up to the maxim 'don't get high on your own supply' and thereby make big money. Steve managed to kick the habit, but kept selling albeit on a smaller scale. The quote is taken from an interview held roughly two months before he became clean, and when I later met him, after he had been drug free, he was fully occupied delivering heroin to a flat in Norrköping's underworld. There is always, no matter what position you find yourself in, someone who can be seen as more worthless than yourself, and when you find yourself in the position you earlier criticized, you can find some other position to project your responsibility on to.

Certain dealers can get upset when they read in the newspapers, 'dealers sell drugs to children in the school playground'. They see it as offensive to their dealer identity and an accusation that they are completely worthless and ruthless. Dealers often claim not to sell to the underaged, and in this way avoid responsibility for destroying young people's lives. However, even if every dealer reasoned like this, the heroin would still reach the underaged. How? By someone else doing the 'running' for the younger ones. The links in the system make it possible to defend oneself against guilt. The dealers are partly free from the responsibility as long as they stick to the logic that says that they cannot be responsible for what happens to the drug after it leaves their hands. They are merely part of a long chain and only take responsibility for the part of the chain where they find themselves. The rationale is similar to one that Hillberg and Bauman describe as used by those involved in the Holocaust:

> Most bureaucrats composed memoranda, drew up blueprints, talked on the telephone, and participated in conferences. They could destroy a whole people by sitting at their desk. Were they aware of the ultimate product of their ostensibly innocuous bustle – such knowledge would stay, at best, in the remote recesses of their minds. (Hillberg in Bauman 1989: 24)

By merely executing a part of the process, the bureaucrats seldom saw the blood their actions had spilled. They could have clean consciences. They weren't 'really' responsible. It seems to be a similar process with heroin supply. In this context, a variation on 'if you can't do the time, don't do the crime' can be discussed, in that the dealers, according to themselves, do not force their customers to buy heroin; it is more a matter of the consumer choosing. This partly explains the existence of the unwritten law of not selling to underage customers. The underage is seen as not having attained maturity, whereas an adult is expected to be able to decide for himself.

The responsibility can be shifted towards those at the top, the dealers, the customers, or the 'horse' itself. Many claim that people become corrupted by the 'horse', that they become capable of conning anyone and betray their nearest and dearest. In this manner, the heroin itself becomes the final resort; when people try to keep their identity clean from different types of attack on their morality. The individual is freed from responsibility and even if he has conned or cheated it is always possible to blame the heroin. The responsibility laid on heroin for immoral behaviour is even supported by the establishment's view of heroin as a substance that exploits heroin users, and renders them victims (see Chapter 1). Steve says:

> I haven't had a problem with any drugs, yeah, a problem, but not really a problem. I can stop using for anywhere from a month to a year, if I want to. But the horse, with that I just lost it. That's why I know that, I'll be . . . like, it's the horse that will be . . . if there's ever a drug I'll get hooked on, that'll be my downfall, that's it.

The heroin users are convinced that it is extremely difficult to stop using heroin. The heroin and what they call 'the hunger' is viewed as a strange force which is difficult to resist, and which calls for incredible will power to defeat. The majority of the heroin users have dabbled in amphetamines and the majority stopped using them. In any event, it was hardly more than a party drug. In the light of this experience, it is unfathomable to the heroin users that the amphetamine addicts cannot give it up. This, too, reinforces the heroin users' identities; they are really strong willed, but have met an unbelievably strong opponent that most would be defeated by. The amphetamine junkies, in contrast, meet a weak opponent, whom they don't manage to defeat. Naturally, you can turn the same rationale on its head and see it from the amphetamine users' perspective, and, in that case, the heroin users end up at the bottom. However, this book is about the heroin users and from their perspective. Heroin becomes a serious subject, which has the ability to change people's personalities (see also Pearson 1987: 15).

By shifting the responsibility to others, on to the top dogs, the system, the customers or the drug itself, the heroin users attempt to separate what they actually do from their self-identities. They avoid having to see themselves as morally degenerate. Many of their excuses are because I am interviewing them – they have met someone who is not part of the subculture and who could have a reason to moralize about their activities. When they meet other heroin users, they don't have to use evasions; there, the rationale which applies is as clear as day. It is about heroin: getting it, selling it, buying it, hiding it, shooting it and smoking it. The rationale is so clear that nothing else matters. Many describe life in the subculture as stressful and that is because of the almost total fixation – 'the heroin mind' – implying that they seldom think about anything else. They are like workaholics who cannot stop thinking about work. As one of the top dealers said in a trial, in the summer of 2002, answering the question why he could have sold so much heroin although it has so many tragic consequences: 'I was like autistic'.

Professional Honour

> Drug dealers organized, planned, and executed their ventures in similar ways to other businessmen. They relied on an occupational body of knowledge which new recruits had to learn. (Adler 1985: 147)

In society outside the subculture it is completely abnormal to deal in heroin. It is definitely not seen as a profession. However, the heroin dealers often have a form of professional honour and pride in their work.

Sam reacted strongly to a letter to the newspaper where a person thought that a 'junkie' stood around and sold drugs to children. 'I took that really badly, I thought about it for fucking days, 'cause it was like the worst thing I'd heard.' He felt insulted. There is a similarity here to how a legitimate professional group would react to a similar attack, as if, say, the Minister for Education said publicly that secondary school teachers were giving low-quality lessons. It was a matter of professional honour for Sam. The attack was taken not as just aimed at dealers, but as an attack on him as a person, because he identifies so strongly with his role as a dealer. He believes his profession is misunderstood. Sam claims that Joe Bloggs thinks that it's easy to sell 'dope', that you just lie around all day, and he cannot identify with this picture of the dealer's conditions; it does not reinforce him in his position. For him, dealing involves huge effort, and this is something that the others also point out: 'It's 24 hours a day, to keep tabs the whole time on who you are selling to, and then to keep tabs on the rumours.'

Recently, he has experienced life as altogether too stressful, and the feeling of being misunderstood by the establishment is obvious. Sam and others have become so involved in dealing that it has become a part of them. The dealers can experience a type of professional honour, which becomes honourable because of the norms inherent in the subculture. Sara criticizes another dealer for immoral behaviour:

A bag should be 0.2 grams, but his were 0.15–0.16, or thereabouts, and he sold a gram for £120. He could have gone down but he sold so much. He doesn't give a shit about who he sells to, so I think he sold to many of the younger ones. He hung around a lot, not with kids, but those who were 15, 16, 17, 18, 'cause he's like one of those who hung around earlier at Film City [in Norrköping's centre].

There are many other examples of the subculture's norms giving rise to professional pride. A dealer told me that he did 'nicer' bags than others, with 0.2 grams of concentrated heroin. He also had a couple of 'regulars' to whom he was extra nice and he told me with a certain pride about a particular event when an old school friend had no heroin and wanted to sell his mother's computer for a couple of bags:

Now when I was selling this week, when I gave away a gram to this guy who was coming to buy a bag, he said, 'Shit, I've got real trouble fixing money for this.' So he came first thing in the morning and bought a bag, and then he was to come and give me his mum's computer for two bags, and I said, 'Ah fuck it, go back with the computer and come back here after.' 'What? But I . . . I haven't any money, I can't buy from you, nothing. I can't borrow 'cause I don't know if I can get money later . . .' 'Nah, but go and put back the computer,' I said, 'and then we can talk when you come back, I promise, you'll make on this,' I said, 'you won't lose or anything,' and then he was a little thoughtful, but it took just a half an hour and he was back.

The dealer didn't trust his friend, but went with him (in a stolen car without a driving licence) back to the friend's home where he said that he put back the computer. The friend was a little irritated and asked why the dealer didn't trust him, and he answered: 'Yeah, but I'm going to give you a present.' In the following quote, the dealer speaks with the same kind of pride that a boss would feel when telling an employee that they're getting a substantial raise:

> When we came home I weighed up a gram for him and said, 'Here's a present. Make it last you a couple of days. At least two days. You don't have to smoke it up all at once.' He was dead chuffed, he nearly hooted and said: 'I'll get you back. Now I owe you a really big favour. Just ask for it whenever you want. Say if you need a new video or stereo or whatever. I can fix it.'

The example above shows that, from the subculture's rationale, it is possible for the dealers to act in such a way that they are judged 'good'. Very few see themselves as really mean. On the contrary, they appear to be 'helpers' and, in a way, the dealer's flats can be likened to pharmacies selling medicine to those in need. The word 'help' is primarily used as a 'masking strategy' (see also Chapter 4) so as not to give the police information which can be used in court, but also has the latent function of making the dealer's activities charitable: the word 'help' legitimizes the continued dealing.

Dealers sometimes see themselves as good pharmacists, in contrast to those at the top who just take in and deliver large quantities. Max complains about one of the top guys, who, according to Max, doesn't know much about drugs. A top guy asked him once if you could mix brown and white heroin, which would almost destroy the white heroin. It would be like asking, in front of a champagne connoisseur, if it was all right to mix fine champagne with a cheap sparkling wine. The top guys lack the professional knowledge of the street dealers, who are often themselves users, and thereby *au fait* with the product.

There are many possible ways, with the help of the subculture's perspective on the environment and its rule system, to handle the threat from established society of socially lowering the status of those within the subculture. The young heroin users know about the establishment's values, but can use the subculture's moral codes to handle them. Or, in other words, the subculture's moral codes are created so that it is possible for its members to identify with it, and handle the criticism that the subculture is subjected to by the larger society.

The Subculture's Perspective

I am on my way to meet Steve and Hanna in Steve's flat, a place I have visited a few times before. We exchange fairly ordinary greetings, like 'how's it going?' and 'how's the writing going?' Steve goes into the bedroom while Hanna makes the coffee and takes out a packet of chocolate-covered digestive bars – they have a whole box full of them under the bed. I'm sitting, talking to Hanna in the kitchen, when Steve comes in. He shows me something that looks like a black sausage; it is heroin in smuggled form. Steve comments that it is difficult to undo the tape, 'Fuck it, it's not usually like this.' Hanna mutters some kind of response.

They talk with me for a while and with each other, as if they are not doing anything particularly special. I stay in the kitchen while Steve goes into the privacy of his room, where he crushes the heroin. Later he will divide it into heaps, with the help of the scales' precision, and bag it for distribution to the flats. I am surprised that they let me see so much; they obviously trust me and know that I will not betray them. I am anxious about being so close to the sale and distribution of heroin, but try to show evidence of strong character and keep chatting. We look at Steve's video film collection and he lets me borrow some of his favourites. Then they ask for a lift to Norrköping's town centre. They say they have some errands to take care of.

We leave the flat and head for my rented car. I drive them through town and now I am really nervous, given the relatively large amounts of heroin they are most likely carrying. I try joking, and say 'if the cops come now, I better just put my foot to the floor!' They laugh in answer, and ask me to stop a block from a place I know well and have visited on several occasions, one of Norrköping's 'all-night pharmacies' – this is a flat, Max's apartment. We decide to meet again in a couple of days; I will ring when I'm in the area. When they've said goodbye, I see them moving in the direction of the address that I had earlier surmised. They are going to deliver the heroin, probably 5 to 10 g, to Max, who in his turn is going to sell it to the bag buyers. Later the same day, I drive three guys to the same place where I previously dropped Steve and Hanna; this is described in the introduction to Chapter 4.

What is interesting, apart from the heightened drama of the situation described, is the calm that both Steve and Hanna display. When Steve opened the packet of heroin and started to weigh it out, it was most reminiscent of an ordinary person unpacking the shopping and remarking on the fact that the milk carton had a new shape. Neither Steve nor Hanna seemed to have any ethical doubts about whether what they were doing was right or wrong. Instead, they did what they were good at, and what they had developed the contacts for – delivering and selling drugs.

In this example, Steve and Hanna display proof of strong character and they couldn't do that if they operated from the larger society's perspective. Their focus is one directional, the game that heroin delivery involves, where what matters is getting the heroin from one flat to another without being caught by the police. They have done it so often that they are far from nervous. It is similar to the focus that occurs in playing a sport, when thought is according to the game's rationale and rule system, where what matters is getting the ball in the net. Steve and Hanna are not occupied with wondering if they are good people or not. Heroin delivery and dealing, like other types of grafting, usually mean being completely absorbed by the game. The interviews I did with dealers were continually interrupted by the mobile phones ringing. If the dealer, for whatever reason, gave up dealing, the absence of ringing sounds was obvious; the silence was louder. The signals of the mobile phones are the rhythm of the dealers, keeping them in motion.

The selling of drugs is not particularly problematic from the subculture's perspective. It can be compared to ordinary society where tobacconists are seldom subjected to persecution, or to the state's off-licences, which, although certainly criticized by the total abstinence movement, are otherwise generally positively viewed by most, even though it contributes to certain problems. In Western society, alcohol consumption is seen by most as less problematic than, say, for example, hash use, because people have been socialized to this interpretation of alcohol. A similar interpretation of drugs occurs in the subculture. Chapter 2 describes how a subcultural habitus is developed, through which what ordinary people see as abnormal becomes normal, and vice versa. The drugs are not particularly problematic as seen through the habitus of the subculture.

A large number of transactions occur every day. The bag buyers buy heroin as often as Joe Bloggs goes to the shop for food, and if this happens often enough, then the buying does not stand out as particularly immoral or strange. The purchase becomes a normal event in everyday life and those who sell probably seldom have any moral or ethical discussions with themselves. They are busy with their customer and delivery contacts, while keeping an eye on debit and credit. They may have had moral doubts in the beginning, but after a while the business has lost its dramatic aspect and they have developed the attributes of strong characters. When I spoke about these things with Steve he suggested that it is like a war; after a while you don't care about the sound of grenades, it becomes a part of everyday life. It can initially be experienced as unpleasant, but after a while it becomes undramatic. It can, nonetheless, be pleasant, when the money starts rolling in and he counts his income, a sign that the business is successful. The enterprise's books balance.

I experienced something similar. When I first saw someone taking heroin my pulse rate was up over 150 beats per minute (see the introduction to Chapter 2). By the time I had seen it about twenty times, I no longer reacted the same way. I could sit and speak to people who were smoking heroin without focusing on the basing. The use of heroin became normal, even to me, although my pulse rate would still be considerably higher than that of, say, Steve or Hanna. Habitus is changed, so as to make it much less dangerous to be involved with drugs. I wouldn't have been able to write this book if I had not managed to distance myself from the establishment's view, where having anything to do with narcotics is viewed as a very serious crime. The development of this perspective is necessary for the young heroin users, partly in order to live with the drama/action in the subculture and partly to counter the criticism directed against them by the established society's representatives.

A Young, Strong and Invisible Character

I am sitting with Ben, who is high, in my rented car. A man passes, about thirty-five years old, with torn jeans and an open jacket, despite the fact that it is cold and windy out. He straggles as he walks, and there is a certain tic-like quality to his gait and head movements. Ben laughs and says something along the lines of 'would you look at that!' in a derogatory tone. His tone shows that he feels himself, somehow, 'above' the amphetamine user. I find the same true for many of the heroin users. Peter describes the amphetamine users:

> You know, down there in the cellars rooting in stuff and that kind of thing. Out breaking into and destroying everything they see. I mean the guy on a bicycle with his rucksack and a screwdriver (for breaking locks), that's the picture of an amphetamine junkie to me.

In this mythical image, the amphetamine junkie portrays anything but elegance. They do not appear well dressed, 'clean' or particularly intelligent. 'Cleanliness' does not mean merely literally clean, but also includes behaving in a 'respectable way'. The amphetamine users are seen as clumsy and not particularly sophisticated in their criminal activities. Many heroin users portray themselves as people to whom breaking into cellars is unthinkable. Sometimes the word 'crazy break' (in Swedish: *tokbryt*) is used to characterize the amphetamine users. This type of break-in is seen as less well thought out and, according the heroin users, a sign of a lack of intelligence and serious desperation. The amphetamine users' character is thereby portrayed as weak, and when the young heroin users compare themselves with them, it becomes, in contrast, reasonable to think of themselves as strong and respectable characters. Richard says: 'Jeez, they are so difficult. They run around and root in things and get these bloody ideas, oh I think they're really trouble. It's this bloody psycho drug they're on.'

The amphetamine users, according to the heroin users, cannot react with the even temper and behaviour necessary for 'ordinary' society. According to Goffman (1959/1974), we act from a 'line' and by that he means that the actor tries to keep his performance together in such a way that the audience knows which role he is trying to dramatize. In order to make this reading of the performance possible, the actor must keep to the line and avoid signs and expressions that would make it hard for the public to know whom the actor is representing (compare to the concept of strong character). The amphetamine user, according to the heroin user, cannot carry off this everyday dramaturgy in the same way as the heroin users. The young heroin users are strictly speaking newcomers to the Norrköping drug scene and, as such, see themselves also as a new generation of drug users. Bauman (1990) writes that newcomers define themselves by describing the established ones as less complete (see also Elias and Scotson 1965/1994). It is the same within the arts, where newcomers, or what Bourdieu (1979/1992) calls 'pretenders', seek out certain flaws in the 'established' players. The new heroin users, in this way, use the old amphetamine users to increase their own sense of value.

An important aspect of the critique levelled at the amphetamine users is that they are old and the heroin users see themselves as young. This can even be seen in their attitude to addiction-suppressing medication. Very few would dream of using methadone, as it would be seen as a sign of serious abuse, age and deterioration. They prefer the abstinence medicine Subutex (buprenorphine), as it doesn't have the same associations. Hanna expresses her thoughts: 'methadone, that sounds bad. It makes you think of old addicts, worn out, who go and fetch their methadone every day, except at weekends . . . I don't know why.'

They create differences in opposition to that which belongs to the stereotypical model of being worn out and aged. Methadone does not correspond to their self-images because it is far too associated with 'failed', worn-out and old drug addicts. The heroin users see themselves as cleaner and fresher, not only in appearance but also in behaviour, than the amphetamine users. The established amphetamine junkies function perfectly as a standard by which the heroin users see their identity as respectable.

The Invisible Drug

The process described above, where the established, worn-out amphetamine 'junkies' provide identities for the heroin users to define themselves against, contributes to making it less difficult to live as a heroin user. Their own stigma is projected on to others. It is a matter of continued belief that their own exterior is not sending any negative signals to the outside world, that one is not a carrier of any obvious stigma. The signs that indicate serious addiction are toned down and lose some of their credibility. To live as a heroin user, when the heroin user is part of an outsider culture, is to try to make invisible what is being thought about the whole time: heroin. The heroin user's self-identity is one of respectability, so that one can be seen out among others without membership in the subculture being obvious. Many of those interviewed say they saw/see heroin as a 'social' or even 'normal' drug and claim that those high can be out among 'ordinary' people without them noticing anything. Below are some descriptions of heroin users:

> . . . someone who isn't that visible. Moves in among the crowd, sort of. I mean, more generally respected in some way . . . you aren't the person you're meant to be . . . You

could be out and be high without so many people noticing it, if you know what I mean. Not like with amphetamine where you go flapping around or behaving in a strange way. You were quite calm, cool. Cool was what you were. (Peter)

I have lived in town, in my own flat, since I was sixteen, so they [his parents] haven't seen, but with heroin you can keep it up for a really long time and no one notices . . . You can keep it hidden for several years, as long as you have heroin all the time. It's when you feel sick that people notice. It's then they think you're taking drugs, but of course it's because you haven't any . . . You can hardly see it in today's users, except for those who look really worn out, those who are really using heavily. You can really do it well. Today there are so many that you would absolutely not be able to see it by, who've been using for several, many years and even so look fairly normal. They look good, and take tanning sessions, and so on. (Ben)

If I concentrate, I could go and meet social services tomorrow and convince them that I'm drug-free, if I just cop on. You might go and get a tan, eat properly and you might not be able to do that if you've been using a long time, that's what's so treacherous about it, that you can sort of hide it for a long time, and that means it often takes a while before anyone notices. (Steve)

The quotations above emphasize the belief the young heroin users live/have lived with – that their use of drugs is impossible to discover. So long as they believe this, modern society's labelling of them cannot occur, because they quite simply don't give society any chance of stigmatising them. They hide their stigma both from others and from themselves. It is a matter of how they believe others react towards them. When they meet others who do not realize they are high, their conviction that they are special and invisible is strengthened.

I worked nights so there weren't that many people around at night. So I just took a half, or maybe two hits to work. So you went to the toilets, and smoked in the toilets, maybe a half, one hit when you began to feel bad . . . they didn't think about it, 'cause 'I'm just going to the toilet', so you were gone for maybe a half an hour, then, 'Oh it was great to sit and shit', you say, 'Yeah, you were gone for a half an hour, it must have been great [in a teasing tone]', they might say.

As long as they can keep their addict's identity hidden from others, they are not subject to any great threat. Many managed to hide what they were up to for several years. Their identity strategies can be seen as 'clean-up work' where, by keeping their external image clean, they create a self-image they can deal and live with. The heroin users can, with the help of a nice façade, create the impression that they do not belong to any problematic societal category – something they themselves to a certain extent believe.

Appearance is important for their self-image. In today's society, where so much is about body and façade, the body becomes all the more important in distinguishing the desirable from the undesirable and the successful from the unsuccessful. The body in today's society is an unbelievably powerful symbol, reflected in advertising, where goods are sold by means of well-trained bodies that are icons for individual success. Our era's bodily ideal strengthens the credibility of their arguments that they are not problematic drug abusers. The owner of a fit young body is not seen as a failure but, on the contrary, as a success.

Heroin is lenient on the body, even if the overdose risk exists, and this knowledge is also used to further increase the worth of the identity. The façade – the body – evinces that they look good, while the fact that they are hooked says something else. To listen more to the superficial evidence of the body is a way of creating a positive identity, and, furthermore, to have older drug addicts and amphetamine junkies to compare to makes this positive identity even more believable. The heroin users can defend themselves for a long time against the image that describes them as physically and mentally degenerate.

The Yearning for Purity – with 'Smack'

'Smack' is derived from Thai smack, which means 'white heroin from Thailand' and is seen to be of extra high quality.[1] Smack has received a broader meaning in Norrköping, meaning, quite simply, white heroin. Many of Norrköping's young heroin users complain of being tired of brown heroin and claim that they would much rather take white. This demand is a result of an increasing number of people injecting, and the brown is apparently less suitable for injecting than the white. To inject brown heroin, acid must be added, which corrodes the veins and means that, fairly soon, the injecting heroin user has to look for alternative veins. Continuous injection leads to marks on the body that can be interpreted as signs of bodily degeneration as well as intensive abuse. Molly has about the same ideas as others about the relation between brown and white heroin:

> The white is much better. Yeah, altogether better, in every way. For a start, it's much, much purer. It isn't as shitty for the body. I think your system gets shitty and then it smells bad when you smoke brown heroin. You don't get that with the white.

It was, to me, quite repulsive to see how the brown heroin is taken up into a vein, like dirty water being transported in the blood stream. Some of the users can feel disgusted by themselves even if, at the time of the injecting, they are focused on getting in the 'horse' and experiencing the wellbeing. To take white heroin is a solution to the dirt problem; it is considered cleaner.

I was with Steve on one occasion when he injected brown heroin. He crushed a rohypnol tablet and then laid it out in four lines on a piece of foil and 'based' them. Then he took a syringe and spent a couple of minutes looking for good spot to inject in. He found one right by his knuckle. He also said something along the lines of: 'Before, my veins were so big, you could have stuck a dart in them.' (He would later get abscesses on his knuckles.) He says:

> I haven't a vein that can be seen, because of the ascorbic acid the veins just disappear, so eventually you just have to use your fingers and look for tiny little veins, it's just . . . it's distracting. That was what I thought when I started myself and saw someone sitting there and not being able to get it into them, they had take out some, get blood, leave a little blood in the syringe . . . fuck it, it was disgusting.

He gets a 'response' (some blood flows into the syringe) and shoots up the contents. After a while his head falls forward and his eyes begin to twitch, but all is as it should be, he is 'well' and presumably feels good. He begins to wax lyrical about smack and claims that 'really good smack' is undoubtedly the best. He and others have tried on various occasions to persuade the bigger dealers to get in smack, but without success.

For Steve and many others, their bodies are turning into proof of intensive abuse, and it is becoming harder to hide this from the outside world. It is also becoming harder to support an even halfway positive self-image. With problems like abscesses on their knuckles, it becomes harder to be invisible among other people. The process itself becomes 'distracting' when some of them are forced to spend a long time looking for a vein, and it can take up to an hour for some of them to get a response. They can hide their bodies, but they cannot leave them.

The evidence of physical degeneration is almost overwhelming and it becomes very difficult to maintain the picture of being clean. The drug use becomes an unpleasant project, where identity is strongly questioned. Most of those who have come to Steve's stage want to give up heroin. Even Steve wants to. He finds it difficult to like himself as an injecting heroin user. His longing for smack is a sign of how central the striving for purity is and how paradoxical the solution to the problem of cleanliness is. To solve the purity problem, which is the result of heavy and intensive abuse, even heavier abuse is embarked on, using smack to hide the growing traces of degeneracy.

The heroin users' self-images are threatened by the spiralling realization of being hooked on the drug, that the drug-using lifestyle is becoming apparent, coupled with the fact that they are getting older. The longer they keep it up, the more ambivalent their self-image becomes and the harder it is for them to find happiness and contentment in the subculture. Many yearn, with nostalgia, for the times when they were recreational drug users who had good times together. Their lives can be described as ambivalent in the sense that they sometimes experience good times and sometimes bad.

We Who Have Really Experienced Life

> . . . when the drug has started to become a central focus of a neighbourhood's youth culture, as it can do, then being a 'smack-head' can even assume something of a heroic status. (Pearson 1987: 41)

One aspect of the stereotype of the junkies is that they are losers and therefore at the bottom of the social hierarchy. Roger however, sees 'getting hooked' as a proof of experience. He says to me: 'Do you remember when there was a whole pile written in the newspapers about smoking heroin having come to town? I had begun before that. I don't know anyone my age who was using then . . . And now loads of my friends do it, but none of them were there when we started.'

Roger was not actually one of the first – many had been using for two years, some even longer, before he began but among his circle of friends he was one of the first. But he was first in a particular group of friends who got into the dangerous and media-hyped drug heroin. He climbed a Mount Everest at home in the industrial city of Norrköping. Roger is naturally aware that established society views him as a loser, but when he is with his friends and when he is high he more often sees himself as an experienced outsider, someone who knows what life is about, a conqueror of drugs.

Others also emphasize the value of having started using heroin early on. Ben emphasizes that he has been into it now for nearly six years. But Max claims that Ben hasn't really been using that long, that for the first couple of years he only used heroin sporadically. Max claims that you cannot count from when you experimented the first time, and that the measurement ought to be taken from the time when the use was regular and frequent. He also uses the expression 'newbies' as the subculture's name for beginners – people who haven't developed sufficient skill or dexterity with criminality or drugs. By using this expression he mentally turns the situation to his advantage. He appears knowledgeable and experienced. This is in line with what Pearson (1987) writes about young heroin users in Great Britain and what Faupel (1991) writes about heroin users in New York. Some of Pearson's informants reported a higher day-dosage than they actually consumed, and some said they started with heroin before they actually did. Injecting heroin was in Pearson's study a proof of experience and knowledge. To 'be hooked', thus, does not have to be discrediting either in Great Britain, the US or Sweden, but can even, from a subcultural habitus, be seen as a valuable experience. Crispin relates:

When I discovered that I was sort of getting hooked, then I thought, 'Fuck it, now I'm a real addict, now I've fallen into that circle, now I've closed the circle. Now I'm bloody well a real addict, now I need horse to survive, otherwise I won't make it through the day.' Then I felt like this . . . Fuck it, I can't explain how I felt, but I felt like an authentic drug addict, even if I didn't inject the shit, but 'Fuck it, now I'm a real junkie!'

The quotation is two-dimensional. One dimension is about Crispin reaching rock bottom, another is that he really knows what life is all about. He has been there and tried everything. He has become a 'real junky' and thereby an adult in the subculture. To be an outsider is ultimately about having experienced what few other people come close to. If everybody had climbed Mount Everest there wouldn't be any great merit in doing it, and it wouldn't function to make an identity unique. To have used heroin is thereby sufficiently conspicuous compared to other people's identities to enable an interesting identity to be created. Being hooked can, thus, from the subculture's perspective, be understood as life experience, even if it also threatens the identity in the subculture. In this sense, being hooked has a divided symbolic significance. The social and cultural contexts decide how an individual's own dependency will be interpreted. With good access to heroin, money and friends, being hooked can be valued positively, but if the heroin user is starting to withdraw, has no friends and has poor access to money and heroin, then the interpretation will be more negative (see Pearson 1987: 140).

The experience that is valued in the subculture is of the dramatic variety. It involves having been 'where the action is'. Having gone as far as to inject heroin every day is a sign of experience, having a history of action, while at the same time showing enough strong character to have come that far. To be a 'real addict' can be seen as final proof of participating in society's borderland for a long time and of having gone the whole way. To be hooked on heroin ought to be seen as the last station on a railway journey, where subcultural capital has been collected. Being at the last station indicates a long journey.

In Chapter 2, I wrote about the language used as being a 'language of action' with words like speeded, high, and so forth. Even the words that characterize heroin use and injecting have this kind of tempo, for example 'shooting up' heroin. Injecting, like a break-in, is an activity with extreme differences before and afterwards, an action event:

1. Get heroin.
2. Prepare the tools.
3. Find a suitable vein to shoot up.
4. Get a response from the vein.
5. Shoot up.
6. Feel the wave/kick/wellbeing come.

For a serious addict this process is repeated several times a day.

Their lives can still be viewed as dramatic, and if we add that as a consequence of their drug use they are hunted by the police, and that there are a lot of hidden codes in their talk, it can be claimed that their lives must sometimes be experienced as exciting and dramatic, even if the excitement can also turn to stress, angst and worry. For some of them, it is almost a merit to be sought after by the police. If the police are interested, then you cannot be insignificant; rather the opposite. That the police are interested is a sign of having experience. Life as a heroin user, in the best-case scenario, can be seen as rich in experiences and dramatic, and, in that sense unique.

Sign of Success

Earlier, I described the body as a powerful symbol and a sign of success or decay. Another such sign is money, which makes it possible to create the illusion of doing drugs with style.

Crispin tried to stop using heroin, but was invited to be part of a deal, which meant that he chose to enter the subculture again. The reason that he wanted to go back to the gang was partly to prove himself to his friends, as a guy who could drive and leave the cops standing, and partly because of the money the deal meant (see the introduction to Chapter 6). One more possible reason was that he longed to go back to the centre of events, to be 'where the action is'. Below, it is the money that is central, and not just the money, but what it represents; a status that can be experienced as successful.

Crispin: I have four suits, two Calvin Klein and then two of those Italian suits that are really expensive. Two of them I traded for and two I bought myself.
Philip: So it's important to look good?
Crispin: Yeah, like when you go out to a wedding or something, to have on a designer suit, as a twenty-year-old, and then there's older young people there, like twenty-six or twenty-seven and they only have ordinary suits. Then they think, 'Fuck, how is he doing for himself?' and that sort of thing.
Philip: Ah right, so you feel a little special?
Crispin: Yeah, you feel a little more special. Like this summer I was in South America and I had a Hugo Boss suit on me, there in South America. The ones who have Hugo Boss and Calvin Klein suits, they're the rich people. So, all my relatives were just a little amazed: 'What, has he got so much money that he can buy . . .?'

He also tells me that he usually asks his girlfriend out to dinner and that he can say to her 'Have what you want.' He dedicates himself to what the classical sociologist, Veblen (1889/1979), calls 'conspicuous consumption' – the consumption of goods that, by their consumption, mark the consumer as successful (see also Bourdieu 1979/1992). Similar conclusions are drawn in Williams' ethnographical study of young cocaine/crack dealers in *The Cocaine Kids* (1989) and in Bourgois' ethnography of Puerto Rican drug dealers in *In Search of Respect* (1996). One of the driving forces behind dealing, according to Williams and Bourgois, is that one can evolve as a consumer and thereby maintain a form of respect. 'Money and drugs are the obvious immediate rewards for kids in the cocaine trade. But there is another strong motivating force, and that is the desire to show family and friends that they can succeed at something' (Williams 1989: 10).

When Crispin's gang steals cars it is nearly always status-symbol cars, like BMW, Audi and Mercedes. The BMW is described in Williams' book as a typical dealer's car. Crispin likes to count the money after a good sale. With the help of money and status objects he can differentiate himself from his peers and create an illusion of success – an illusion that is possible to maintain by selling heroin. Money and consumer goods make it possible for the possessors to believe that they have moved in the social space, the hierarchy of which society is constituted. They are, using the title from Bourgois' (1996) study, in search of respect.

Crispin was relatively successful as a dealer, and in a week he could sometimes earn up to £2,500, but even those who weren't as successful at selling would sometimes dream about a life with power and money. Veronica, who lives at bag level, has pawned her parents' belongings and her mobile phone in order to buy heroin, but even so she has about £8 left over. From a heroin point of view, she ought to keep it to put towards buying more heroin, but she doesn't. The money is wasted on slot machines. The slot machines may give an economic payoff, which can be used for more 'bags'. Playing the machines may also give the illusion of wealth, a chance visit to an imaginary casino. The heroin user who gambles on slot machines is doing drugs in style.

Roger, on the occasion described in the introduction to this chapter, was feeling happy despite the fact that he had recently become homeless. His good humour was partly dependent on the fact that he was high, and partly dependent on having done a good deal, which had secured his own heroin access for a day or two. He had been able to buy a gram of heroin for eighty pounds and had split it into bags, of which he had sold three for £100. We talked about it:

> *Roger*: Then I had £20 in my pocket, and I got two free bags. There was a profit there, already, and if had sold the other two then ... if we say that someone rang me and said 'Can you help me with two bags?' [and I responded] 'Of course' then I would have earned eighty pounds in maybe half an hour. So just look at the money there's in it.

He was as pleased as a salesman would be after a particularly good day. The pleasure is also because it is 'good' heroin he has got his hands on, and for a well-evolved 'heroin mind', good heroin means happiness. The dream of success can be kept alive by small profits, like one day earning £80 and living that day as a 'king-for-a-day' (Svensson 1996). To spend time at the slot machines losing money one day, only to have to pawn a mobile phone the next, is nothing abnormal for a young heroin user.

Money has a magic that is nearly as powerful at the drugs. Roger is highly ambivalent about his own situation and describes how he would like to solve it:

Roger: My life doesn't feel too good right now. I have problems with my girlfriend. Home is shot to hell. I want my own flat. I live drug-free a lot. When I'm clean, I have more money. I buy clothes and feel good. I buy things. It makes me feel good . . .

Philip: What's an ideal life? How would you like to live?

Roger: How I'd like it to be?

Philip: Yes, use your imagination.

Roger: [Laughs.] How much imagination can I use?

Philip: Try it. You can invent as much as you like.

Roger: Eh, how would I like my life to be? [Silence.]

Philip: Imagine.

Roger: I would definitely like to have money, I think most people would, and a sort of good job. But it's not something I have the energy to invest in, a good job that is, it feels impossible, I will never have an ordinary job, so I don't know what the fuck . . . I would rather not, but I could do more business and earn money, but I don't really want to get involved. But I could make big money and buy myself a Mercedes [laughs]. But, nah, I could go that way, but then you end up sitting in the clink doing hard time.

Buying things makes Roger feel good, something he shares with many others exposed to capitalism. Money has an extremely powerful value and is a substitute for happiness, and the heroin users are far from on their own in their attitude.

People today are imprisoned in dreams of consumption, which lead to a continuous search for new objects to consume and new needs to satisfy (see Campbell 1989). According to Bauman (2000), the market creates these needs and the media ensure that few escape the market's pitching of dreams of success, which also become the consumers' dreams. By dealing in drugs the heroin users can try to realize their dreams of success, without having to do it the hard way – they take 'the fast reward system'. With the help of money and goods, they are capable of creating the illusion of a different environment, they can be who they want to be if they believe in the goods' magic and that those who own the goods partake in this magic. The goods can be likened to amulets that bring happiness and success.

Style and success can even be implied with the help of the right drugs. Smack has a higher value than brown heroin, and that is because of the white heroin's exclusivity. That which is expensive and difficult to obtain becomes surrounded by myth and gives status to those who, against the odds, manage to obtain it. Steve says: 'It is significantly cleaner. It is, more or less, like a wine connoisseur who drinks a good wine and then drinks a cheap wine, you can compare it to that, there really is a big difference.' It is about showing who they want to be with the help of consumer goods, someone with style and success. The experience of being successful, however, is not permanent; signs indicating that they are unsuccessful destroy it – for example withdrawal, where their situation is experienced as anything but stylish, threatens the illusion.

The Threats to Identity

In this chapter I have discussed and analysed how the young heroin users try to create respectability in order to deal with the threats which form against their identities. Ultimately, it is about what makes drug taking, according to their perspective, a relatively rational undertaking, despite the fact that it is condemned by the surrounding society.

That most of them have begun to use heroin in such a way that it is seen as heavy and intensive abuse places pressure on their ability and the subculture's ability to create positive identities. The threat to their self-image has to be neutralized and made less threatening if they are to preserve their self-respect. These threats can be divided into three categories.

1. The threat that says that they are 'morally degenerate'. They are able to fend off this threat by operating from the subculture's morality rather than that of established society. The subculture provides alternative codes of honour, which mean that the heroin users, if they can live up to these codes, experience a form of pride and thereby a reinforcement of their identity. To have coped with the police and to have had praise from their friends are examples of this type of reinforcement, where the subculture rewards the type of behaviour that protects it. A type of professional honour develops in the subculture, where the alternative knowledge that is created provides more or less the same type of reinforcement as people in 'ordinary society' experience when they are good at something. The heroin users have developed a way of thinking about drugs and criminality that is specific to the subculture, as a result of the alternative socialization they have undergone. The subculture's perspective is focused on heroin, and its members are so occupied with grafting and thinking about heroin that any tendency to reflect on the moral consequence of their dealings with heroin is rare.

2. The threat that says that they are 'physically and mentally degenerate'. This threat they can handle as long as, when they look in the mirror, they see relatively young and well-trained bodies, which in comparison with those of other drug addicts seem more or less untouched. Even their way of moving among ordinary people and making their stigmas 'invisible' to them reinforces that they have not changed noticeably. The authority the well-trained body represents has great importance for how they judge themselves. This fixation on the body can also make them stop using heroin. As they get older, the bodily decay is more apparent and when they begin to inject it becomes much more difficult to maintain a 'clean appearance'.

3. The threat that says that they are 'losers'. According to the subculture's logic, experience of drugs is valued as an important life experience, as subcultural capital. The pioneering heroin users emphasize that they were first, and in today's culture of individualism there is kudos in having been the first with a particular discovery or exploit. In this sense, an experience of originality is created, which the subculture can interpret as positive, but which for society in general is negative. The heroin users can use status symbols to portray their own identities as success-ful. They detach themselves from ordinary young people and partake of the subculture's rewards: money, consumer goods and drugs that convey status. They demonstrate, in this way, that they are more capable than many of their peers.

In this chapter I have tried to show the perspectives the young heroin users employ when it comes to judging their own actions. At the same time it is import-ant to point out that their self-images are marked by a powerful ambivalence. Their participation in the subculture can be seen as a roller-coaster ride, and when they leave the subculture what they remember most is the excitement and drama. After a while, it becomes particularly apparent that they cannot experience action in the same way as they did in the subculture. The tempo is slower, and many who try to stop participating describe the experience as extremely tedious. From the sub-culture's perspective, life as a heroin user is not always miserable. There are sometimes light moments, provided by successful deals, fast money, exciting burglaries, strong fellowship, successful emergency strategies against the police, extra high-quality heroin and powerful drug kicks.

At the same time, there is a reason why the majority of them say they want to stop. I believe the main reason is that they are scared of physical, social and bodily degeneracy, coupled to the fact that it is difficult to cope with the experience of being dependent. Many of those who are today between twenty-four and twenty-seven are trying to stop, but they find it difficult to leave the subculture completely. At lot of it is about learning to live in a society that is not characterized by the type of action they are used to, while for some, in particular, it is the lack of rewards that they are used to. Some dealers who try to stop find it difficult to get used to living on £800 to £1,000 per month. They have got used to the flow of money that characterizes the subculture. To get money once a month or every fortnight is of significance to the larger society, which values waiting for and deferring rewards.

Society sends heroin users a mixed message. On the one hand it says, 'you shouldn't use drugs', because drug use conflicts with the good behaviour and discipline necessary to an ordered society. It is important for society's members to be productive, and whatever threatens this characteristic of production is fought. If everyone used drugs, the factories would stand idle. On the other hand, we should consume, say both the media and the corporations. This is the voice of capitalism, which does not concern itself with people's drug habits, but is interested in having people consume, that the wheels continue to turn, and with increasing speed. What is important is not producing, but experiencing, and in this case the young heroin users are exemplary.

Note

1. This connection between smack and Thai smack is most likely specifically Swedish. I have heard it from both Norrköping and other Swedish heroin users. Otherwise, smack can be used to describe heroin in general – white, brown and black. See Stewart (1987).

–6–

Who is Directing?

The Collection

Enrique is trying to quit heroin. It is evening, and he is on his way from his flat in the suburbs to the hamburger bar, when he hears a car horn blowing. 'Who the fuck is that?' he thinks, and doesn't recognize the car. He continues walking and the car suddenly approaches again and brakes in front of him. 'What the fuck is it now? Is it the filth? Cops in a new car, after something?' He is nervous, but in order to calm himself thinks, 'Fuck it, I've nothing on me, I don't need to be nervous.' But it isn't the cops; it's a friend that Enrique's hung around with since childhood.

Louis: Yo, long time no see!
Enrique: Fuck you; you scared the crap out of me.
Louis: You remember you owe me a couple of favours?
Enrique: Well . . .

But his friend reminds him of the two occasions he has helped Enrique out of a hole. Enrique remembers and realizes what he has to do, he must help his friend and thinks: 'The world goes around, he helped me, he has a right to demand I return the favour.'

Louis: I need one of those two favours tomorrow. I need you to drive me to Stock-
             holm, me and another guy, Hugo.
Enrique: Fuck it, is he going too?
Louis: Yeah.
Enrique: Okay, what are you going to do there?
Louis: We're just fetching some horse.

Enrique imagines it's a matter of 10 g to 15 g and that's not, in his view, so much. Heroin is something with which Enrique is pretty familiar.

Enrique: Okay, I can drive the car, but is it clean?
Louis: No, it's this car, here; we've just taken it.
Enrique: The fucking thing will be hot by tomorrow, then.

Louis: Yeah, so . . .?
Enrique: Then how the fuck are we going to get out of town?
Louis: It'll be fine, we know how you drive, you can do it, you can leave the cops standing.

Enrique is a little flattered but still ambivalent. He knows he is risking a lot, but he has mixed feelings. His decision is coloured by the good times he has had with the gang and the strong social ties that have been formed. He knows it is wrong. He also knows he cannot escape his friends and thinks, 'Even if I tried to give up and stay away from them, they know where to find me when it comes down to it.' He even feels he doesn't want them to go without him; he wants to be 'where the action is'.

Enrique: Okay, but if we're caught, I'm not going down.
Louis: It's cool. We won't rat on you.

Louis and Enrique decide on a meeting place for the following day, and Louis jumps back into the car and takes off, burning rubber. Enrique's girlfriend has heard the conversation and says in a worried tone: 'You shouldn't do it!', but Enrique says, in a serious voice, 'Yes, I have to, old friends, collecting debts, favours I owe them, so it has to be done, it's that simple. You know how it used to be, it works the same way now.' Enrique arrives, and the two others are sitting on the sofa in Louis' flat.

Enrique: How much are we fetching? Five to 20 grams?
Louis: No, 50. But we'll take the train back, so you can drive back right away.

Enrique thinks that it's a bit too much, but he has already made up his mind and doesn't raise objections. Anyway, he can't pull out at this late stage. After they have smoked, they leave Norrköping and head for Stockholm. They have brought sweets, soft drinks, and, of course, heroin with them – 'snacks' for the journey. Enrique stays within the speed limit. He doesn't want to get stopped by the police. The police would see that they were high and also wonder why they had so much money with them. The guys get anxious in the car. 'For fuck's sake, sit still!' says Enrique. They stop by an exit and take out the heroin and the foil (smoking in a moving car is almost impossible). They take several hits and become a little calmer. Meanwhile they have reconsidered.

Louis: We've changed our minds, you'll have to drive us back.
Enrique: No way! The deal was I drive you there, then you take the train back.
Louis: Yeah, but we'll give you 10 grams if you drive us back, payment for the risk.

Enrique knows that money is valuable and that heroin equals money. Besides, he has had money worries recently after giving up much of his dealing. He values heroin highly, as something worth taking risks for, and so he accepts the offer. Enrique may not be completely comfortable with this, but at the same time, he is beginning to feel that the gang are back having an adventure again. His pulse rises; he is part of it once more. They pass many police cars along the way and each time their pulse and adrenalin levels rise. The guys are excited and agitated and want Enrique to drive faster. They are running late, they have stopped along the way for heroin and refreshments.

Louis: Come on, step on it, we've to meet the man in an hour for fuck's sake, we've an hour to go before we get to Stockholm.

Enrique: Fuck off, I'm doing 110 kph [the speed limit] like it says, and I don't give a damn, you'll just have to ring him and tell him we'll be late, because I'm damn well not going down.

They arrive in Stockholm and get to the meeting place. But 'the man' isn't there. They wait for a half hour, and then for an hour. Louis and Enrique begin to get edgy. A few police cars pass by. Enrique and his friends have a talent for sighting police cars, like bird spotters with rare birds; their attention is also focused on discovering possible plain-clothed police; they are nervous. 'The man' finally shows up and the goods are exchanged for cash. The tempo rises once again when Louis comes back from the rendezvous with 50 g of heroin and just says, 'Drive for fuck's sake!' Enrique's adrenalin flows and he shivers all over, thinking 'What if the filth were to give chase right now, how fucking cool would that be, to just press my foot to the floor, go right through the city, break every red light, the works.' However, leaving the city is problem-free.

On the way back they stop once again, to smoke. The tension has made the hit feel even better and more necessary. The contrast between tension and calm makes a heroin high even better. They pull back on to the motorway again. Enrique feels tiredness creeping up on him; the horse is like cotton wool wrapped around his brain, his eyes are closing and he is finding it hard to stay on the road. The journey is in danger of becoming fatal, but they are still calm.

Enrique: Fuck it, I'm getting tired.

Louis: Yeah, I knew you would be, so I bought this for you.

Louis throws a gram of amphetamine to Enrique who doesn't hesitate. He is tired and wants to be on top again, so that he can stay on the road. He snorts a half-gram, two lines, immediately. He can feel his nose seriously sting, but after a short while, he becomes more alert. The 'shit' has put him back on track. They continue back to Norrköping with the most precious thing a heroin addict can dream of: goods that are easy to sell, and that will quickly put Enrique back in the black again.

A Staged Reality

The subculture is heavily influenced by film, especially by American films but also Swedish films. *The Collection* is a reconstruction of a couple of conversations with Enrique and is heavily reminiscent of a gangster film. This is no coincidence. Enrique's world is the gangster's world, with the gang's symbols round his arms, just as in the film *Blood In Blood Out,* where the gang's symbol was tattooed just over the thumb.

Blood In Blood Out: Bound by Honour (1993). Director: Taylor Hackford. Starring: Damien Chapa, Jesse Borrego, Benjamin Bratt. About three cousins who, during their teens, are members of a gang, Vatos Locos in East LA. The gang defends its territory against rival groups. One of the gang members, Miklo, saves his cousin Paco from being shot by a rival gang member, with the result that Miklo gets a long prison sentence. A series of events in prison result in Miklo becoming further involved in crime while his cousins on the outside develop in different directions. Paco, the former gang leader, becomes a policeman while Cruz becomes a heroin addict. Their different situations test their former loyalties.

One of the addicts from real life has a photograph of the gang, nicely framed, hanging in pride of place in his flat. In *Blood in Blood Out* the artist and, later on, heroin addict Cruz paints a picture of the gang. What the creed, 'the world goes around' means to Enrique and his friends is that everything comes back, that is, if you have paid for someone once, or helped them with a problem, you can count on the favour being returned. It is a question of the gang's honour – the members are *Bound by Honour.*

The world had gone around, and Enrique had to go to Stockholm. A favour is returned by a favour – a common theme in many American gang films, which picture brotherhood as 'one for all, all for one'. The group is more important than the family, or rather, the gang is the family. The social ties are clearly expressed in a number of places in *Blood In Blood Out*. Paco will not leave Miklo, who is injured and bleeding, despite the approaching police. Paco is confronted at one stage by his mother who questions the gang's values and instead wants him to think more of his family. He answers, indicating his friends: 'this is my family'. Enrique and Crispin wear the gang's symbol in the form of tattoos and feel like a family.

As with the mafia families, no outsider can be present when business is discussed. When Miklo, from the film, receives his tattoo there is no doubt; this is a proud moment. The gang shout out 'Brother, Vatos Locos, forever!' Miklo who has distanced himself from his white father, is as proud as can be. He feels he has finally found a family. The rest of the gang shout 'Vatos Locos for ever, Viva Vatos Locos!' Paco says to him, 'Now we are brothers even in death.' There is a strong parallel here with what Enrique and Crispin have to tell me, which Enrique expresses when he says to his girlfriend: 'You know how it used to be, well it works the same way now.' Enrique usually speaks with a more reverent tone when he talks of the gang's honour – the gang represents what is most sacred to him.

Enrique has been involved in about ten joyrides (car chases involving the police). He says this with a certain amount of pride. Car chases are a regular occurrence in American gang and gangster films. In *Blood In Blood Out* there is a joyriding scene. Miklo, Paco and three other members of Vacos Locos believe for a minute that they have managed to lose the police. Paco shouts proudly to the others, 'That was a real Chicano curve!' and someone shouts, 'The cops can't take Chicano curves!' The gang are jubilant. They have fooled the police and the feeling is like no other. Enrique feels something similar when everything has worked out for the gang.

Enrique: We stole mostly sports cars, Audis and BMWs and sometimes it was fun to be chased, we thought, 'Shit, this is just cool' and driving with your foot to the floor, just driving away from the cops, that was the best feeling in the world . . . It was that kick: 'We got away! Yes! They know nothing about cars, they can't drive, shit I'm the best, I drove the car, and we got away, guys, thanks to me' – That sort of thing.

There is an obvious parallel between Enrique's words and the film world. There are no great differences. In Enrique and Crispin's world their own experience and that of the film world are merged. The car chase becomes part of an *action story* featuring the group's strength and superiority in relation to the police, who ought to be fast drivers. They conquer a difficult opponent, which makes the experience and the victory that much greater. They have have done just as in the film.

The favourite films of Crispin and Enrique (among others) were *Blood In Blood Out, Boyz 'N' the Hood, Menace II Society* and *New Jack City*:

Philip: Were there other films that were especially important for you?
Crispin: Yeah, the gang films. We tried to learn a little about how the gang stuck together, what they did together and how they looked after each other and those kinds of things.
Philip: It became your thing in a way, the gang?

Crispin: Yeah, it was when we went out together we decided everything together, for example: 'You watch my back, I'll watch yours', we've always been those kind of guys . . . The two of us, we always looked after each other, us two. 'You take care of me, so I take care of you', and then each of us, we look out for one another, so . . .

Philip: You were watching to see if anyone came?

Crispin: Yeah, sort of. If you get into a fight I'd jump in right away and watch your back so that no one would come from behind and hit you or anything.

Philip: But, do you think it was so tough in Norrköping that you needed to?

Crispin: No, probably not, but we believed it at the time.

In the film *Menace II Society*, something similar is expressed by the main character Caine: 'My older cousin Harold hung with us. He lived in Long Beach. He was a real gangster. He had a Beamer [BMW], a pad and money. When he was around I didn't have to worry. He had my back and I had his. We looked after each other.'

The strategy of watching each other's backs is not actually necessary, but serves to fulfil two functions. The first is that the unity of the group is strengthened; they show each other that they are ready to sacrifice for each other. Each time they cover for each other, the social bonds are strengthened. The second is to create a daily environment that is as action-rich as possible. The ritual dramatizes the daily environment, and makes it like the fictitious world.

Menace II Society (1993). Directors: The Hughes Brothers. Starring: Tyrin Turner, Jada Pinkett, Bill Duke and Charles S. Sutton. 'Caine is a small-scale drug dealer who wants to escape from his world's confines, but it is all he knows.' Both his parents, a dealer and an addict, die and it is difficult for him to leave his surroundings where he is continually confronted by weapons and vendettas. The film is particularly violent and brutal.

Boyz 'N' the Hood (1991). Directed by John Singleton. Starring: Ice Cube, Cuba Gooding Jr. and Morris Chestnut. The film is about three young men who live in a poor area of LA where crime is pervasive. The theme is ultimately the same as in *Menace II Society* – about being drawn into the world of gang crime and the attempt to escape it. In contrast to *Menace*, this film is more tragic than violent.

New Jack City (1991). Director: Mario Van Peebles. Starring: Wesley Snipes, Ice T, Chris Rock, Mario Van Peebles and Judd Nelson. Wesley Snipes plays a crack dealer, Ninio, who is expanding his enterprise and trying to be king of the street. Ice T and Judd Nelson play policemen who are trying to put Ninio behind bars and who infiltrate his inner circle in order to do so. The film is violent.

By imitating the American role models, they try to make their lives dramatic. They use the expression 'cops', like most of the other heroin users, instead of 'police', as it sounds more like something from an action film, and also because it clearly indicates their identity as criminal outsiders.

Through this type of idealization (Goffman 1959/1974) the heroin users become like characters in a film where they can, with the help of the media's role models, script, and retrospectively, review their actions. After almost every event, the group members gather to talk about what went down. The group has complete control over the interpretation of events when it comes to reconstructing them. On these occasions they also share out heroin and money and go over their finances. The gang's success is thereby materially tangible. Sometimes even the gophers (hangers-on who do fetching and carrying) partake, to collect the heroin for either delivery or resale. The gophers fulfil two functions:

1. They make it possible to avoid keeping too much heroin at home, a security measure.
2. Having a gopher strengthens and idealizes the image of a successful dealer and crime boss. The dealers become more like those of the film world. The gophers can be seen as the admiring audience, the Bens/dealers as stars. The stars need an audience in order to define their success. (Ibid 1959/1974)

Roger spoke about the first time he took cocaine; he and a friend each obtained a little mirror in preparation (others tell a similar story). I asked why they wanted to use mirrors and not something else with a flat surface. He answered that he didn't know why. When I asked Enrique about this he said he had seen it in a film. He didn't know anything more about the purpose of the mirror, just that it should be a mirror. John also used a mirror, but when thinking it over, didn't think it had any particular function beyond that of a flat surface on which to lay a line of cocaine. Snorting cocaine becomes more *real* if done as it is done in the films. It must be done according to accepted use, in order to seem authentic. The mirror is a consequence of global media.

A researcher in youth culture, Ziehe (1993), claims that youths today are self-reflective through a 'media package', which they have internalized from watching film and television. This media package indicates what is possible, desirable, and so forth. In Roger and Enrique's media package there is information about the relationship between mirrors and cocaine, and this makes it possible for them to dramatize the role of cocaine user.

They learned how the gang functions through films. They picked up on and imitated those aspects they found useful with regard to their identity construction (see Hall 1980 and Fiske 1989). Media provide a 'guarantee of authenticity'. When the gang acts in a way similar to occurrences in film they experience themselves as a genuine gang. Gang life is dramatized in order to correspond better to the fictitious reality, and where danger has a central position in films, that danger becomes synonymous with real. To live dangerously is to live authentically. It is also a question of 'staged authenticity' (MacCannell 1976), where the actors in the subculture, with the help of images from film, stage the events occurring in the subculture. In doing this, they use signs to idealize their acting.

Knowledge of the correct symbolism is found in their media packages. If they wish to portray themselves as a dealer they can acquire the correct façade: good suits, mobile phones, gold chains, drugs, visits to restaurants, slicked-back hair (prevalent among the South American users and dealers), BMWs, special jargon, secrecy when dealing (to prevent detection by the police) and money. These symbols are all tools for constructing the façade that is necessary in order to make a believable attempt at becoming the role as dramatized in films.

The French sociologist Baudrillard (1983) states that we live in a time where the borders between the imaginary/filmic and reality are increasingly obscured through the globalization of media in the Western world. He speaks of hyper-realism, and living in an 'aesthetic hallucination of reality'. There are many indications that the border between reality and media reality is gone, or to perhaps express it better, reality has become like the fictitious, where certain people are using the media's frames of reference to define their identity.

Films produce a belief that different types of transaction and behaviour are associated with a desirable identity. Desirable and undesirable outsider behaviour are distinguishable through the medium of film. A style and a repertoire of behaviour are constructed by the group, through which the members are enabled to experience power and a clear identity. It is therefore not strange that many choose to become familiar with these particular gang films, as they provide solutions to the need for identity and belonging. They can identify themselves with the liberation from establishment values and parents that are portrayed in these films.

In accordance with the search for coherence between the media and the real they seek and adopt behaviour that lessens the distance between the two worlds, as their behaviour is something within their control, while that portrayed by film is not. Dangerous and forbidden behaviour is desirable, and is given a high value. Life is dramatized in order to make it genuine, and also in order to make it more closely correspond to the film's rhythm and themes. This is a positive process in the sense that it strengthens their belief in their own identity: they become important and authentic. The films supply the behaviour and style stereotypes, which contribute to aestheticizing the overstepping of boundaries. They are not only outsiders; they are now 'aestheticized outsiders'.

The Picture of Success

Philip: I wonder where you learnt that it was cool, if you know what I mean, to take drugs?

Crispin: It probably had a little to do with the gangster films we saw. Like a gang had a lot of drugs or money. They did drugs, had the coolest cars and chicks, that kinda thing. The other gangs respected them just because they had more of those things, it was there we got some of it . . . Well, mostly we got it from films and those kind of things.

Few heroin users read books to any great extent. Most have only read somewhere between one and five books, and it is often Tolkien's *The Lord of the Rings* (1959). They all like music, but music that defines the subculture cannot be identified, not in the way that films can. To a large extent, the users say that they are interested in films and, in particular, films about outsiders, who attempt in different ways to be successful in a world where they are shut out from the possibility of a decent chance at life.

The films deal with a concept of success like that which is described in Chapter 2 and called the 'fast reward system', a shortcut to power and money. Most of them have seen the film *Scarface*, which is a story about a Cuban's road to success in capitalist America.[1] Tony Montana arrives in America as a criminal accompanied by his close friend Manolo. Initially, they are treated like dirt by the American authorities. They are given jobs at a diner, but soon come in contact with the American Mafia. By playing the game and taking risks Tony Montana becomes, in time, the King of Cocaine. He gets everything he wants, a fancy house, great cars, and a beautiful woman. A classic line from the film occurs during the following scene: Tony is driving with his friend Manolo, having been to see the Mafia boss, Frank, who lives in a large luxurious house with a beautiful woman, Mia. Tony is envious, and on the way back he tells Manolo how he sees life:

Tony: I want what's coming to me.
Manolo: What's coming to you, man?
Tony: The world, chico, and everything in it.

Tony also advises Manolo on how to pull chicks: 'In this country, you gotta make the money first. Then when you get the money, you get the power. Then when you get the power, then you get the woman.'

This need for money and power is a recurring theme in the film. This film has had imitators; watching *New Jack City*, one is struck by the parallels to *Scarface*. It, too, is a film about the criminal path to success, the fast reward system, in a capitalistic society where some are much better off than others. *New Jack City*, however, deals with Afro-Americans. The film's central character, Ninio, is a flashy dresser, a graceful mover, has 'chicks', nice cars and a fleet of employees to aid him. He is ambitious, he wants to be New York's biggest crack dealer and in order to get there he will use all means at his disposal. It is the realization of the American dream, but in an alternative way; not through education, high school and college, but by being streetwise and strong in character.

The Swedish film, *The Seekers* (In Swedish: *Sökarna*), was popular among the young drug users. A strong theme in the film, as in *Scarface* and *New Jack City,* is the path to success via crime. Crime is portrayed in the film as a reasonable alternative for the characters that have grown up in Stockholm's poor suburbs. The main characters, Jocke and Ray, join forces with an older criminal and become career criminals. Their dream is to make big money, become powerful and get 'chicks'.

Sökarna (The Seekers) (1993). was made by Daniel Fridell and Peter Cartriers. The lead roles were played by Liam Norberg, Ray Jones II and Torsten Flink. The two friends, Jocke and Ray, grow up in a poor Stockholm suburb under difficult circumstances. Their fathers are completely absent and there do not seem to be any adult role models to look up to. Through violence and crime, Jocke and Ray manage to make money and gain power, but the path is not problem-free.

Money and consumer goods are very important in this film (as they are in the two previous films). As their criminal activity increases, so does their income. Money is transformed to success symbols like champagne, cocaine, Rolex watches, Armani suits, and attendance at celebrity events, and so forth. Jocke and his friends start to look more and more like successful consultants. On one occasion, early in the film before they have made any money, Ray and Jocke are leafing through pornographic magazines, and Ray says: 'I wonder who gets to get those chicks?' Jocke replies: 'Those with money, cash' (my translation).

This is strongly reminiscent of *Scarface*. In the mid 1990s, John, a heroin user from Norrköping, and his friends dressed in the same way as the characters in *The Seekers*, which seems to indicate that it had an impact on the creation of their identity. Characters like Jocke and Ray were role models for John's evolving identity. *The Seekers* managed to make the latent message of *Scarface* and *New Jack City,* about an alternative career even clearer to the Swedish heroin addicts. Because they spoke Swedish and were active in a Swedish environment, it was easier to identify with the film. The 'fast money' and 'power through drug dealing' correspond to many of the young heroin users' career projects; the subculture values the same aims as the fictionalized media world. The films describe lawless enterprise, and making one's own luck through criminal enterprise.

The films mentioned above have inspired the creation of the subculture. Most of them were released in the first half of the 1990s: *Boyz 'N' the Hood* in 1991, *Blood In Blood Out* in 1993, *Menace II Society* in 1993, and *The Seekers* in 1993. The majority of the heroin users were between 11 and 17 years old at the time and involved in what in Chapter 2 was called 'separation'. The films have influenced the subculture and made it possible to chisel out the identities that the members of the subculture would make their own. The heroin users wanted to separate themselves from the mainstream, the question was how to symbolize this separation. The media provided much of the answer, and could supply the cultural forms necessary to aestheticize the separation, give it character and authenticity. Money and status goods became the ultimate signs of success, and crime and drugs became the ultimate signs of separation. Through imitating these films they could both live up to the demand of the post-modern – to experience and consume – and also separate themselves from modern society's demand for discipline.

The Establishment's Degeneracy

The films also provide the argument that the heroin users' identity is no worse than that of those who submit to societal law and order. The representatives of established society, as portrayed in these films, are often perverted, dishonest and selfish. In *The Seekers* the picture given of adults verges on the absurd. They are either corrupt, unrealistic/out of touch, alcoholics or deranged homosexuals. There are no 'good' adults in the film. The only teacher with a part to play is homosexual and performs a striptease during a lesson when egged on by the pupils. The headmaster, on one occasion, is masturbating during a parent's visit. The establishment is portrayed as sick and, in contrast to this, the gang's activity seems sound. The gang as a micro-society appears to be much more honest than established society, and membership of the gang is described as almost necessary given that society is splintered and incapable of taking care of a large portion of the younger generation.

Good is not found among the representatives of the establishment but rather in Jocke and his gang (if it exists at all). When Jocke hits someone it is usually justified. He beats up the headmaster, who has assaulted his little sister. He beats up a couple of skinheads who had shouted *sieg heil* and taunted people in the underground. He beats up a rapist in jail and a media celebrity who tries to assault his girlfriend. Most of what he does has an external rational explanation. Jocke portrays good in a perverted world where everyone seems to be out for themselves, including those whose duty it is to look out for others, like teachers and the police.

The prison guards in the film *Blood In Blood Out* are brutal and every bit as evil as the prisoners. In *Menace II Society* the main character, Caine, and his friends are captured by the police, beaten and then driven to a Mexican ghetto where they are left by the police with the specific intention that they will be beaten again, 'let the trash take care of the trash'. The reason they are stopped is because Caine had a nicer car than someone like him should, which irritates the police. This theme with evil *rule enforcers* is also found in the film *Pulp Fiction* (very popular among heroin users), where only one policeman appears, and he rapes the Mafia boss Marcellus in the basement of a weapons shop.

Pulp Fiction (1994). Directed by Quentin Tarantino. Starring: John Travolta, Samuel L. Jackson, Uma Thurman and Harvey Keitel. The film could be called episodic, where seemingly unconnected segments are woven together. It is about the underworld and two central characters are Vincent and Jules, two hit men who work for the Mafia boss Marcellus. Other characters are also woven in and out of the action, often in an unexpected manner.

Natural Born Killers is a powerful critique of society where nothing is portrayed as good. Everyone, including the police, prison authorities and journalists, is perverted. Human existence revolves around recognition, fame or notoriety, and for that they are prepared to do just about anything. No one is prepared to do anything to create a better society. Everyone is more or less equally selfish. Modern media consumers, and the producers of it, are portrayed as perverted. The media's driving force is far from contributing to an improved society, to create saleable drama, and what could be more perfect than to make a documentary soap about a pair of serial killers who have fallen in love with each other. The film satirizes both the media and the double standards that are part and parcel of shows like Ricky Lake and Jerry Springer. In a sick society, Mickey and Mallory are not much sicker than anyone else. In capitalist society, everyone is out for themselves and solidarity and altruism are dispelled.

Natural Born Killers (1994). Directed by Oliver Stone. Starring: Woody Harrelson, Juliette Lewis, Robert Downey Jr and Tommy Lee Jones. The original screenplay was written by Quentin Tarantino. The film is about a young couple, Mickey and Mallory, who fall in love with each other, kill Mallory's parents and take off on a serial killing spree. (More about this film in Chapter 7.)

These films can strengthen the experience of moral levelling, the idea that no one person's morality is any better than anyone else's, all are more or less equally poor or equally good. Established society's representatives are weeded out, to the advantage of the thinking and logic that rule the criminal subculture, a different normality.

This dissolution of different types of polarity, for example between good and evil, or the normal and perverted can, by itself, be interpreted as a sign of the post-modern. The films describe something completely at odds with modern society's spokesmen, for example the schools, who see their duty as continuing to reinforce belief in modern society's morality. The school system's latent function is to see to it that the upcoming members of society learn to believe that the established order is good. While school and modern society's voice says, 'honesty is the best policy' and 'study now, and you will be rewarded in the future', the films, part-icularly Tarantino's, are saying something completely different: 'honesty no longer exists' and 'take what you want, otherwise someone else will get there before you. Live for the present! Carpe diem! The future is now!' The films help those who live with ambivalence to work this out, even if only for the moment. The subculture's morality is legitimized by undermining establishment's. It becomes easier to live as an outsider with these films in mind. It becomes more difficult for modern society's representatives to legitimize their norm as the good, natural and authentic one.

The Drifter

To many the drifter is a description of a hash smoker, but others see it more as a way of life and the adoption of a position whereby, through action and attitude, people show that they have chosen another way of life, an undetermined path where they allow themselves to drift in their surroundings rather than planning a course of action.

A drifter is relaxed and takes things as they come, and the life of the drifter can be described as a collection of 'nows'. The modern person's life, in contrast, is future oriented and, in order to cope with this, he must plan. Planning has no great role in the drifter's life and, therefore, those concerned represent modern society's anti-heroes, a personality who refuses to participate in the timeframe and discipline expected of people in modern society.

The drifter seldom knows, and doesn't care to know, what shape tomorrow will take. Pleasure and relaxation are central. Work and family are less important. Money is not saved for future investments, but spent. Like much else, it goes 'up in smoke'. Even when money is running out, and the drifter has just pawned his or her parents' heirlooms, the drifters can stand at the slot machines and keep putting in the coins.

Drifters do not have to be drug users, but it is likely that they are. The drifter has a positive attitude to the effects of drugs. Drugs are one of the main symbols of the drifter, because these, more than anything, symbolize the 'live now' attitude. The 'now' is clearest when things are happening, either in their surroundings, or their perception of their surroundings. Drugs are often intimately woven into the drifter's sense of identity.

The drifter type is often found in the films named by the heroin users. One classic film series of this type, which those who have been involved in the scene for a long time are familiar with, are the Cheech and Chong 'cannabis comedies'. In these the audience follows two brothers, Cheech and Chong, through various experiences; musical performances, UFO's, drug-induced states, lows, etc.[2] The films portray an attitude of aimlessness and lack of planning, a drifting in the present where experiences are created and reinforced with the help of drugs: LSD, magic mushrooms, marijuana and cocaine among others. Seen from a conscientious perspective, that of an obedient and upstanding citizen, Cheech and Chong are almost totally irresponsible and obnoxious.

When drugs are taken in company, reaction and conversation can occur without any of it making sense. This is another ingredient, and characteristic, of the drifter in films. The participants are freed from the seriousness involved in living in a rational modern culture, where they are expected to have aims and opinions expressed through everything they say and do. Ideally, the drifter has neither aims nor opinions, which is the major difference between him and his antithesis, the modern sensible person who has a reason for everything and who thinks before he or she says or does anything, in order to ensure that what he or she says is in keeping with what is going on. Cheech and Chong are, in this way, not unlike Vincent and Jules in *Pulp Fiction,* who often talk about nothing at all. They talk about what a Big Mac is called in French, or how a foot massage can be construed as a sexual come-on. They say nothing about the future or politics. They seem to live in the present, as do certain of those whom I've met. They like to talk about nothing, and the point in talking about nothing is nothing, it's pointless. The conversation has no higher aim or purpose, it is just talk.

The films can also capture what the drifter sometimes experiences, a twisted perspective on the present. I asked Hanna what she thought of *Pulp Fiction* and her rationale follows:

Philip: Have you seen *Pulp Fiction?*
Hanna: Yeah, I like that one, too.
Philip: Yes, most of those I've spoken to like it.
Hanna: Yeah, yeah it's great. I don't know if Steve has told you that . . . We've even dropped a little acid and stuff you know, has he told you that?
Philip: Not really, maybe hinted.
Hanna: Yeah, there was a summer where we did acid together. It was me and him and a really good friend of ours then. It's got to be the right atmosphere when you

do acid and that, you shouldn't be . . . it just ruins it a bit if the weather's bad, it ruins it if you're bothered about something, so everything should be great for it to work best, and stuff. But I never thought it was going to be like that, 'cause it started when our friend came and began to hassle and said, 'Come on, we'll do it!' and we just [said] 'Nah, not today.' We sat and sunbathed on the porch and thought that 'this can't go well now that he's been at us and hassled us until we go along and give in' . . . you get just a little bit like, 'nah.' But, anyway, it was probably the first time, it was one of the first times, yeah, it was the first time I did acid and it was like a whole new world opened up and you can't like, describe it, 'cause if you've never taken it, you can't understand it . . . First your mind is so open, like so different. We'd much more fun than before we were gone . . .

She continues to tell me about that particular LSD experience until I asked how she could make the connection between acid/LSD and *Pulp Fiction*. She answers that it is due in part to there being drugs in the film, and in part to the film's structure:

. . . that the film comes together like that in the end and the beginning. Where it begins, it comes back on itself in the end like, anyway. That's when I started thinking about it [laughs] . . . It's a little acidy, the way the film is built up and comes back on itself like that. You think a little that way, maybe, when you're high . . . so I started thinking about acid. Then . . . it is heroin that they're snorting, and in the film it's pretty disgusting when she overdoses and they're going to stick the syringe in her chest.

Tarantino's films are to the heroin users' taste partly because they portray a twisted perspective on existence, with extreme amounts of action. Hanna can relate, from her own experience, to the film, which corresponds with her interests – twisted and extraordinary experiences. A heroin-using couple I interviewed often put on the music from *Pulp Fiction* when they have acquired their smack. Shooting up a fix to the beat of the music apparently makes the experience more satisfying; it frames and gives it an aesthetic form.

In *Pulp Fiction* the spectator is thrown from one experience to another; sometimes the change is so fast, it's hard to keep up. The time sequence is widely distorted so that the spectator can find it difficult to follow it, that is to say, the time is non-linear, which is in keeping with the drifter characteristic. A drug user can feel that the film portrays a believable perspective of the present and that it is therefore something they can relate to. The unpredictable happens, as with an acid trip, where the beautiful can become terrible and the calm can become sharply dramatic. The film captures Hanna's perspective:

1. The period before the high; in Hanna's case in the garden, in *Pulp Fiction* in the café.

2. The period during the high; for Hanna it involves a disorganized adventure where 'a whole new world' is opened up to her. In the film, it is the drama and disorder that define the film; disorder in the form of murder, drug-induced states, homosexual rape, overdoses, and so forth.
3. The period after the high; when the drug has lost effect and where everything goes back to normal, that is, in the film the starting point, the café.

Even the film *Natural Born Killers* is reminiscent of an LSD experience, as is the film *The Doors,* where one of the themes is in fact LSD and the experience of moving between different realities. Jim Morrison's life as an addict and musician is portrayed as he seeks the twisted and the abject using LSD, mushrooms, cocaine, alcohol and heroin to get him there. He, like Cheech and Chong, is seldom clean and goes around on a constant high. The drifter experiments when he or she wishes to experience something. This desire to experiment, which is described in Chapter 2, is also described in films.

The heroin users like the films that correspond to their desire for action, and in the interplay between film and reality, the drifter is born and develops, modern society's antihero.

The Doors (1991). Directed by Oliver Stone. Starring: Val Kilmer, Meg Ryan and Kathleen Quinlan. The film is about the Rock group, the Doors, and especially their myth-surrounded lead singer, Jim Morrison. We follow Jim Morrison from his days as a young poet, through many rock events and drug experiences, until his death in Paris in 1971.

The Losers' Drug

Heroin figures in many of the films described but, unlike cocaine, it is not portrayed as associated with success. In *The Seekers,* cocaine is most important. Jocke and Ray deal cocaine and also start to use it. A friend of Jocke and Ray's becomes a 'horse-head'. The horse-heads are differentiated both in elegance and speech from the more elegant cocaine users, Jocke and Ray, who are recreational users. Gustav is filthy and hasn't washed his hair in ages, while Ray and Jocke are clean and very well dressed. The portrayal in the film of heroin and heavy drug use is that it is both dangerous and leads to loss of social status.

- In *Scarface,* Tony Montana loses control as he begins to use cocaine too frequently.
- In *New Jack City,* the crack-heads are portrayed as anything other than happy individuals, rather they are shaking shadows of their former selves.

- In *Blood In Blood Out,* Cruz's heroin abuse leads to his younger brother finding his syringe and injecting an overdose. The heroin is also responsible for destroying much of his creativity.
- In *Menace II Society* the main character's mother is an injecting heroin addict, which is described as decidedly unglamorous and tragic.
- In *The Doors* an increasingly intensive abuse leads to Jim Morrison not only losing control of his career, but also of his body and health.

The exception to this, of the films I have researched, is *Pulp Fiction* where John Travolta, to throbbing music, injects a fix while driving a car. It plays almost as if John Travolta is actually high for real when he does it. There is no moralizing undertone, or hint of downfall caused by heroin. Vincent seems capable of taking care of his work as a hitman without any great difficulty. His heroin use is of no great consequence in the film, merely one of the many indicators of Vincent's identity.

The film *The Seekers* also presents a less problematic picture of heroin than many others. Jocke 'shoots up' towards the end of the film and appears to slur a little as if 'beautiful'. However, it is shown as a one-off event. Afterwards, he is still the elegant, smart and impulsive Jocke, who works out.

A theme in these films, symbolic of success, is about how to avoid becoming hooked, to show force of character confronting drugs – to live with drugs and criminal behaviour without being caught in the addict's trap. Using cocaine now and then is one thing, crack and heroin on the other hand are seen as particularly problematic. This corresponds well to how the young heroin users try to hide the fact that they are hooked and look for different extenuating excuses. None of the heroin users intended to become hooked, it was rather the effect of an incremental need and also miscalculation. They would really rather use the drug for recreational purposes. The addiction itself is problematic, not just from the modern viewpoint, but also from the image-fixated post-modernist viewpoint. Recreational and experimental drug use, along with dealing, are not problematic from the post-modernist viewpoint, as one can still present an identity that is successful and autonomous. Those who are hooked are often filthy, sweaty and anything but elegant. Cruz, the artist in *Blood In Blood Out,* experiences this alteration when he becomes hooked. He transforms from a creative, stylish, elegant outsider into a worn-out model of degeneracy and downfall. The addict cannot live for the present but instead only to acquire more heroin.

The films have not only contributed to reinforcing and influencing Crispin, Enrique and their friends' outsider identities, they have also contributed to slowing down their development as drug users. The film *Trainspotting* disgusted them, while at the same time they agreed that it was very good. Crispin says:

Trainspotting actually became a warning that we shouldn't . . . we were a little scared that he shot up, he had an overdose and that, it was that which scared us into 'Shit, don't shoot up.' 'Cause it had come up in the group you know, 'Should we try shooting up, it seems to make you a little higher than just smoking it?' so there was some talk about that in the group, but when we saw that film, well after that, we talked and just said, 'Ah fuck it, we'll stick to smoking it instead.'

Trainspotting (1995). Directed by Danny Boyle. The original novel was written by Irvine Welsh. Starring: Ewan McGregor, Ewen Bremner and Jonny Lee Miller. The film is about how Mark and his friends live a life centred on heroin and the various dramatic, often darkly comic events, that occur. It is also about how Mark tries to break free of his life as a heroin user. The film is both absurd and realistic, a black comedy.

The films have not, with a few exceptions, sanitized addiction or heroin. On the other hand, they have contributed to making drug use less taboo-ridden and more 'legitimate'. The films function as the voice of opposition to the schools' anti-drug teaching, and if a person is occupied with separation they are probably more likely to listen to the films' message than that of society's representatives – in the same way as they would rather listen to the older criminal mentors.

Who's Directing Whom?

The young heroin users have, since secondary school, undergone the work of building up an identity, where films were an important influence and parental instructions less so. The films supply the form and the ideal which is necessary for the heroin users to know the freedom that is part of alternative socialization and separation. As they become internalized in the heroin users' self-reflection/media packages, the films have contributed to an aesthetic form of separation – the separation thereby becoming authentic. The films are a parallel reference world, which can be used to create identity in a dialectical process between practical and fictitious reality, where the practical experience deepens the interpretation of the film, and where the film is an interpretative framework which defines the practical as authentic.

The films have inspired the creation of a subculture and made events and objects interesting and legitimized them. It is like a little boy putting on a shirt with 'Beckham' on the back and almost feeling like him. The shirt and the game become magic – he becomes a genuine football player. In the subculture, you dress yourself up in the symbols that make you believable in the part. Instead of football shirts, you dress in drugs, experience jargon, criminal jargon, and so forth. With the help of the media, the subculture is idealized, the environment dramatized and identities become authentic.

The films provide support for the breaking of different taboos that regulate coexistence in the modern world. Modern society's taboos are weakened by being presented on screen in such a way that they can be identified with. Taboos can, in this fashion, be changed to something almost worth striving for, of merit. The breaking of taboos becomes less of a big deal and is not experienced as quite as problematic if there are media role models. Taking drugs becomes a way of being cool.

Seen in relation to earlier chapters, the interpretation of the films becomes an argument in direct opposition to established society's viewpoint on criminality and drugs. Drug use during the 1950s and through to the 1970s was constructed as a serious problem in society (Lindgren 1993). Before that, drugs had not been an important concept in people's consciousness.

Established society has contributed to what could be called a marginalization and stigmatizing process where the drug addict has been portrayed as indolent, problem-ridden, of weak character, and so forth. The drug addicts' identity has not been seen as quite human. The films, however, show another picture of the drug user, where drugs are symbolic of a type of success or a post-modernist 'live for the now' concept. The addict is no longer the worn-out, long-haired, filthy figure, which functioned as the stereotype, but rather another picture is emerging where drugs symbolize something else – celebratory, successful, youthful. Drugs are being divorced from their symbolism of social disqualification, and the stigma is dissolving.

Heroin, and other drugs, have thereby become socio-culturally prepared and charged and can be used by those who for some reason or another wish to create an image of themselves as independent. The post-modernist stance weakens the validity of modern culture's denunciation of drugs as taboo. To use is still stigmatized from modern society's perspective, but from a post-modern perspective it is merely a possibility, a way of living adventurously, specially and richly experiencing life.

Film and reality occupy a dialectical relationship where reality is transformed in order to conform to films, and films are made to liken reality. In 1986 Terry Williams wrote *Cocaine Kids,* where we follow and share the lives of some young cocaine users. What Williams describes had become a problem in the US (see also Bourgois 1996). Minorities had found a path to success, but an illegal one. With reference to similar groups, and with experience of living in a segregated American society, films like *Boyz 'N' the Hood, Menace II Society* and *New Jack City* were made, along with others not mentioned. Some of these films, obviously, are not portrayals of reality, but rather dramatized aspects of it. The films' tempos are, for instance, faster than reality. Films that mirror increased segregation were also made in Sweden, and *The Seekers* is a good example. This was most likely dramatized not only from real experience of Sweden but also from films like *Scarface* (which in its turn is a remake of a gangster film of 1932) and *New Jack City*. The films are created through drawing from authentic social problems, but they also represent other media constructions. What occurs in the films' world has an effect on what happens in the subculture, but not in such a way that the subculture becomes a 'copy' of the film. Rather, they provide a source of inspiration – the subculture's activity acquires a filmic form. In this sense, the subculture becomes like film.

Notes

1. The film was made in 1983 and was directed by Brian de Palma, with lead roles played by Al Pacino, Steven Bauer and Michelle Pfeiffer.
2. The first film was called *Up in Smoke* and was produced in 1978 by Lou Adler, starring Cheech Marin and Tommy Chong. It was followed by eight more films, the last made as recently as the early 1990s.

The Subculture's Gender Code

Hanna in Business

Hanna wakes up at around ten o'clock in the morning because her mobile phone is ringing. She understands almost straight away that it is Jeff, a friend of hers since they were children, who wants to buy, not just for himself, but also for his friends, whom Hanna knows as well. Since Jeff and his friends have become dependent, he, or one of his friends, has a habit of ringing almost every morning. Hanna is his only means of buying bags. Hanna also sells to a guy in a smaller town nearby, by the gram, which he in turn breaks up into bags and sells on.

Initially, these friends had hassled Hanna to help them get heroin because Steve, her boyfriend, deals in slightly larger amounts. Steve, however, does not want to deal with Hanna's friends. He doesn't really trust them or believe they know the rules. However, Hanna has carefully shown them the ropes. She has tried to impress on them the care that is necessary when it comes to handling heroin.

'Can we meet?' asks Jeff, and Hanna answers: 'Yes, but in about three hours. I have just woken up.' Jeff replies: 'Can't you make it earlier?' Hanna gets a little irritated and thinks that they are always putting her under pressure, but that in spite of that, they are her friends and she wants to help them. She says, mostly in order to keep Jeff calm, 'Okay then, two hours, where we usually meet.' She knows however that it will take more time than that. 'Okay', says Jeff. Hanna, who is using heavily just now, feels she needs a fix herself first, in order to be calm. Sometimes she thinks of doing the drop first, so that she can be more relaxed when it comes to the fix, in order to get more out of the hit. Her boyfriend is still asleep, but she tells him she has to get up and get ready. Steve mumbles some kind of answer. He seldom gets up before eleven o'clock. Hanna injects a fairly small dose of heroin. She used to smoke, but having tried injecting, smoking seems almost meaningless. As she is going out to deliver, she doesn't want to take too much. She will have to save the serious high until after she has done what she is coming to see as almost a job, and which is becoming with time more and more troublesome. This is in part due to the risk involved and in part due to the fact that as her dependency on heroin has increased, the selling has become both a more disturbing but also a more necessary part of her everyday life. She has learnt the art of peddling from Steve, partly by giving him assistance, partly from what he has told her.

When she has had her fix and tidied up she goes out to the cupboard where, apart from 5 g of heroin, there is a heap of scrap, a lawnmower, some windscreen-cleaning fluid, old hosepipes, engine oil, tins of paint and other stuff like this. It is a good place to store the heroin, as the police would find it difficult to find anything there, and the different scents could distract a sniffer dog if the house were searched. They have more heroin, 20 g, hidden behind one of the council's water pumps about 300 m from the building where they live. Steve and Hanna operate by a type of distance principle when it comes to where they keep their stash. The further away it is, the greater the chance of the police catching them when they leave the hiding place, and the closer it is the more chance there is of the police, if they find it, connecting it with them. Small amounts are kept closer to the house, and larger amounts are kept further away.

Hanna takes out the 5 g that have been put behind a broken sander, which is never used. The heroin cylinder, about 2 cm in diameter and 1.5 cm long, is carefully wrapped in cling film, to prevent any damp getting at it. She goes into the room where Steve is still sleeping and, with the back of a knife, crushes off a little piece of heroin which she thinks will be enough for five bags, that is, about a gram. She takes out their scales, a Metler, a precision instrument capable of weighing one-thousandth part of a gram. Bought retail, these scales would cost about £4,000, but are mainly used by laboratories. Steve got the scales when he broke into a place where he had been tipped off about a safe. The safe turned out to be too heavy to take (it was a metre wide and almost two metres high) so he had to make do with the more manageable scales. Having Metler scales that weigh one thousandth of a gram makes dealing with heroin more pleasant, in the same way that a fast computer with a good Internet connection makes surfing more enjoyable. It also provides a certain sense of status, giving a sense of credibility.

Hanna then gets a bus timetable. It is printed on a type of paper that is especially suitable for folding into the bags that the heroin is placed in. It is glossy, which means the heroin doesn't stick to it, and it is thick enough to be strong, and is easy to handle. She cuts out five squares and folds them up like envelopes, and then puts the paper on the precision scales, and resets it to zero. Then, with the help of a knife, she adds what she reckons is a bag amount. The scales show 0.2 g, so she takes back a little, making it 0.19 g, and thinks 'it's still a decent bag, others just put in 0.16 gram, or make six bags from one gram, and I never cut it.' She goes through the process rather casually. She has, after all, been doing this for almost half a year now, and this is not entirely unrelated to her own increased usage. She uses about a gram per day.

When she has made five neat packages, she wipes them clean. She does not want her fingerprints discovered if the police should catch any of her friends. Then she takes care of what is left of the heroin, rewraps it in the cling film, first twice, and then one more time just to be certain. She puts it back in behind the sander in the cupboard. There's a lot to think about. Afterwards, about an hour late, she goes out to meet Jeff, who has already called her twice to see what is happening. She had put the bags into an empty photographic film canister together with a couple of one-crown coins, to weigh it down so that she can throw it far away if the police try to catch her. It isn't necessary; the drop goes smoothly, though, lately, she has felt more uncomfortable and frightened about getting caught. The police have been close a few times, but she has always managed to get rid of what she was carrying. When Hanna gets home again, there is another call from a guy she delivers to. He wants to buy a couple of grams. Steve is awake and in the shower.

A Protracted Ritual of Masculinity

The intro with Hanna questions the discourse which claims that women drug users are less competent and more passive than males. Taylor (1993: 152) writes in the ethnography *Women Drug Users* the following to describe her informants: 'They developed sets of skills which afforded them satisfaction . . . Shoplifting, fraud, dealing with drugs, all require a variety of skills if they are to be carried out successfully.' For Taylor and Rosenbaum (1981) it is of major importance to write about women drug users in a way that contradicts the discourse claiming that they are 'pathetic, passive, psychologically or socially inadequate' (Perry 1979: 1, in Taylor 1993: 3). In this chapter I will discuss the gender politics of the subculture, focusing extensively on how the subculture and its central activities are gendered. I will also discuss how the code of gender relates to the popular films in the subculture and research about addiction.

Men dominate the subculture of heroin users in Norrköping; not completely but to a large extent. Reading other ethnographies of drug cultures (for example Adler 1985, Faupel 1991, Svensson 1996 and Bourgois 1996) I get the picture that masculine dominance is very often the case. Even Taylor, who intended to give a different picture, sometimes supports this. She writes for example: 'male partners acted as a role model from which the women learned the skills and knowledge required to purchase, use, and recognize psychical effects' (Taylor 1993: 34). This doesn't, however, mean that women are totally passive and controlled by men.

I have asked the young heroin users to evaluate roughly how many women versus men there are in the culture and the majority believe it is about 90 per cent men, 10 per cent women. According to the police about 20 per cent of heroin abusers in Norrköping are women. (Women represent about a third of all drug addicts in Sweden (Nordegren and Tunving 1997).)

Partaking in the subculture can be seen as a protracted ritual of masculinity. The ritual means that ambivalence and doubt are washed away through creating imaginary distinctions between what one wants to be seen as and what one does not. Thus, constructing a definite masculinity is done both by acting according to what is seen as manly and by defining clearly the feminine, which, if the purpose is to raise the status of masculinity, must be devalued and separated from the manly. When it comes to disarming the feminine, men in the subculture have help. Both the media and the establishment, including research, contribute to a powerful stigmatization of the female drug user (Taylor 1993 and Rosenbaum 1981). This is described further on in the chapter. Despite this, there are active women in the subculture, like Hanna, who transgress the boundaries of what is expected of them, who become 'abject' (Kristeva 1982) in the sense that they embody a duality, which both society and the subculture have difficulty accepting. In the coming sections I present different themes with the intent to describe participating in the subculture as a 'protracted ritual of masculinity'.

Men in Action

The subculture contains a series of the attributes that in the past century and even earlier have been associated with tough manhood. These can be summarized by four terms; action, outsidership, strong character and material wellbeing.

The term 'action' encompasses the idea of tempo changes, from calm to danger-filled activities, from rest to action, and is a way of creating for oneself a socio-cultural free zone in relation the formal and rule-bound school culture. The passion for tempo is also expressed in anything that can raise it further, such as drugs that can very quickly create changes in the environment, and fast cars and action films. The heroin users like things that are fast and irregular, the elusive and the sudden. It is about not letting life become fixed, but staying in continuous motion and on course for new experiences, both uplifting and tragic. The subculture allows men to reach 'rock bottom', in order to get up at nine afterwards, to commute between triumph and defeat.

In the subculture's terminology there is an 'aesthetic of tempo' (see also Chapter 2), including a marked emphasis on change and movement. 'Speed', 'chase the dragon', 'hit', 'shoot up', 'cop chase', 'break-in', among others, are phrases that express this. The interest in cars is great, not just in this subculture but even among many other criminals. The youth culture researcher Bjurström allows cars and their quality of movement to symbolize masculinity: 'The underlying opposition between motion and the stationary, which this symbolism expresses seems without exception to contribute to drawing the line between the masculine and the feminine' (Bjurström 1995: 217, my translation).

The cars I hired were often commented upon, and, in hindsight, I realized that many of the interviewees were very interested in cars and particularly high-performance action cars: Audi, BMW, Porsche and Mercedes. I also heard stories about car chases. One of the top dealers has a Porsche, of course not officially owned by him, despite the fact that he has no driving licence (and hardly any official income). It is apparently sufficient for him to look at it from time to time in order to feel good. The fast car is proof of strong control (Bayley 1986 and Bjurström 1995). It expresses power and that the driver is as strong and fast as the horsepower under the bonnet permits. With the car, you can escape from almost anything, but control is necessary in order to do so. By identifying yourself with fast cars you create the illusion of control, of being able to command great movement and power.

Motion is also of central importance to those living at bag level – to move from flat to flat, to do break-ins, to keep grafting. Even this vagabond lifestyle has historically symbolized manliness and been an ingredient in male youth culture, for example the beatnik ideal portrayed by Jack Kerouac (1958/1998) and in the films that I have written about earlier, where the young men are often on the move, in the street, fighting or in gun battles, in the car, on motorcycles, and so forth. Women in these films are often placed in the kitchen, at a makeup table, or portrayed as trophies (standing beside the slot machines and pinball machines) or in restaurants – the men are occupied with action, the women with preparing themselves to be objects.

Movement is a sign of being a drifter, comparable to Cheech and Chong who are on the way to nowhere, often in a large van. This characteristic can be drawn from the suburban gangs who drive around in American cars and taunt rival gangs, and also from the films *Pulp Fiction* and *The Doors,* where the actors when not physically in motion are mentally so – high or about to become so. This is particularly obvious in the alternative road movie, *Natural Born Killers,* where Mickey and Mallory murder people, often quickly – they shoot from the car. Shooting from cars is not at all unusual in other American gangster films. The subculture's tempo is similar to that of the film world. For the bag buyer it is about being continually in the chase after new heroin and for the dealers it is about continually ringing telephones, fetching and delivering and what strategies to use in order to avoid the police – about always being a step ahead, giving it a competitive character and thereby tempo in relation to the police.

The men are portrayed as adventurers in motion, and, throughout history, adventurers have most often been associated with masculinity (Elsrud 2001). The masculine monopoly of the adventure strengthens the possibility of using motion as a sign of masculinity.

The Man as Outsider

To be an outsider is to be unlike others. To be a genuine outsider is to be on the brink with respect to the justice system, someone who doesn't follow the straight and narrow, but who has appropriated an identity which stands out in relation to the identities that are in line with established society's demand for respectability (Becker 1963/1973). An outsider appears independent of others' approval and in this way symbolizes strength and power. Drugs, violence and criminality are possible symbols with whose help outsidership can be idealized, and there are plenty of these symbols in the subculture. To see things that others don't, to know the subculture as well as the ordinary world, characterizes the life experience of an outsider.

All heroin users will, with hindsight, want to stop using heroin. At the same time, many cannot imagine a completely law-abiding life, and claim that in the future they would buy stolen goods, and participate in break-ins or similar activities. The majority of them have difficulty imagining a completely action-free future.

Ben stopped using heroin, but he did not stop living like a criminal. In fact, he progressed in crime and committed a number of armed robberies under dramatic, action-film-like conditions, despite the fact that he didn't do such things during the period when he was using heroin. He still wanted to preserve the identity reinforcement provided by being an outsider. He had become used to this identity, and it was difficult for him to accept an identity as a well-behaved member of established society. He wanted to be in motion, hunting and fleeing, and be clearly defined as an outsider, through his actions.

Roger was in a secure children's home but longed to get back to freedom, and I asked him what he longed for most. After a certain hesitation he answered that he missed his friends most and doing break-ins. Breaking in gives such satisfaction and such an identity profile that the longing for this was almost greater than the longing for drugs. He was driven by a need to define himself as an outsider.

Enrique, who tried a number of times to stop using heroin, told me that he had started a course and had many new friends. He told them almost immediately that he had used heroin. When he talks about this he sounds almost proud. He shows the others that he is a genuine outsider, someone who has really lived the dangerous life on the outskirts of society and who has come through it. He defines himself as an outsider. On one occasion, Roger and I passed by a number of sixteen- and seventeen-year-old youths who were standing and talking outside the library in central Norrköping. They were Latin Americans and seemed to be influenced by hip-hop, with the caps and over-large jeans. Roger said, as we passed them, 'they're young' and laughed, and, thereby, defined himself as more experienced, as an outsider, as someone who has really lived. Roger is only twenty-one, but he has been 'there' – he is already more adult than the adults. And 'there' is the outskirts of society, on the border between life and death, balancing but still alive.

The male outsider is a central character in films. The ordinary people are there – they get shot in the supermarket, they go past on the pavement, they are the extras. Those who are seen and defined in the films are the unusual – the outsiders – who think, plan and act. Many films describe men with miserable backgrounds as having addictions, being criminal and so forth, but also as developing strategies for handling life's problems. This aspect, of having reached rock bottom and then moving up, according to the logic described in this chapter, can be an advantage – outsider experience has been gained, and therefore you're not just anyone.

Men of Strong Character

The strong character has been described earlier and it is about reaching a condition of rationality where feelings are not shown and control is kept in extremely stressful situations. Action environments are the ultimate test of strong character. The encounter with the police is central even here; not to snitch and thereby be soiled by the androgenous/gayness, to be a real and complete man and show strong character. Existence in the subculture can be seen as a continuous test of capability. One mistake, one careless word, can give rise to suspicion, as can associating with the wrong people, or giving away when questioned by the police. A strong character is necessary to succeed in living in the subculture. Proper behaviour is rewarded and favours are returned, but behave badly and you will be labelled as weak, lacking in character, as a slimy creature not worth anyone's respect, a snitch, someone with a 'screw up label', a rat or a blabber mouth.

The strong character is fostered in the subculture through action and risk and considered necessary, while existence in ordinary society is seldom so threatened. To give oneself away or to be nervous in a decisive moment is seldom as serious in ordinary society as it is in the subculture, where it can lead to loss of freedom, having to spend every day in remand, modern society's entrance hall to long-term imprisonment. In ordinary society, you almost always get a second chance, but in the subculture it is difficult to make a comeback if you, for example, sample the goods, and neglect to pay. That is a way of failing the subculture's test; showing strong character also means not letting your own drug consumption come before business. Character is put to the test and only the strong pass. But masculinity must be proved time and time again. Crispin tells how they tested the gang's runners:

> They had to show that they could be trusted, that you could give them a little horse, so they could come back with the money, that kind of thing. They maybe had to steal a car or break into a little kiosk to show that they were worthy of going out to deal, 'cause it wasn't just . . . you couldn't just barge in and say: 'Yeah, I want to begin selling for you guys', we didn't know then whether we could trust them or not. You have to show that you are good, that you are good enough for us. Maybe we said: 'Yeah, we want you to break into that kiosk there, and you bring maybe ten cartons of cigarettes here, ten cartons and a crate of lemonade or whatever.' And so they came back with it and we read

in the paper . . . you bought the paper the next day to check like, because they came back at night, the same night that they did it, they came back with the stuff, so then you thought: 'You don't get the stuff now, you'll have to wait till tomorrow, till we have read in the paper or heard something on the radio, or whatever.' You knew that it was in the paper if anything had happened. So then you read it, then you knew something had happened, that they had done it, then you knew that, 'Okay, you're good enough.' First you gave them maybe six to eight bags, then with time they got more and more. When they showed up with the money and showed that they hadn't had trouble with the police, and then they got more and more. Yeah, show that you can behave, that you are worth being one of us, so to speak.

Living in the subculture can be seen like a trial where your character is put to the test; some pass, others don't. Brian told me that he believes that those who choose to leave the subculture are those who realise that it is awful. Another way of looking at it is that those who think it is awful cannot manage to live in the subculture, as they haven't developed a sufficiently strong character.

Men as Materially Successful

Ben told me that he stole a gold ring for a girl he had recently met. She was shocked, but told him she had never met a guy like him. Many want to be chivalrous towards women, by showing a façade of material wellbeing and thereby receiving reinforcement as men, more or less like in the film world where money gives rise to power and 'chicks'. It means being elegant in the right situations. Enrique speaks about being out at restaurants with his girlfriend: 'We went out to eat in restaurants every weekend and it was £30 to £40 every time we went out to eat, and we ordered a bottle of wine and drank a little, ate steak, and things like that. We went there and back by taxi, and I had a wad of notes in my pocket.'

The bundle of notes that were acquired through heroin selling made it possible to act like a successful man. Jocke, in the film *The Seekers,* kept a large number of notes in his trouser pockets and could spend a lot of money and thereby show riches. Or like Ninio in *New Jack City,* who could buy the cars he wanted and get the women that he looked at. Enrique told me that two of his friends in the gang tried to stop using heroin, which also meant that they had to stop selling it:

Philip: Did they come back to the gang?

Enrique: Yeah, they came back, they missed the gang of friends, so to speak, and they couldn't stay way from the drugs either, because there were drugs there the whole time in that group.

Philip: Right.

Enrique: And they missed that thing with having money in your pocket, because we had money the whole time because we were selling, then you have money and drugs which you can use yourself, like.

Of those who have stopped using heroin, some describe that one of the difficult parts is not having money. Max told me that he wanted at least £2,500 per month, but it is hard to find that kind of salary if you are lacking in education and training. Money is a symbol of masculine success and can be used to dress the set for different types of manhood rituals, with the help of which a belief can be created in the polarized gender code, reinforcing masculinity.

The polarity is made obvious, men have the resources, the women are 'treated', and the male identity is strengthened. In Chapter 2, I described how some of those who participated in the criminal subculture could earn more money than their peers. It isn't the money that is sought after; rather it is that many long for objects that indicate status, power and freedom. In capitalistic society, money in your pocket is a sign of success and, in this way, money can be seen as an important ingredient in the male rituals that occur, where distinctions are created from both women and less successful men. The rich are capable of moving with elegance in casino-like environments, which are like the film world's simulated reality. Supremacy becomes credible. With money in your pocket you cannot be a failure, at least not if you live in a capitalist society.

Character Weakness and Passivity

That only a minority of heroin users are women can be understood by studying how the subculture interprets women who transgress the boundaries for how women are expected to behave. To be a female heroin user in Norrköping is harder than being a male one, as they not only are forced to live with the prejudice of established society, but also that of the media and the subculture. The criticism against female heroin users that can be drawn from the material consists of:

1. Female drug users are seen as less smart and less strong in character than the males.
2. Female drug users are seen as less clean than their male counterparts.
3. Female drug users are more sexually impure than their male counterparts.

These three points of criticism are related to each other and contribute to giving credibility to the image of women as being of lower status. If this picture is believed to be true, then as a man, one's own identity is both lifted and purified. In order for the male rituals in the subculture to have the desired effect – to underline men's higher status and power – it must be defined against something else, in this case the feminine. The male outsider's tempo, autonomy, character strength and ability to cope are clearly defined in contrast to how femininity is constructed.

Hanna says: 'For a girl I'm really equal to the other guys, so to speak, if I'm in a room and three or four guys are there, they talk just as if I was a guy.' Hanna considers herself fairly well respected by the guys and this is necessary if she is to succeed in the subculture, as most are men, especially those who hold the kind of positions that she needs to respect her. At the same time it is clear from the phrase, 'for a girl' that she considers herself somewhat of an exception. Not all the girls enjoy the same respect, and Hanna has not been given it for nothing. On one occasion a male dealer was taken into custody and the police 'took in' several people in order to collect evidence and testimony against him. Even Hanna was taken in and questioned.

> He [a male friend] thought I'd give myself away. It isn't usual, especially with girls who are being questioned for the first time that they cope so well as I did. It is like victory, or, yeah, like, 'what a great girl she is' among those people, 'really good at keeping her mouth shut, and says nothing, she can really be trusted, like' and those kinds of things.

Girls can almost be excused if they 'squeal', as, according to the myth, they cannot be seen as being as strong in character as the guys. Hanna says:

> It is almost an unwritten rule that you shouldn't tell everything to a girl, and that. 'Cause you never know, it might be a short relationship and then, when it's over, maybe she'll run round telling what she's heard and seen and everything like that. Steve began trusting me very early on and telling me things. I mean if I were to tell everything I know about him, he would get life!

Hanna and other girls have come to know the unwritten rule, that as a girl you risk being left out of the planning, because you are not seen as being as smart as the men. For Max, who is long established in the subculture, it is clearly apparent that girls lack many of the characteristics that would place them among the resourceful in the subculture.

> Yeah, I don't think it suits a girl to do drugs. Girls can't do drugs because there's this tougher mentality when you're using. 'Cause you have to be protective about what's yours. Right and wrong and that, you have to be able to refuse. And that gets to be enough with the girls, and it doesn't suit them at all, and being tough and the trouble and all that, like. It's not particularly feminine at all.

He claims that much of the subculture's activity is masculine, and that requires strength, being tough and hard, where you are expected to be able to defend yourself and act so as not to be swallowed by the subculture. Women in the subculture, in that sense, are almost misplaced. What Max describes can also be seen as an identity strategy where, by undervaluing the feminine as something incapable of being of worth to the subculture, he makes the subculture out to be extra hard and rich in action, and its character of male ritual is thereby strengthened. It is as if he says 'In order to live in this world you have to be a tough bastard and women aren't tough.'

Female designations are used in the subculture's terminology to describe the feeble and weak, whereas the male stands for the strong and the solid. Enrique relates that after he had taken a break from the circle of dealers and using heroin, he came back and smoked with them. As he hadn't used for a while his body was no longer as tolerant and showed it. He says:

> I felt really high, but they, they thought like this, 'Fuck it, have you become a wimp?' and they just sat there on Monday night; 'Have you become a weakling?' and blah, blah, blah, and 'Fuck it, you're like a cunt, like a chick, for fuck's sake, throwing up as soon as you've smoked half a hit', and so on.

The quotation underlines how, through female designations of the weak, in this case reduced heroin tolerance, their own experience of strength and manliness is raised, as if they thought that 'a real man should be capable of taking heroin.' There are parallels here to alcohol use, where the thing is not to vomit, for by vomiting you risk being seen as weak. There is a relatively high frequency of use of tough jargon among heroin users, as if they are continually occupied in recreating their own feeling of manliness, and where the polarity between the masculine and the feminine is continually reconstructed in everyday speech.

Girls are portrayed as more passive than boys, who can refuse things, mark their territory, and so on. The polarity is made obvious and the men become strong at the cost of the women. Max and Enrique are not alone in their opinion; several of those to whom I spoke expressed similar thoughts:

Philip: How do the girls graft?
Roger: I don't know that there's that many that live by . . . yeah, maybe stealing from home, they take their own money, and I don't like that. If you're going to be a heroin user, and take it all the time, then the first thing that happens is that you never have enough money, if you sort of, if you borrow money the whole time, like twenty pounds here and twenty there, and buy a half bag at a time.

The attitude that girls are bad at grafting is clearly portrayed here. They do not live the action lives that are otherwise preferred by many, but manage almost like ordinary members of society. Women are seen as unsuccessful outsiders. It is as if Roger is saying that women do not handle action as well as men. In doing that, further credibility is created for the assumption that he as a man knows how to handle action in the subculture. The type of myth that has been presented so far is that women are weak in character and that they lack the capacity that men are assumed to have when it comes to dealing with action. These kinds of myth have real consequences, as it becomes more difficult for women to be taken on by the more experienced mentors, or as partners, for example, in break-ins or drug dealing. However, this drawing of the boundaries between the sexes on the basis of the polarities, 'strong character – weak character' and 'active – passive', is not the only one, as it seems even in general that drug-using women are seen as unclean and dirty in comparison to men.

Drug-Using Girls Are Dirty

Roger: Yeah, I don't like girls who use. I think that it's sad that, you know, now, that I'm not a grease ball or anything, I wash, but you know when you've been using, you're . . . you're not the cleanest person in the world, right. Like, a girl . . . they are really, they should . . . they have to look nice and fresh the whole time, almost, so it's a little mangy, scruffy I think. But I don't know any prostitutes.

Philip: Do you know any girls who use?

Roger: Yeah, but there's no one that I would want to be with, or anything like that, I couldn't cope with that.

Women should be clean and fresh according to Roger. In a time when women are expected to shave under their arms, their legs and even their genitals the drug-using girls appear even more unclean. In the quotation above, it seems to be a matter of projection, where he moves part of his own dirt over to the drug-using woman and does not want to be in too intimate contact with this outcast from the subculture, both woman and drug user. This way of seeing the women of the subculture is also found in the quote below:

Philip: What do you think of girls who use drugs?

Crispin: Yeah, that I don't like. I don't like that at all. It is okay for a guy, that's normal, but girls, that's pretty unusual. But it is more common now that girls actually use. There's a fair few girls smoking heroin and shooting up and things, but I don't like it.

Philip: What is it that you don't like about it?

Crispin: It's not like a girl thing. I think it's more a male thing to do drugs and that it isn't something for girls. Girls should mostly . . . okay they can stick to alcohol, but not too much either, but that's more their thing I think. Alcohol, and not drugs. I wouldn't actually like to be with a girl who did drugs.

In Crispin's world, women have a much more restricted freedom than men, when it comes to transgressing rules of purity. Drugs sully their identities, but, most of all, their drug use questions the order of things – it threatens the male bastion that the subculture is. The borders are made more diffuse by these double creatures who engage in activities symbolic of men, but who are equipped with the wrong gender. A female drug user would never be accepted in Crispin's group and, apparently, it is a matter of 'purification', where they try to keep the sacred, the group, clean. Similar values are to be found among the majority of those I interviewed. Ben expresses some strong opinions on female drug users:

> I think drug-using girls, that's just (he laughs) . . . they are really the lowest. Girls who do drugs, that's, well, they aren't exactly at the top of the heap, if I think about amphetamine junkies and that, they are really disgusting girls, they are repulsive, unsavoury girls. So a drug-doing chick isn't really anything great.

The myth of the unsullied and pure woman is also found among young people other than those in the subculture. In a report about young people's views on moonshine I interviewed thirty young people, both boys and girls, about their drinking patterns. To drink moonshine was seen as an entirely male activity and the women who drank it risked being classified as unwomanly and even loose (Lalander 2001; see also Järvinen 1991).

There is a parallel here to what happens in the subculture, a mixing of symbols that questions the established symbol combinations, and, thus, the order of things. Women are not expected to 'take in' elements in the body that are associated with danger and lack of self-control. The mouth is one of the body's entrances to the outside and when she takes in something which shouldn't be taken in, she is seen as an ambiguous figure who has crossed the boundaries. She is interpreted as impure by the classification schemes, which make male drug consumption a sign of action and adventure, but female drug consumption a sign of impurity and degeneracy. To further strike down the female threat to the subculture, it can be maintained that women engage in unclean sexual activity – prostitution. This makes the female position as a drug user highly dubious and impure.

The Myth of the Whore

> I know six girls, I think, who use or have used, one of them has been off it for two years, but had a little relapse. And she was the world's biggest slut, a total slut. Nearly all the ones I know, the girls, are sluts, and change guys because one minute this one has horse and then they live with him, screwing and smoking together. Then suddenly he's gone down or he doesn't have money for horse any longer, then they split suddenly. Suddenly she's with another guy who's sitting pretty. Then they, well, they become sluts, it is a shame to say, but it's actually true, it happens to them, with the horse. (Ben)

Hanna heard a lot of rubbish about herself because she hung around too much with a guy who dealt: 'They see me all the time with different guys, and now there's a load of shit going round, I can imagine, Peter said something like, "Are you with him or what?" "Nah, I am not." "Yeah, but you're screwing him, anyway?" but I am definitely not.' Hanna tries to defend herself when she hears such accusations, she doesn't want to be seen as a whore, but even she has internalized the male gaze when it comes to evaluating other girls:

> Yeah, but it's just that . . . as soon as some girl is with a guy who deals they start suspecting them straight away, I was like that too. I mean when I met Jeanie, an old friend of mine, at home with a guy who deals, I started thinking just those sorts of things. It gets like that, you just simply think that way.

When I ask the women about prostitution, I get a different picture than I do from talking to the men. The women do not consider that they are with the guy because he has heroin, but because they love him. And who can really decide what is love, and what is heroin dependency? I have met several heroin-using couples and their relationships seem characterized by love; they care about each other, and need each other to deal with loneliness. They often try to agree together on how they are going to stop using drugs. It has also become known that some women are as good at taking care of the heroin business as men, but that, because they work in pairs with a male, they are often interpreted as not helping so much and the man is seen as the enterprising one. Nevertheless, it also happens that women do try to sell their bodies for heroin:

Philip: You must have sold to girls?

Enrique: Yes, of course, we had customers, that is, girl customers. It happened several times that they maybe didn't have the money, and: 'Can I borrow a hit from you?' 'No, fuck no, you can't, you have to have the money to buy one.' 'Yeah, but if you can have sex with me, can I borrow one then?' It has happened that you get offers. It's been offered to me, several times from girls who use heroin, or who have used sex, if I lend them a hit, but I've always said 'No', because of my girlfriend.

Philip: It's tragic that they should be so hooked.

Enrique: But no one in the group has ever said 'yes' to that. They've said, 'no, fix the money, or there won't be anything. Fix something as security, then you can borrow, something that's worth at least £40, then you can borrow, but don't come trying to offer me sex, because I don't want that.' There's no one in the group who has ever said 'Yes' to something like that. They'd rather say, 'Get something as security that's worth forty pounds to pawn, then you can borrow.'

Much of the desperation that many customers can feel when they have no means to get heroin comes through above. There are young women in Norrköping who are prepared to exchange their bodies for a hit, but I have not spoken to anyone who has acknowledged doing it. Enrique says that no one in the group has said 'yes' to sex. It would mean 'sullying' the group to have sex with a heroin-using girl, despite the fact that they are themselves users. By only having sex with drug-free and 'clean' girls, Enrique is capable of making his own identity cleaner. The drug-using girl who offers her body is seen as a lot more reprehensible than a man who is dealing heroin. The logic of a subculture can be difficult for other people to understand.

A Simulated Gender Code

In the films *Scarface, The Seekers, Menace II Society, Boyz 'N' The Hood, Pulp Fiction, New Jack City* and others, it is men/boys who act and who are the thinking criminals. Men are portrayed as the clever ones, and women are characterized as 'those who wait' for the men to come.

A very popular film with the subculture's members, amongst others, is *Pulp Fiction*. Here, it is the men who show strong character and the women play more passive or less participatory roles. At the beginning and the end of the film we see the hold-up partners, Yolanda and Pumpkin, a woman and a man in their early thirties, while they are planning a crime. Yolanda listens to what Pumpkin says and follows his instructions. It is he who is the actor, the clever, the cunning one. They decide to rob the cafeteria they are sitting in. However, it just happens that this is where the character-strong hit men, Jules and Vincent, are eating. Yolanda and Pumpkin end up at a disadvantage, as Jules takes over control, in an ice-cold manner (strong character). By the end of the scene Yolanda has been reduced to a tearful child who answers Pumpkin's question, 'Still calm, little pet?', with 'I have to pee, I want to go home.' Yolanda behaves throughout in more hysterical fashion than the men and is anything but a strong character. She is the undeveloped criminal, the one carrying the 'screw-up label', that you would really rather not have anything to do with.

Another woman in the film, Mia, is the girlfriend of the Mafia boss, Marcellus. As his girlfriend she has a certain status, but she gets it because she is his girlfriend and not because she has earned it herself. Even so, she shows a certain amount of self-control when she hangs out with male characters. Mostly she is seen with Vincent, whom Marcellus has ordered to entertain her. Vincent is very nervous about the meeting with Mia and is afraid that he won't be able to control his urges. He has to go to the bathroom and remind himself that he ought not to have sex with Mia, as it would mean his death to have sex with the boss's girlfriend, who is seen as Marcellus's possession. While Vincent is in the bathroom, Mia finds his 'extra good' white heroin, which, due to inexperience, she lays out in two lines and snorts, only to later succumb to a serious overdose. This way she is also the stupid drug user, who cannot tell the difference between heroin and cocaine. Vincent, because of her, ends up in a difficult situation and has to drive her to his dealer friend that he bought the heroin from. He asks the dealer: 'Have you never given adrenalin?' The dealer rages at Vincent and answers: 'No, my friends don't use with kids.' Vincent and the dealer manage, with the help of the adrenalin injection, to bring her back to life and when she gets back home she is like a disobedient little girl who has been corrected. She is dishevelled, with her mascara running and looks anything but sensual, after having met the heavy drug, heroin.

In the film *Scarface* women are portrayed as sex objects to a great extent. Tony and Manolo often talk about how they are going to get women as status symbols and 'screw' them. The picture of women is that of sex symbols. In the quote below Tony is involved in a discussion with the Mafia boss Frank and his friend Manolo. They are sitting at home with Frank in his fashionable duplex, which has a glass lift. Frank's girlfriend Elvira is young, beautiful and sexually challenging:

> *Frank:* Where the hell's Elvira? Go get her, will you, Ernie. The broad spends half her life dressing and the other half undressing. [All laugh loudly.]
>
> *Tony:* I guess you gotta catch her in the middle, hunh? [Frank laughs.]

Elvira makes an entrance and in the glass lift she turns and shows her elegant but revealing dress, in a decadent pose. Tony is impressed and starts to think, 'I want her'. Tony lets himself be impressed by all the status symbols that Frank, the Mafia boss, has, and in the course of events, he makes sure he gets them. Women appear in the film world as objects/icons who are used by men to present themselves as successful. It is also clear from the film how 'chicks' are connected to power and money.

Tony Montana becomes a big-time drug dealer and with that comes money, power and 'chicks'. He steals the boss' wife, Elvira, but both she and Tony begin to use greater amounts of cocaine, despite the rule 'don't get high on your own supply', which is expressed in the film. In the second half of the film, Tony shows in various ways how tired he is of her using cocaine, despite the fact that he himself uses a lot. His trophy, which should show his rise in the hierarchy, is beginning to lose value. Her drug use increasingly becomes a threat to his status and identity. Tony begins to see the cracks in the façade he has built up. He shouts at Elvira and accuses her of being an ordinary addict. To be involved with a drug-using woman is not desirable, but rather indicates that he has sunk a long way. This is strongly in keeping with the subculture's view.

In *Menace II Society*, the mother of the film's leading character is a heroin user. On one occasion she is in withdrawal and asks her husband, Tat, for a dose of heroin. The drug dealer Tat is busy playing cards with his friends.

Mother: Haven't you finished?
Father: Let me clear the table first.
Mother: I've been waiting all day.
A Friend: Your woman looks a little tired, Tat. Tat's probably been using her all night.

She gets a fix from the father, who then says to a friend: 'Give it up now!', referring to the card game. The mother is shabby and hollow-eyed and thinks only about heroin – a tragic figure, a wreck of a mother. The father is portrayed as the autonomous and active one, while she is the dependent and passive one. In the film *New Jack City* the picture is similar, even if some of the girls are armed with automatics.

The women in the film *The Seekers* are neither active nor criminal, and those portrayed are waiting for their men, to get out of jail or to come to see them. Jocke, the main character, is jealous and suspicious that his girlfriend is 'easy'. He beats up a couple of men who appear to him to be a threat against the purity she represents. At the end of the film, the innocent and morally pure girlfriend is shot, which is supposed to be all the more tragic in that she as a woman has had so little to do with the 'tough' world peopled by men. Women are portrayed as those to spend money on, but they should not use drugs and they should guard their sexuality.

It is difficult to interpret the films in any other way than that they support and contribute to reconstructing the gender code which the subculture supports, and make it even more credible. There are, however, films that give another picture. I will return to them a little later on. Women have not only the subculture against them, but also the subculture's main source of inspiration, the simulated media world. As if that wasn't sufficient, established society contributes in different ways to burden the young women who have fought their way into the subculture.

The Establishment's Perspective

> On the drug scene sexuality is not based on mutual feelings and respect, but on power and exploitation. He not only uses her body as a source of income, he may well demand that she participate in an increasing number of extreme sexual variations; not because diversity and rejuvenation stimulate mutual pleasure, but as an element in a relationship built upon contempt, exploitation and submission . . . Regardless of whether a girl chooses to go from one partner to another, or she tries to stay with the same man, the end result is usually the same: she has many partners and also works on the street. (Goldberg 1999: 143)

This type of information is also found in two well-established Swedish reference books. The following is from Nordgren and Tunving's *A–Z of Drugs*:

'Around 70% of the female drug users, particularly those dependent on heroin, are "self-financing" through engaging in prostitution' (1997: 36). In *The Swedish National Encyclopaedia* one can read: 'The female drug users, who often prostitute themselves in order to get money for drugs . . .' (1997: v. 14, p. 30) It is true that prostitution is much more common among drug users than among 'ordinary' people, but it is a long way from clear that all or most drug-using women are prostitutes (see also Kristiansen 2000: 36). Taylor writes about these kinds of conclusions:

> Most of these conclusions have been based on interviews with women in treatment. It has been argued, however, that the form of questions in many such interviews reveals stereotypical assumptions of acceptable feminine behaviour . . . Where studies have investigated the social setting of women drug users, they have usually concentrated on one aspect of an illicit drug-using lifestyle, and as a result are similar to treatment-based interviews in that they ignore the social setting and social relationships within which drug use takes place. (Taylor 1993: 4)

In the opening quotation from Goldberg, women are portrayed as very passive, and it is almost a law that the boyfriend dictates the conditions. To balance this we can put forward the research of Taylor, among others (Rosenbaum 1981, Ungmark 1992 and Trulson 1998), that describes female drug users as active and enterprising. Likewise, women in these references are seen as reflective and enterprising, and not merely as objects, waiting to be taken care of, or to be exploited by, men. The texts where women are seen as passive and lacking in 'smarts' contribute to the reconstruction of women as passive, as victims of men's need, while the men are portrayed as much more enterprising and cunning.

Women are, thus, labelled as bad from three perspectives: the subculture's, the media's and that of established society. For men, it is expressly a matter of one perspective, which means that they have other possibilities – to be positively reinforced as drug users and criminals – compared with the women, who are exposed to a triple pressure of shame. The myths are so powerful and agreed upon that the 'loose woman' and the 'enterprising man' are experienced as natural, eternal and constant, rather than as the social constructions that they really are.

The mythology of the male versus the female has consequences for how men, in contrast to women, see their own abuse. The female heroin users generally expressed more 'shame' about their abuse than the males, most likely because of the factors I have described above. Shame is a feeling that is ultimately about fear of outsidership and loneliness, of being unloved and undesirable – a fear of not being perceived as a good person. The men could also describe being ashamed of being dependent and of injecting, but this was more tangible among the women. Hanna describes how she mostly took her injections in the bathroom: 'I didn't want people to see while I was sitting and fixing, I think it's really disgusting. It feels really humiliating, even if the others take it the same way, I didn't want them to see me.'

The guys could sit outside and, without any obvious shame, search for a blood vessel to inject into, while Hanna mostly injected alone, behind a closed door. In the sight of others, the undesirable identity would be even more obvious, that of being a bad woman, a long way removed from the archetype of how women should be: beautiful, pure and maternal.

Molly reacted in a similar fashion when I was there. She never injected or smoked heroin in front of me; at best she could manage to take a quick 'snort'. Not all the girls were like that, however. Veronica could smoke in front of me without any great difficulty. The majority of the guys had no problems with it at all, and there were even those among them who really wanted to show me and who spoke in detail about what they did, without any kind of sign that could be interpreted as shame. I talked to Enrique to see if one of his friends would consider being interviewed by me. The friend said, 'But does it matter if I come high?' Enrique replied: 'Nah, not at all, he isn't bothered by it. You can probably smoke as well, if you want to.' His friend: 'Nah, I wouldn't ever dare to do that, he could be drug squad.' For the guys, it is the fear of being caught, and not the shame of smoking or injecting in front of me that is problematic. I conclude that it is more shameful for the young women to use heroin, as it so much further from the subculture's, the media world's, and established society's myths about men and women. The men, on the other hand, are not subjected to 'the triple pressure of shame', but are legitimized by both the subculture and the world of film.

Real and Simulated Women Who Transgress

I just thought it was exciting and daring. Maybe if I had met a guy that was into something exciting and daring in another way it would have been totally different. Do you know what I mean? I think there was always this wee bit in me that wanted to do something exciting. (Rose, a drug-using woman from Glasgow, in Taylor 1993)

Molly told me that, when the drug life was best, she could feel like Modesty Blaise, a female cartoon character who defies the boundary definitions between the sexes. She is good at hand-to-hand combat and often defeats men, without any effort worth mentioning. Her partner in arms, Willy Garvin, calls her Princess and desires her more than anything else. However, she is no ordinary princess who is waiting for her prince but makes it her business to create adventure. The occasion when Molly compared herself to Modesty Blaise was when she and a friend were going on a short holiday together, with drugs in their luggage and wanting to experience a good time together. Modesty Blaise is free. She goes where she wants to, and does what she wants to; no one can stop her. She is in all likelihood what many women want to be; free, able to command and act indifferently, but still lovable and desirable, and feminine. Hanna told me repeatedly that she likes the film *Natural Born Killers*.

Philip: Are there any particular films you like?

Hanna: Yeah, there are lots, like *The Doors* for example, I like that a lot and *Natural Born Killers*. I am completely hooked on that, I can watch it again and again. I'm the kind of person that can watch films that I think are good as many times as I feel like, it doesn't matter how often . . . Yeah, lots of those kind of films, it might be Mafia films and, yeah, drugs and gangs, gangster films, too. Mostly those kinds of films. I hate comedies. I don't think they are at all funny.

I hadn't seen the film *Natural Born Killers* at the time of the interview, but when I did see it, the first thing I was hit by was how brutal it is. The main female character's parents are shot to death, and then the couple take off into freedom and carry out a bizarre type of activity – a pair of artistic, sensual murderers, rather than ordinary serial killers. They kill a large number of people, often with a smile upon their lips, and they sometimes use the murders to score witty points, against each other and society. The girl, Mallory, is at least as capable of initiating and participating in the murders as her boyfriend. Both of them are seriously dangerous to their environment. Furthermore, they leave someone alive after each murder in order to witness their deeds.

The film described above is unusual in several respects, one of which I will concentrate on. A woman executes what, from a historical perspective, has been seen as the most masculine type of activity – serial killing. In this way the film is different from other films like *Silence of the Lambs* and *Seven*.

Hanna has been attracted to outlaw-type guys and I think her life, metaphorically expressed, is about making a film of herself. She is a little like the lead character, Mallory, from *Natural Born Killers*, who on one occasion says to Mickey: 'Every day is an adventure with you.' However, like Mallory, she is often the one who begins the adventure, and she hates anyone messing with her and dealing with her as if she were stupid. Mallory not only does what Mickey tells her to, but also acts independently. On one occasion she meets a young man in a workshop and exploits her femininity to get him to perform oral sex on her:

Mallory: Lick me!

(*He starts, only soon to discover who she is – an infamous serial killer*)

The Guy: Fuck, you're Mallory Knox!

(*Mallory kills him with several shots and then says:*)

I've never been licked that badly. Don't be so eager the next time.

Hanna wants her life to be exciting and dramatic, and to choose a normal nine-to-five job strikes her as impossible. She is tattooed and tattoos have in the Western world long been a male province and have symbolized 'movement and boundary transgressing adventure – a longing for the dangerous, different and wild, the informal and the culturally original' (Birgitta Svensson 1998: 42). During the past twenty years, tattoos have in the meantime become more usual even among women. Tattoos can, in Hanna's case, be seen as symbols in the same adventure category as crime and drugs. Mallory also has a tattoo, of a scorpion, on her stomach. Hanna is searching for activities and objects, loaded by danger and outsidership, and she does not allow the guys to steer her but chooses her own path. In the film, Mallory was to a great extent a prisoner in her home until she could free herself, and here is something that Hanna can most likely identify with; breaking free of family, for better or worse, and not being the passive woman who is subservient to men, but being involved in making decisions herself. Even if she doesn't want to copy the film, it symbolizes who she wants to be: free, independent and strong, uncompromising, someone who sees things through to the bitter end. Being with dangerous guys means she experiences existence as more exciting than if she went out with guys who stay on the right side of the law. Hanna and Molly demonstrate that there are possibilities for women to create a position within the subculture, while at the same time illustrating how hard it can be. The society we live in worships adventure, experiences, kicks, and sensations, and even if it is mostly men who seek out dangerous situations, there are women who do so too. The author and former heroin user Tam Stewart (1987: 39) writes: 'Girls crave adventure, too. Many are not afraid of a challenge. Some set out to emulate the boys.'

However, because this type of activity has mostly symbolized maleness, these women become a threat to a masculinity that is actually rather fragile.

A Fragile Masculinity

In Figure 7.1 I have sketched what can be seen as masculine and what as feminine in the culture, primarily from the male point of view.

Based on this polarity, which has support in both established society and the world of film, masculinity is created with the help of rituals. However, the polarity is based on belief, and as such is neither absolute nor final; the rituals must be continuously repeated. Besides, a whole lot of threats to this interpretation are manifest, and the primary threat is that there are women in the subculture who do more or less the same things as men – women who ritualize masculinity. Female heroin users ought also be seen as a possibility for the men in that the men can project negative qualities on to them. The female heroin users in this way fulfil the same function as the amphetamine addicts.

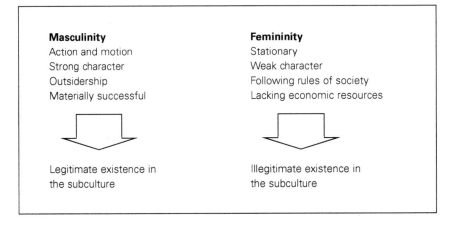

Figure 7.1 The significance of gender in the subculture.

In order to deal with this threat, a morality is created where the feminine is denigrated, causing the masculine to increase in worth. The enterprising, drug-using woman is, from the subculture's, the media world's and established society's perspective, an abject creature, who questions the premises of both the subculture and established society, and is therefore a dual threat. The female drug user who is also a professional criminal questions the gender code. Women are therefore mostly viewed as if their participation in the subculture is an exception. The men create the differences and distance themselves from them, as if to show that they don't really want to associate with them. In this way the men can, at least temporarily, deal with the threat that is formed against the subculture. If the women are made weak, dirty and loose, then the men's identities appear less open to censure. The female drug user is objectified, a target on to whom others can project their own dirt.

The subculture is created in opposition to modern society's demand for order and discipline with time. The point in joining it was to approach the 'other', which established society's representatives try to prevent. However, the gender code seems to be similar in the subculture, in films and in larger society and the portrayal of women with respect to men in the subculture is not in contrast to society in general, where, for example, a drunken woman is far more problematic than a drunken man (Frykman and Löfgren 1979/1987 and Järvinen and Rosenquist 1991). It becomes possible here to speak of a 'masculine hegemony' (Connell 1995), that encompasses the subculture, the world of film and established society.

This hegemony is reconstructed in such a way that a certain type of maleness is naturalized as the most acceptable, while anything that threatens it is fought against. In films, research, the pub (Järvinen 1991, Sulkunen et al. 1997 and

Lalander 1997, 2001), in male sports, in newspapers and in conversation between people, the picture of the male as the strong and powerful in action, and the female as weaker (more fragile) and more passive, is reconstructed. In this chapter I have shown that research and the general society often convey the same picture as the films and the subculture, which makes the argument that woman is an object seem almost natural. The gender code in the subculture is, thus, socially and culturally pre-prepared, which enables men in the subculture to use women as objects to project upon, and by which their own identity can be purified. However, the hegemony is never total but is continuously threatened. Female drug users in this sense portray not only a threat to the subculture's men, but also to society's masculine hegemony in general.

Accordingly, the subculture's masculinity is fragile. Apart from the threat from women, the following can be mentioned:

- The desire for sex decreases in proportion to the increase in heroin dependency, while potency and interest decrease proportionally. The heroin users do not associate as much with women, which makes it difficult to play the materially successful man in front of an audience. Some of them take Viagra in an attempt to remedy this lack of sexual prowess.
- Becoming 'hooked' and focusing their lives on heroin makes it difficult to maintain a picture of autonomy and freedom. Life for many becomes exceedingly regular, with maybe three occasions everyday when they shoot up heroin.
- Good finances become worse when almost all money goes on drugs. The picture of someone materially successful becomes harder to maintain.
- The majority lose their driving licences or their competency rating, which is necessary in order to get a driving licence. This is a hard blow if they are to maintain the image of a 'man in movement'. This is a serious motive for many to stay clean, as after a certain period of being provably drug free, they may be able to renew their competency.
- As a result of the drug dependency, the majority, sooner or later, show weak character, by either not paying back debts or telling the police about the subculture's activities in order to prevent a too serious withdrawal (in custody). This means that they have failed in one of the criteria required for manliness.

It thus becomes more difficult for men in the subculture, as they enter an increasing dependency, to maintain the image of being the continuously moving, successful outsider man, even if the majority try. This makes the masculine jargon even more important in order to smooth away the setbacks that actually exist. For women, the transgression is even greater and, for most of them, harder to take, as they, to a larger extent than men, must fight against the subculture's and society's gender code. Women are the real outsiders to a greater extent than the men.

–8–

The Whole World Is Yours

Role Play

Certain aspects of the subculture can be viewed as theatre, or as a living role game. However the difference between a role game and the activity that takes place in the subculture is that the participants in a role game can go home after the game is over and also that the power relationships in the role game are temporary and fictitious. If you end up in jail in a role game, you are released when the game is over, and if you are the king, you get to take off your crown after the end of the game. However, in the subculture's action, if you are caught with 10 g of heroin it will be a while before you are let out into the free world again, and if you overdose there is a risk that you will never again wake up. In the subculture, you play for real and the consequences of the game are extremely real.

The better the role game is, the more you can distance yourself from life outside it. A really good role game can mean that you almost become the role you are acting. When identification with the role becomes strong, you may have 'crossed over' to the reality of the game and left behind the dominant everyday reality you otherwise live in – the game becomes reality. Role games make it possible to construct a temporary identity from the game's idea and rule system. In the role game, the weak can be the strong, the shy the outspoken, and the frigid can be sexually debauched. In this sense the role game is like what Turkle describes in the book *Life on the Screen* (1996), where people who socialize via the Internet can create their own identities whatever way they like; they can even change sex, start falling in love and form new friendships; everything is possible. The Internet can in this sense function as an opportunity for those who are otherwise stigmatized by being, for example, overweight and make possible the construction of new identities.

On the Internet your social history, your body and other types of limitation do not fix you. There are parallels there to the subculture: even if it is to a great extent a face-to-face culture, you can create your own life history and identity together with your friends, as the actions that are valued in the subculture differ so markedly from those valued in the surrounding society. The things one has done in 'ordinary' society are relatively uninteresting to the subculture and do not contribute to a base for judging whether a person is successful or not. Personal history is erased in favour of the 'action history' acquired in the subculture. There are also similarities to other global cultures here, like the backpacker culture where the travellers free themselves from their local, social and cultural ties and create a new identity as backpackers (Andersson 1991 and Elsrud 2001). The subculture provides the opportunity for a fresh start.

Five of those whom I interviewed have been interested in role games in the form of both computer games and conventional games. These and others were also interested in Tolkien's *The Lord of the Rings* (1959), where mystical creatures live in a mystical world. None of them, however, have tried playing real role games. Roger told me what he thought of *The Lord of the Rings*:

> *Roger*: Yes, it was good. Seriously good. I read it and was hooked straight away. I love that kind of thing. I played role games when I was younger, Dungeons and Dragons and that kind of thing, if you know what I mean?
>
> *Philip*: Yes.
>
> *Roger*: They are real games. I like this kind of thing with dwarfs and elves and giants and a bit of wizardry, magicians, that kind of thing. You sit there with a piece of paper and a dice. There's a lot of imagination, like there's a game leader and he sits and tells you about the adventure and what happens. He needs an amazing imagination.
>
> *Philip*: What do you think it is that you like so much about it?
>
> *Roger*: Well, I haven't thought about it, but it could well be that . . . yeah, like that I don't like reality, that's probably why you drift. To get away from reality like, I mean, it's not up to much, I think [he laughs]. I don't think so. It's probably because it isn't reality the whole time, not like the news, you just . . . (he whistles, and makes a sweeping gesture with his finger that signals that he disappears).

The longing for another world is shared by many of Norrköping's heroin users and drifters. By participating in the subculture and using its symbols, they can create an adventure. Many use the word 'world' to distinguish the subculture from the 'ordinary' world. There is thus a feeling among the young heroin users that the subculture is enclosed and autonomous. Molly told me that sometimes she would look out of the window at the 'ordinary' people on their way to work and feel that they lived in another world. This experience of alienation becomes possible because of the subculture's illegitimacy and the police surveillance, as well as the status of drugs in modern society, that of being taboo ridden and dangerous. The illegality makes it possible to stage an authentic 'pretend world' in the real, modern world. The modern, thus, cooperates to create relatively autonomous worlds where people can go in order to approach the other, the abject, and that which has been rationalized away. The subculture, in this sense, can be viewed as an enclave in which the 'other' in relation to the modern can be sought.

To participate in the subculture's game no school results or work experience is necessary, it is sufficient to be a drifter and to like the idea of the game. The point in playing is nothing other than playing, and this is an important point. If there were definite purposes or goals, the game would be far too much like life outside it, the modern, and the game would forfeit its exclusivity.

To compare the subculture to a game is in keeping with what both Goffman (1967) and Katz (1988) write about gambling. Gambling is a prototype for 'action'. Drug-related activity can be viewed as gambling, which becomes clear if the speech is examined – such terms as 'cop chase', 'hooked', 'gain' (profit), 'runner', 'link'. Furthermore, there are a series of risks involved in the game, like the overdose risk, the risk of being captured and the risk of losing face. It is necessary to have a strong character, a type of poker face, when in contact with other players and opponents, where a variation of *Call My Bluff* often has to be played. There are also prizes in the form of money and drugs, and thereby power and status.

Gaming is an autonomous world with its own rules and its own codes. Many of the rules that apply on the outside are thrown out and replaced by others. The rules serve the purpose of defining how the players should act and react towards other players and the outside. If some of the expressions I came across are examined, the parallels to the world of gambling become apparent. Someone spoke of playing chess with the drug squad; many others spoke about trying to find out what strategies and technical equipment were available to the police, and in Chapter 4 a lot was said about how the players are careful about which ways they chose through town. It is about moving through the playing field without being taken and punished. The parallel to playing games is therefore striking.

The game's players are first and foremost those who deal and use drugs. I call these 'players'. The opposition is both the police, who should be seen as established society's representatives, and other players who are both players and opponents. Even the 'audience' should be defined. In this case the audience are the players, as they observe each other and themselves, the opponents and the 'outside'. The actions on the playing field are of interest to the outside, as they are seen as problematical from different points of view. The media, researchers, social authorities and police pay attention to what occurs on the playing field, even if they mostly only see certain aspects of it. It is important that the outside pays attention to the game, as it helps the players to see themselves clearly. The attention from the outside also helps to give the game an aura of secrecy.

The playing field is not, as in ordinary games, limited to a fixed area, but is spread throughout Norrköping, and the procurement of substances/game markers occurs with the help of technological equipment, primarily the mobile phone as well as face-to-face meetings in flats, where money and goods are exchanged for substances. It is possible to be on the playing field even if you are at home in your parents' house. The push of a button on the mobile phone is sufficient; you are plugged in. Players can visit the family home in order to transact, which makes the home a part of the game. The mobile phone is very important as it increases the tempo of the game and contributes to maintaining a spread-out playing field. Much of the game happens at a distance with the help of modern communications equipment.

The family home can also be a place where the substance is taken as well as a place where dealing occurs, and in these cases the family home is a part of the playing field. The playing field is 'where the action is', and by that I mean the type of events that make the subculture specific in relation to the outside. As these types of activity are illegal, masking activity is engaged in against the opponents, as these are the representatives of the outside.

The specific events that occur on the playing field do not often look particularly spectacular – a guy stands talking on a mobile phone, another spends a long time in the toilet. You have to be knowledgeable and have gaming experience in order to draw the conclusion that the game is afoot. This is a conscious move on the part of the players, to conceal from the outside what they are occupied with, and this also provides the game with an extra dimension of secrecy. The game becomes worth playing and, as only the players participating know what is going on, an experience of exclusivity is created. The playing field is diffuse and to the uninit-iated does not look like anything special, but for the game's participants it is clear and tangible. Few of the game's participants can distinguish the whole playing field. This is a consequence of the secrecy.

Learning the Game and Progressing

In keeping with other games, there is a lot to learn. I have called this action skill, knowledge of how the action can be maintained in a way that minimizes the risks and makes a certain amount of control possible. In Chapter 2, I explored 'alter-native socialization', which involved developing a type of knowledge of criminal activity, drug use, the effects of drugs, and so forth through practical means. This helps create a special perspective on existence, a 'subcultural habitus', where you learn to interpret different sorts of situations and to react based on the inter-pretation. You also learn to create action. A necessary condition for being able to create action is having learnt to handle risks. The pedagogical situation during alternative socialization is almost perfect and ordinary school could learn quite a lot from this. Education in the subculture occurs through events and quick rewards, which functions like a 'carrot' to further learning. The knowledge is also not abstract, but something experienced, which is made one's own. This is possible when the feeling that one has chosen to go to the alternative school exists. The knowledge is extremely useful later on, when it comes to grafting – creating resources for obtaining drugs with. Money is needed to play the game. As well as learning from mentors and friends, the films produced at the beginning of the 1990s are also useful, as well as the alternative sports engaged in, like Tae Kwon Do and kick boxing. The lifestyle takes shape and contributes to an action lifestyle/player style where the central focus is a matter of dealing with risks and creating drama.

An important criterion for status among the players is to have lived the action because this shows that you are a genuine outsider, someone who does not follow the straight and narrow, leading a life like Joe Bloggs, but rather someone who has chosen a more dangerous and individual path in life – someone who has defined himself or herself as a player. Drug use symbolizes action, as it involves challenging danger and daring to subject the body to a change from one state to another. Drug experience also involves learning about dosages, combinations, choosing the correct time, place and surroundings. Using drugs is criminal and disapproved of, according to established society, and this also constitutes it as action. Drug use can also be defined as action because it gives rise to tempo changes in the environment and drastic changes between different perspectives on existence.

Drug use is a sign of experience, and experience is the most obvious marker of the alternative lifestyle. In this sense, drug use can be seen as 'experience capital' in the subculture, with whose help one can obtain status (Bourdieu 1979/1992 and Thornton 1996). To learn about drugs through testing should also be seen as a way of showing cultural belonging, as well as a way of creating an identity and a position in the game.

The action skills are carved into the players' consciousness and create a perspective from which they see the world. The drug's symbolic worth in the subculture is diametrically opposed to that in modern society. This is learnt in the subculture. It can be compared to how the majority in established society view alcohol – if alcohol consumption is kept within reasonable limits it is completely acceptable, alcohol is rendered undramatic. The more you play, the more the risks are downplayed while, in tandem, the skills necessary to deal with them are learned. Besides, the players protect each other against risk, which further strengthens the belief in the new perspective on existence. The group, through seeing and discussing films, conversation, jargon, and actions, communicates this new perspective. This perspective, or subcultural habitus, and associated actions become the 'correct' one. It is a matter of the production of the subculture's 'belief' (Bourdieu 1979/ 1992) where the cultural view the players develop becomes the dominant one – they are socialized into the game and the game becomes more real than the reality outside it. The game has been naturalized.

The Desirable Adventure

> There is a need to explore and see other things . . . Yes, I think it is very much this thing with adventure that I feel. I feel that I want to have done many different things. Experiences! Excitement, and all that . . . But it is also the challenge, to test yourself, to experience. (A backpacker in Andersson 1999: 104)

> So, it's fun, if you're smoking, to go somewhere. It feels like you're in an adventure, that you're out on an adventure, so much can happen, so much happens all the time. (Roger, a 'horser' from Norrköping)

The alternative socialization means that you get used to living in a 'fast reward system.' The game contains dramatic changes and provides fuel for restlessness. The thought that you need not wait is engraved on the players' consciousness, with the knowledge that changes in perception can happen at once. Life becomes a series of experiences, in contrast to the routines modern society expects us to live with. The knowledge that change can happen quickly makes the game worth playing. The plot of the drama is mainly about creating 'now' experiences.

The first quotation above is from a culture where 'now' experiences are viewed as central – the backpacker's culture, a global culture whose members leave their everyday lives in order to live in other social and cultural contexts from those to which they are accustomed, for long periods of time. As they travel they experience freedom from the culture they are leaving behind, and this is also a point in backpacking. This passion for adventure can be seen as a reaction to the modern, which is described by many, both backpackers and heroin users, as humdrum, predictable and boring. In Chapter 2, I described how the apprentice heroin users enter the subculture and create it as transcendental in relation to the formal school (the long arm of modernity). A space and time of one's own is created in the subculture, and the members experience a feeling of control over their existence. To travel and to use drugs are therefore related strategies for dealing with life in modern society. Like gamblers, the drug users create the great adventure on home territory, and existence becomes a game and an adventure.

The game is in keeping with the global media's emphasis on adventure, experience and sensation. Life should be dramatic, where adventure is chosen over staying put in the modern and following the path of deferred rewards. The game creates the opportunity to rise to the challenge of the post-modern, to experience, create sensations and satisfy needs, like the Coca-Cola advertisement: 'create your adventure'. Joe Bloggs's imprisonment in planning, daily, monthly, quarterly and yearly, is kept as far away as possible. Joe Bloggs, according to the message of the post-modern, is the antithesis of adventure. The young heroin users do not want to be prisoners in the modern, but rather 'choosers' and consumers. Bauman writes:

Everybody may be *cast* into the mode of the consumer; everybody may *wish* to be a consumer and indulge in the opportunities, which that mode of life holds. But not everybody *can* be a consumer. To desire is not enough; to make the desire truly desirable, and so to draw the pleasure from the desire, one must have a reasonable hope of getting closer to the desired object. This hope, reasonably entertained by some, is futile for many others. All of us are doomed to the life of choices, but not all of us have the means to be choosers.

Like all other known societies, the post modern, consumer society is a stratified one. But it is possible to tell one kind of society from another by the dimensions along which it stratifies its members. The dimension along which those 'high up' and 'low down' are plotted in a society of consumers, is their *degree of mobility* – their freedom to choose where to be. (Bauman 1998: 86)

The young heroin users try to change themselves to choosers in the sense that they oppose the order which, from their point of view, they would otherwise be doomed to live with. They choose not to follow the modern and slow path to becoming choosers; they want to choose at once. By joining the subculture on good, post-modern grounds, they try to create mobility in regard to experiences of consumption. They have learned, from the media and each other, other ways of life than the one that school teaches. There are fast ways, shortcuts, to happiness. You do not necessarily have to be on good terms with established society, which still purports to be modern. The subculture is locally tied to Norrköping, even if it has its counterparts in other places. The subculture's members travel in the local, but it is also as if they were somewhere else. In this sense the subculture has made it possible for them to solve a particular stratification problem that is part and parcel of the modern/post-modern society. They have, like the cocaine- and crack-using young people that Williams (1986) studied, become good consumers.

Bauman (1998) distinguishes between two worlds in post-modern society. In the 'globally mobile's world' people travel to other countries and cultures to experience different types of sensations that are desirable in a post-modern, globalized, culture. If existence at home is felt to be altogether too boring, then it is no great problem to get on a plane to some other country and use your money to experience something else. You can simply rewrite your history in the face of something new and take with you the pieces of yourself that you wish to keep, and put together the old and the new into an identity that you can be satisfied with. However, in the 'locally tied world' this is not so easy. For these people, *the global space* is not as accessible. They are forced to stay in the local, which becomes extra painful because of '. . . the obtrusive media display of space conquest and of the "virtual accessibility" of distances that stay stubbornly unreachable in non-virtual reality' (Bauman 1998: 88). The locally tied also want to travel, or to take part in the experiences that the aesthetically produced reality provides for them. They become backpackers on home territory, in the industrial town of Norrköping, where they travel in a world that is different, because it is secret and invisible, and in some way without history. They travel in a world where they sometimes experience the extraordinary, even if they haven't moved particularly far. Bauman writes about the opportunities for travel for those who live in the locally tied world: 'The second travel surreptitiously, often illegally, sometimes paying more for the crowded steerage of a stinking unseaworthy boat than others pay for business-class guided luxuries – and are frowned upon, and, if unlucky, arrested and promptly deported, when they arrive' (Bauman 1998: 89).

In Williams's (1986) study of young crack dealers it was portrayed as reasonable to start selling drugs in order to get some of the goods which were seen as important. However, one could question if young people in Swedish society need to do this, as the majority are relatively well off materially, here. On the other hand, Sweden is not an isolated paradise that globalization and post-modernization hasn't reached, but rather a society where films, advertising and other post-modern sources of information show how life could be lived. The discrepancy between one's own life and the life portrayed visually is great, and creates a sense of loss, and an imaginary poverty, which results in many longing to surround themselves with status goods and to enjoy the desire for these goods, in order to experience freedom while showing themselves to be successful and to define themselves as unique and independent of others. You do not have to be poor in order to feel poor, it depends on what comparisons you have. The game, like the films that inspire it, is about 'consumerism', to leave behind the ordinary, to have a bundle of notes making a lump in your pocket and feeling that you can buy what you want creates an illusion of success. It is not to be wondered at that a certain few chose to create this opportunity in a way that is not deemed legitimate by the modern – you quickly become a perfect person, one of the 'desirable'. The temptation is there and it adds fuel to the desire and some turn this desire into action. When they have once enjoyed the fruits of consumption they find it difficult to live any other way.

Consumption and experiences are at the centre of contemporary Western societies. The subculture's consumerism is about trying to define themselves as good members of society: people who have the means to live in the way recommended. The subculture is not completely an antithesis of modern society but only of some aspects of it – those that deal with deferred rewards, planning, discipline, and so forth. Other consumer-related aspects are very positively received in the same way as they are by other members of society, who dream about the big win or the fast car (cf. with Campbell 1989). Subculture is, thus, created both as an antithesis and as a consequence of the modern. In the subculture, there is a passion for modern technological developments in the form of fast cars, computers, mobile phones and other such equipment. In this sense the subculture is 'hypermodern' and keeps abreast of the times. It is on the same level as other cultures that defend the fast, the communicative, the mobile and the adventurous

– for example, stock-market speculators, gamblers, hackers and backpackers. The modern defends a certain order, which the subculture makes a lifestyle of transgressing. It is against this order that the adventure is interpreted as interesting.

Togetherness and Reintroduction

Maffesoli (1996) writes about 'neotribes' and means the new social groups that arise in a pronounced, globalized consumer society where it is difficult for an individual to maintain and deal with an individual autonomy, and therefore use consumer goods to indicate similarity to other people. Neotribes are different from what we usually mean when use the word 'tribe': people who are bound together by a common history, common mythology, gods and legends. Relationships between members in a neotribe are built upon similar consumer preferences; they show a similar consumer lifestyle, and that is true for the young heroin users. In this way, neotribes have a short history and there is no genealogy to provide the tribe's history and character. Neotribes are ultimately created by changes in consumer society and its members adapt their façades from interpreting the media, rather than from stable and historically based values of how life should be.

Both Maffesoli (1996) and Bauman (1991) write about the 'togetherness' that arises in the post-modern society in order to deal with the loneliness that people lacking in history and living in a global information society experience. The subculture makes it possible to experience togetherness quickly, and this becomes extra strong because of the inherent secrecy (Maffesoli 1996). The small group is encapsulated in relation to the outside world and only the closeness experienced in the group is of importance. The drug ritual operates in such a way as to separate the participants from the rest of society. It makes it possible to create an illusion of sameness, while quickly building up a group identity, where the group members are separate from others. The group can be seen as an opportunity to create a different order, a microcosm where the aspects one perceives as being missing can be filled in. The group becomes an area for adventure and an approach to the 'other', which the Western world's rationalism has pushed aside. In this sense it is not a superficial neotribe, which merely shares consumer preferences, but also an existential problematic they try to deal with via consumption and action. They try to make themselves a tribe in the real meaning of the word, and, through their experience history, they bring legends to the group and the culture. They create a clear cosmos with definite poles, the police and themselves, which means they live in a definable cosmos where they experience a strong sense of belonging.

According to Weber (1934/1992), modern society compromises a 'disenchantment' of the world, a 'demystification', as a consequence of science and rationalism's expansion. Ziehe (1993) continues this argument, but writes about a form of demystification and pre-consciousness that happens when children and youth, early in life, find out everything about life's mysteries through the media and a less taboo-ridden school. This results in some trying to invent mysteries in life. By mysteries I mean ideas and objects that cannot really be defined, ideas that there is something to discover beyond the reality in which we live, something society is incapable of defining and that makes life special and worth living. New age and new spiritualism can be seen as answers to what is lacking in the modern. We live in a time when witches and goblins have been rationalized away, but at the same time there is a longing for what these objects represented.

Goblins and witches were earlier times' labels for the 'abject' (Kristeva 1982), they were both human and something else. Drugs, during the twentieth and twenty-first centuries, have come to symbolize the abject, both the contemptible and the desirable. This meaning has been strengthened by popular culture's expansion, and combined with tempo, transgression, other reality, death, hell, paradise and more. Drugs ultimately symbolize the unpredictable, the uncontrollable, the other, and can, thereby, replace witches and goblins. Through drugs you can succeed in regaining part of life's mysteries, and this is ultimately reached through their antithetical relationship to modern society. What frightens some may attract others. When you approach the other in relation to modern culture, you can really experience that you are fully alive, that life becomes mystical. Proximity to the other creates a feeling that all is not understandable, systemized, rationalized and ordered, but the experience of an existence hiding other as yet not experienced dimensions.

When it comes to heroin it is a matter of approaching death, but not as we mostly perceive it, a threatening extinguishing of reflection and consciousness, that everything becomes merely black, but rather an approach to what death symbolizes in our culture, something else. The other is fascinating as it is not predefined and ordered. Death fascinates and some wish to approach it, though few want to die. Formula one racing drivers do not in all probability long for death, but rather want to live an intensive life where the other is present in the form of death. Knowledge that death, the greatest challenge of all, is present, makes it possible for the present and, thereby, life to be experienced more strongly. It is a matter of 'potentializing' (Ziehe 1993), where life is intensified and condensed. I would like to compare it to a flat with different rooms.

Furthest in is the room of death; no one has come out of it to tell us what it is like to be there. In the modern we react with both fear and angst or fascination if we catch a glimpse of it. However, the rooms around it crackle with energy, which arises because of the proximity to the room of death. To spend time near that room is almost like conquering death – or life. Heroin, like formula one racing, and Mount Everest, is of interest because of its proximity to this room. Life energy and now experiences become total when in proximity to modern society's ultimate other. Those who survived the *Estonia* disaster (the car and passenger ferry that went down in the Baltic with the loss of 900 lives in 1994) became interesting people to the mass media. Their identities seemed charged with energy. They had been there, in death's waiting room, without having to enter.

To live near the abject conveys the experience that life is not predetermined, because if it were so, then living wouldn't be any great idea, at least not if you live in the post-modern where variation and change are seen as important qualities of life. The 'extraordinary experience' is created when, with a certain control, the indefinable is approached, that which is impossible to understand. It is the same with rock music that constantly composes themes of the 'other', the undesirable (Sernhede 1996).

The young heroin users are far from alone in encouraging the other, which has crept into its hiding places during the modernization of the Western world. The young heroin users are 'seekers' who try to find another and more mystical existence than modern society can offer. They want to find themselves between waking and sleeping, high, in a dreamlike state. The God they create for the tribe is that of extraordinary experience, the drug experience or kick, where everything is perfect. However, God does not often show himself.

When the Game becomes Unpleasant

The game continually delivers new challenges and the participants learn to appreciate and handle this. The players develop a 'playing competency', that is, a capacity and skill for handling action. The paradox is that the better you get at dealing with action, the less action you experience. In the beginning the competence is a condition for experiencing existence as dramatic, but the more you become used to adventure, the less attracted to it you are. The earlier occasions that were eventful and dramatic become relatively dull. It is as if Columbus were to sail to America for the hundredth time and say, 'Wake me up after you've gone ashore and come back, and we'll go home.' Time does not stand still, and the pulse rate does not increase. This is a description of the development from 'drifter' to 'strong character'. The drifter is the one who is still playing and enjoying living with uncertainty. The drifter is fascinated by excitement and adventure, he or she energizes the environment and the game is fully charged. However, in order to survive the game it is necessary to develop the competency that is associated with the strong character. The well-developed strong character no longer experiences any great adventure or sensation and is, in Simmel's (1903/1981) words, almost blasé. The blasé attitude is a way of dealing with things which grows in urban, eventful environments, where impressions are so many that the individual is forced to develop a psychological defence.

The strong character is an expert at the game, whereas the drifter is a player who plays and is fascinated by the novelty of the game. If you have played a computer game so often that you easily reach the higher level, the inner world via the other worlds, then it is no longer interesting, as you know what is coming next during the course of the journey. The drifter on the other hand is a new player, occupied with action – by moving through society's borderlands, playing at resistance to the establishment's order, and to him, the game is still relatively unexplored; new forms, sensations and computer game worlds can still appear. The strong character knows the game's rationale well and few new sensations appear and his pulse no longer rises. It is no longer a question of action but rather of acting or reacting and a competency that is similar to 'going to work' – a lack of the dramatic. The heroin experience also becomes anything but an adventure after a while; it no longer provides any great kicks. The professionalizing of the subculture's activities makes the game lose much of its earlier lustre. The other is no longer the 'other', but rather the 'normal' from the perspective of the strong character, and has, thus, lost its power to fascinate. The strong character tries to approach the other by maximizing the drug experience and potentializing the now, but these attempts to maximize do not stand comparison with earlier drug adventures. The strong character plans so that nothing unexpected will crop up, and in this sense has more difficulty living in the now. The young heroin users joined the culture and felt that they escaped the discipline of the modern, only to find it necessary to plan existence for themselves, in order to keep their opponents at bay.

Action involves experiencing events as voluntary and not directed by powers that you do not have the ability to control. As a result of the game's logic, and the experience capital provided by drugs, you become dependent on being drugged. The drug gives rise to change and drama and you want to try everything. The player begins to use the most dramatic of all drugs, heroin, and falls in love with it. Other action substances pale in comparison, and an experience of lack of problems, harmony and great sense of wellbeing is created. However, with heroin in the body, the game almost becomes uninteresting. Other action events, like break-ins or shoplifting, are no longer any great pleasure, but rather a necessity in order to provide the means to obtain a hit. The experience becomes 'the only thing that means anything is getting a hit'. Eventually you realize, although you try to tell yourself that this is not the case, that you are hooked.

The game becomes serious. You do things that previously would have been interpreted as unsuccessful. You are anything but free. You also begin to be nostalgic for the 'good old days' when you 'played' together. Once you become addicted to heroin both the modern and the post-modern reject you. From the modern perspective, you are a failed person who cannot accept responsibility for yourself, and from the post-modern's perspective you are a loser who cannot cope with living a varied and changeable life. The chapter on media discussed how films portray a tragic picture of those who are hooked. They are no longer travellers in experience, but tragic figures who have fallen victim to their own needs. Life begins to be seriously ambivalent and they try to find good excuses for not seeing themselves as useless individuals. Many excuses can be found in the subculture, which is, partly, built as a protection against the accusation that one is morally degenerate. In this instance it becomes suitable to reconstruct heroin and make it into a power beyond the individual's control, and in this way protect one's identity against accusations. To appear a free individual is very important in both the modern and the post-modern. In the modern you are expected to be a responsible individual who produces, while in the post-modern you are expected to be a flexible individual who consumes, so that you can seize the day instead of being seized. Giddens (1992: 76) writes this about addiction: 'Every addiction is a defensive reaction, and an escape, a recognition of lack of autonomy that casts a shadow over the competence of the self.' The 'lack of autonomy' is a threat to identity; another threat has to do with social bonds. It is more fun to do drugs with others. Together, a faith in the secret and specific existence that drugs and criminality involve can be created.

However, heroin is so expensive and so desirable that trust becomes a problem. The social bonds are weakened and the participants in the game become suspicious of each other. Players with a common history 'blab' about each other, and people who were previously playing partners try to cheat each other. The participants in the game finally do not know when something is said in earnest, or when it is a case of bluffing. Playfulness has become suspicion and undemanding togetherness has become caution. The earlier hash smoking can be likened to children hiding in a dark cupboard without the adults' knowledge, and their mutually experiencing a strong social togetherness on account of being cut off from the surrounding world. However, when they become hooked on heroin they look at each other with suspicion, and the strong social togetherness that was there in play and adventure is blown away. It is no longer a matter primarily of people who meet each other, but players, who often play games of bluff with their former friends. The game is serious, and may the best player win. In this instance, many players wish to leave.

There is also a power dimension to the playfulness, which indicates vitality, but by developing a serious dependency, going over to injecting and getting older, the vitality dimension is threatened. The body displays something else. What is being done can no longer be interpreted as playing but is in every respect serious. Previously, money in one's pocket was a sign of success. However, as a heroin addict it is often a question of being able to collect enough money to pay for the day's dose.

The argument above displays how the social action experiences are eroded and how the players end up fighting to get these back. The argument can be summarized in three points:

1. Tired of the game. The game has been learnt so well that it no longer gives rise to any sensations.
2. Threat to identity. There is no longer the experience of being someone who chooses, but rather one of being a prisoner of need. Added to this, the body begins to be visible evidence of failure.
3. The social bonds are weakened and threatened and the experience of collective transcendence is made difficult.

They sometimes look longingly back to the exciting times when it was mostly a game, and sometimes they play the slot machines or take a little cocaine or smoke some hash to try and recreate the feeling of the time that has gone – a nostalgia trip to try once again to experience existence as rich in action.

One Push of a Button Away from the Game

The modern state sees the game as a threat and therefore spends a lot of energy fighting it, but is at the same time involved in defining and creating the playing field. If the game did not have autonomy it would not be a game. Bauman (1991) claims that the post-modern involves a 'pluralizing of authorities', for better or worse. Established society's tip on how life should be lived is one among many codes, but they are contradicted by the messages promulgated through the media. The most important aspect of being a successful consumer is how you present yourself in the 'now'. Experience and body become more central than education and future. Without the expansion of the post-modern consumer society the game would be judged absurd. If the state's hegemony were total and individuals in society only thought in the state's terms, it would be irrational to play the game. However, the young heroin users have listened carefully and created a lifestyle of the 'now' and consumption, which in the end has hit back against them and shown itself to be anything other than a place of freedom. The moral is as clear as it is in the films *Scarface, New Jack City* and *The Seekers*, where those who long for quick success in the end meet their downfall.

The game is constructed in relation to the modern, but takes its inspiration from the post-modern and takes on, like backpackers, hackers and stock market speculators, the characteristics of a 'now' culture. The game is inspired by, and linked up to, a post-modern simulated reality whose normality is in line with the game's. The simulated world makes the game less problematic in relation to the outside. It is a matter of a consumer's world, where happiness is consumption and experiences, not working towards a better society. In order for the consumerism to function, the society's members must focus on the now. Consumerism is fed by the consequences of modern society in the form of strong discipline, where every individual watches over himself and others (Campbell 1989, Bauman 1991 and Maffesoli 1996).

It is difficult, but not impossible, to integrate into ordinary society after having played for some years. After a while of keeping away from the game's symbols, the negative aspects of the game have become toned down, and what is remembered is the excitement, the sociability and the secrecy, among other things. By having lived outside the game, the game is often renewed again. There is a belief that that is where the action is; the subculture is, in the memory, refreshed in the same way that the body recovers. Some who try to stop using heroin continue to play the game. They might take cocaine, hash, handle stolen goods or continue drug dealing. Others might gamble on horses, slot machines or the football pools. However, for those who have also isolated themselves from the subculture, when they stop using heroin, there is often a longing to go back. They long to break the routines of everyday life, to go out on an adventure and to use the specialist skills they have obtained. They know that the other world still exists. Time outside the game is experienced by many as empty and linear, when nothing happens. It is a time of waiting, of future and of history, an angst-producing time of painful self-reflection and a feeling of having wasted one's youth. However it can also be a time of happiness and curiosity. They often long to be surrounded and cherished and thereby not to have to think of the future.

With today's technology, the possibilities are simplified of having a short flash back to drug use, despite the fact that an hour previously you were determined not to relapse. You might see a film that reawakens the need, or maybe feel anxious and alone. One touch of the button on your mobile phone, and the words 'can you help me?' and you are back in the game again: the flats, the public toilets, the friends, the enemies, the lack of problems, the angst, the shame, the feeling of well-being, the sweats, the money, the destroyed veins, the drama, the worry, the occupation, the stress, and the feeling of being somebody or nobody.

Appendix – Method and Researcher's Reflections

A Moral Decision

> If one is effectively to study adult criminals in their natural settings he must make the moral decision that in some ways he will break the law himself. He need not to be a 'participant' observer and commit the criminal act under study, yet he has to witness such acts or be taken into confidence about them and not blow the whistle. (Polsky 1969: 138 in Taylor 1993: 17)

The present research project has been seen as morally suspect. In the beginning of March 2000 a number of Swedish newspapers wrote about the project, but didn't as such describe it, rather focusing on the 'morally doubtful' aspect of Bengt Svensson (my collaborator in the bigger heroin project, which is described briefly in the preface) and myself wishing to be present when 'young people got high'. The Norrköping newspaper *Folkbladet* had placards broadcasting this news, and the national newspapers, *Kvällsposten*, *Metro*, *Aftonbladet* and *Expressen*, all wrote about it. Everyone focused on the fact that we were 'going to watch'. We had been transformed into voyeurs who exploited young people in the name of research. I was at this time to meet with some social welfare secretaries in Norrköping to discuss the project, but the newspapers had already approached them first:

> Researchers want to watch as young people abuse heroin
> (Headline in *Folkbladet*, 6 March 2000)

When I arrived at the appointment I was met by an icy silence, no smiles and no greetings. Someone said, 'What we read in the paper is not what you told us about earlier.' It appeared they chose to take the newspaper's line. I told them about the project and few questions arose. The FMN (Organization of Parents Against Narcotics) was telephoned by the local newspaper *Folkbladet*, which wanted to hear attitudes to the fact that researchers were 'going to watch'. The FMN chose not to give any comments, as it wanted more information on what the research was about. I called the organization and offered to give a talk. After the talk, I received many favourable comments to the effect that what we were doing was good. I had already started conducting interviews before the placards and I do not believe the media attention disturbed the opportunity to do the research. I asked some of the young heroin users what they thought of my wanting to observe as they used heroin, and they thought, on reflection, that it was the only way to understand, without using oneself. But, what is it that is so remarkable about watching while someone uses heroin?

It is probably about transgressing a boundary of respectability with regard to how one may act as a researcher and adult citizen. It is within the boundaries of respectability to observe withdrawal, abstinence, when drug users are in hospital and so forth, but not when they are actually using heroin. The researcher who is in a place where heroin is being ingested is something alien, which questions the boundaries between the established and the subculture, the order of things. The mass media's interest clearly shows the taboo status of drug use in established society. I, however, find it necessary to observe, as the study to a great extent is about understanding drug use.

Another objection to watching as the informants use a dangerous drug like heroin could be that you ought to contact the authorities in order to provide help. To counteract this objection, I just wish to say that in that case the research would have been impossible. I would only have been able to interview those who had stopped using narcotics.

The main ethical principle I chose to work from was to guarantee the informants' anonymity and thereby ensure that the research results would not be used against the persons studied. Data were kept securely and tapes, after transcription, were destroyed, so that in the future they could not be used as evidence in trials.

Sample and Time

In order to partake in the study the only criterion was to have used heroin in Norrköping during the 1990s. The first contacts I made with the heroin users were through an alcohol and narcotic agency in Norrköping, NOA. The decision to use them was made as I realized I didn't have the channels to get in touch with the heroin users without help. I didn't, like Adler (1985), have a smuggling and dealing neighbour or, like Jackson-Jacobs (2002), have drug-using classmates. Nor did I want, like Whyte (1943/1993) and Bourgois (1996), to spend a few years living close to the informants, hanging around in their blocks and thus creating contacts. This was also impossible because I simply did not know where they lived. Therefore, I followed Faupel (1991) and Taylor (1993) and used social workers or treatment staff to create contacts.

The staff at NOA asked the young horsers if they wished to allow themselves to be interviewed and also if they wished to give me their name and telephone numbers. Almost everyone who was asked was willing to participate. In one month

I had interviewed ten young heroin users and, through these, I received more contacts, arranged by those I had interviewed.

Before the summer I had done some sixty interviews, and I had made a number of observations with twenty young heroin users. Of the twenty-five who have been interviewed, thirteen were recruited through NOA. Three were contacted through a Youth Agency and the remaining nine through those that I interviewed. The majority of the interviewees are of Swedish origin, while some came to Sweden as children. Eighteen of the interviewees are men, seven women. They are aged from seventeen to thirty and the average age is twenty-three. The majority were born during the second half of the 1970s. Of the twenty-five interviewed, fifteen have been using heroin during 2000. Seven of the remainder have been heroin-free since the end of 1999 and the remaining two stopped using heroin two and four years previously. Of the twenty-five, I had more contact with ten of them, whom I met between four and thirty times. Eight of them are Swedish, two have other ethnic backgrounds, two are women. Of these ten, eight had used heroin to a large extent during 2000.

During the year 2000 I did most of the ethnographical work in a rather intensive manner. I have, however, continued to meet and to interview the heroin users in the years that have followed. I have now made a total of about 150 interviews and met heroin users around 300 times. The last two years it has been more a case of friendly meetings with for example Max, Molly, Steve, Hanna, John and Ben, who have been extra important as informants. I have, however, sometimes conducted interviews with them and also written down field notes.

Gaining Access

Gaining access has to do with the ability to create an impression that one is a person who can be trusted, and also a person who will do something valuable with the information obtained from interviews and observations. The maintaining of access has to do with how motivated the informants are to talk about their lives. The researcher, thus, can be seen as a motivator, and if the informants find it motivating to go on with the collaboration they do so. If they don't they may not answer the phone, fail to show up for interviews and bad-mouth the research to their mates. Fortunately, this didn't happen, at least not to the extent where it became a problem. I discuss possible reasons for this below.

Adler (1985: 19) writes that 'trust is not a one-time phenomenon, but an ongoing developmental process'. This is especially important when it comes to criminal cultures in which you, as a researcher, can't guarantee 100 per cent immunity to the informants, and when what they say and do in front of the researcher can, if the researcher has doubts, lead to imprisonment (Agar 1973). The researcher may be called as a witness in a trial without any kind of rights to withhold secretive information about drug dealing. It is therefore very important to 'make a moral decision' about how to act if this would happen, because it's almost impossible to do ethnography on criminal cultures without witnessing crimes. My decision was, as I wrote earlier, to keep the rule of anonymity out of respect for my informants, no matter what. In some cases this was a difficult task.

On one occasion an informant's parents came home while I was doing an interview and, most likely, thought that I was a shady figure, maybe a dealer. This was also probably due to my age; I'm about ten years older than the average age of the informants. The father asked me who I was and I said my name without mentioning what I was doing there. He was really upset and shook my hand while saying to me 'I'm John Johansson and work at the post office [assumed name and occupation]. Who are you?' I answered: 'I'm Philip Lalander, researcher of youth culture.' Two of my informants were standing just beside us, and they didn't interfere with our conversation. The father later checked out my credentials. I couldn't tell the father that I was writing a book about young heroin users, simply because that would have been like telling him that his son was a heroin user.

I found this situation ambivalent as I had to compromise with my values on how one should act in society, and also on how I would have reacted if I were the father and one of my children were involved in dangerous activities. I would certainly be suspicious towards a man, ten years older than my child, who acts in a secretive way in my apartment, unable to express the real purpose of his being present. The two informants, however, knew that after this incident they could trust me.

Another important aspect in the process of gaining access and trust was to observe how the informants used and dealt with heroin. Adler writes, in *Wheeling and Dealing*, about a situation in which this aspect was very clear:

> Then one day something happened which forced a breakthrough in the research. Dave [the smuggler] had two guys visiting him from out of town and, after snorting quite a bit of cocaine, they turned their conversation to a trip they had just made from Mexico, where they piloted a load of marijuana across the border in a small plane. Dave made a few efforts to shift the conversation to another subject, telling them to 'button their lips', but they apparently thought he was joking . . . Later, after the two guys had left, he discussed with us what happened. He admitted to us that he was a member of a smuggling crew and a major marijuana dealer on the side . . . From then on he was open in discussing the nature of his dealing and his smuggling activities with us. (1985: 14)

I didn't experience the sort of breakthrough Adler experienced, but the more I saw and got to know, the more they told me and showed me. To be present where drugs were used meant it was very important that I did not belong to any authority but was an independent researcher. These occasions can also be viewed as tests. If no police came after I had visited then I was seen as OK. Had the police made a raid shortly after I had been there, my research would have been ruined, or I would at least have run a serious risk of being suspected of 'snitching'. I was occasionally anxious about this.

The problem with using NOA for contacts was that the young heroin users would associate it with authority and that they, therefore, might worry about having what they said used against them. For that reason, I avoided, as far as possible, using the NOA premises as an arena for conducting interviews. Most of the interviews took place in the informants' flats, in cafés, outdoors or in my car. I believe it helped them accept me to see me in their environment on their conditions.

When I presented my research to them I, intentionally, used the word 'book' and not 'report'. It is more interesting to be in a book than in a report that perhaps only a few people will read. The word 'report' is more associated with authorities than the word 'book', which can be connected to independent authors.

That I came alone and was not afraid of them also can have contributed to my being accepted, as social workers most often work in pairs when making home visits. Furthermore, I used only my own telephone when I called them, despite having access to NOA's telephones. My intention was to show, in every possible way, that I was an independent researcher. As the vast majority had mobile phones, and these display numbers, this, too, was important as they could decide if they wished to answer me or not. I also decided early on to have as little as possible to do with the police. I had one meeting with them in January 2000, and then no further contact. At this meeting the head of the drug squad said to me: 'I wouldn't recommend you to do what you plan, visiting them alone in their flats.'

During the interviews I avoided asking about names and places, because these types of questions can be viewed as 'cop questions', reminding them of an interrogation. When we talked about criminal activity, which we did most of the time, I asked follow-up questions about their experiences rather than asking them to reconstruct how the crime occurred. I think they noticed this, and drew the conclusion that I couldn't possibly be 'drug squad'. The thought occasionally occurred to some of them, though. Hanna said on one occasion: 'Imagine if you were a cop, then I would be in a really bad way.' However, she was probably only playing with the thought. I answered: 'If I were a cop I would be very icy and skilful, and besides that, one who had written a PhD thesis on young people's alcohol habits.' She believed me.

In order to create trust and motivation it is of major importance to treat the informants with full respect. Before entering the field, I actively tried to work on my own prejudices on drugs and drug use, which can creep into speech and in this way create a barrier between people. I did not for example use words like junkie or addict and I did not presume that those I interviewed were criminals or in any other way stigmatized. I saw them as fellow human beings who had experiences to convey. My strategy was similar to one used by Faupel in *Shooting Dope*:

I explicitly placed them in the role of a teacher who was to assume that I knew nothing about crime. What would I have to know? What skills would I have to learn? How would I go about committing such a crime without getting caught? (1991: 17)

This strategy requires a willingness to listen to the informants' stories, motivating them to express their point of view. I have never worked in the treatment system. The closest I have come is a period during the beginning of the 1990s when I worked as a youth and community worker. My thinking was not therefore impaired by any treatment discourse, where I would see them as presumably in need of help.

Another aspect of motivation has to do with the possibility of creating a belief that participation in the research project is highly important. The first interviews, with each person, always started by my explaining the project and informing him or her about anonymity. I also had a copy of my earlier book with me, *The Genie in the Bottle* (1998), and a copy of Bengt Svensson's *Speed-freaks, Junkies and Others* (1996) and was (almost) always well prepared with a tape recorder, batteries, opened tapes, and so on, as would be expected of a professional researcher. The point was to strengthen the fact that I was an independent observer and that by showing I had already written a book to make it credible that I would write another. They met a real researcher and knew that what they had to say would lead to concrete results. As previously mentioned, I often used a hired car, which may have given them the impression that the research project has good finances and, thus, is important.

I also believe that my knowledge of Norrköping improved the motivation to participate in a two-way-process: I understood them well and they understood me. This was partly due because of the accent and partly because of the solidarity created by having lived in the same town. I could use my knowledge of Norrköping in conversation with them as a way of breaking the ice. When they mentioned a street or a place, they knew that I knew what they were talking about, and this made the interviews a lot smoother than if I hadn't had that local knowledge.

Few other researchers would have been able to discuss the now-disbanded ice hockey team The White Horse with them, as well as the teachers in my old school Djäknepark School (some of the teachers I had were still working). I also understood certain words, without having to ask what they meant, words like 'grann' (beautiful) amongst other particular Norrköping words that I had used myself. As I understood, they could speak more freely. They did not have to think about translating for me. I also had the advantage of not being too old (thirty-four) and the interviewees were on average eleven years younger than me.

However, I sometimes discovered that I had been living out of Norrköping for a long time, as when I was fixing a place to meet Roger and he said: 'I'll see you in Domino's'. 'What's that?' I said. 'You don't know Domino's? You said you knew Norrköping.' What I didn't know was that the department store Domus had changed its name to Domino several years previously. He said to me: 'Was it the Stone Age when you lived here?' I laughed a little self-consciously and so did he.

A technical aspect simplifying the ongoing process of access was the use of the mobile phone and the car. I am fairly certain that this study would have been a lot harder to carry out ten years ago. As everyone was equipped with mobile phones it was possible to reach each other no matter where anyone was. If someone did not come to an arranged meeting I could ring up and perhaps fetch the person with the car, which was also a necessary detail in the research. We would sometimes arrange a meeting for a certain time, but mostly we used a form of flexitime. This has to do with the bag buyers' mobility, as they don't really know where they are going to be in advance. On these occasions I needed the car in order to move quickly between one place and another. The car was also used as a way of establishing contact, and I often hired an Audi or a BMW that was in keeping with their interest in power and performance. They seemed to like travelling in these kinds of cars, and if we had nothing else to talk about we could at least talk about the car's details. Sometimes, I gave them lifts to different places, which also strengthened the relationships.

A last aspect of creating trust and access presumably has to do with how my character was interpreted in different situations. In order to create trust and motivation it was of importance that I was calm. The informants often describe me like that, 'you're so calm.' I was forced to display a type of strong character, even while I was on some occasions nervous, particularly when hearing about serious crimes. However, it mostly felt that I wasn't 'reacting', that I was relatively relaxed when meeting them.

Observations, Interviews and Feelings

Even if the majority of the research was done through qualitative interviews, the observations made were invaluable for obtaining a more thorough understanding. There are different kinds of roles a researcher may take. Adler (1985: 11) acted from a 'peripheral membership role' (1985: 11), using cocaine and marijuana at parties with the informants, but was not involved in the drug traffic. Sometimes, during the research, I thought that 'maybe I should try heroin, or at least have a joint with the informants.' I didn't, though, come close to realizing my thoughts, for several reasons:

- The risk of loving the rush. If I had tried, I might have discovered that it was the best thing that had ever happened me.

- My unique position in relation to them as a researcher would have been erased. They would probably have ceased to trust me. I would also have been dependent on them for dosing and instructions.
- My own health and concern for my family.
- The risk of undermining the credibility of my research. It would be difficult for me to defend myself against the public and established society's representatives.

Another reason is that the experience that heroin gives rise to cannot be completely rendered in text form. The experience transcends attempts at textual reconstruction (as most other experiences do) and it therefore becomes less important to have experienced the rush myself. If I had experienced it, I still wouldn't have been able to describe it. My experience would probably have dominated the text. I do not think the book would have been much better if I had tried heroin.

Adler (1985: 24) writes about her smuggler and dealer study: 'Quite frankly, it would have been impossible for a nonuser to have gained access to this group to gather the data presented here.' For her research that may well have been the case. I believe, however, that it is a matter of trust and that this trust can be realized without having to act the same way the actors do. My role of research, drawing on Taylor (1993), can be seen as 'participant-as-observer'. This means that I participated in the interaction, joking, making small talk, and so forth, but didn't do like the actors did when it came to using and dealing with drugs. Taylor (1993: 13) writes: 'I wanted to be accepted as an acquaintance, if not a friend – a relationship not likely to be fostered by continuous note-taking.' Like Taylor I wrote up field notes at the end of the night. Most often I used a tape recorder to make it smoother.

The observations during the year 2000 were mostly made in connection with the interviews. The two latest years, though, have mostly involved a kind of participant observation. Mostly the informants have used heroin at such close intervals that a three-hour interview was done with heroin smoking breaks or they smoked during the actual interview. Sometimes their voices had a metallic quality on the tapes, which is because they were speaking through the foil straw. They have also told me during these observations what they are doing, why they are doing such and such and what the various parts are called. We have spoken about the ritual while it is being performed. Most of the interviews were individual, but some were conducted with pairs.

By observing I have been able to see what their homes look like, what sort of music and films they like, and so on. The observations have given me the opportunity to nuance my understanding of these people and at the same time to question the stereotypical picture of the drug user. Sometimes I have brought chocolate or buns with me, and sometimes they have provided them. These small gestures were of importance in creating a feeling of mutual respect and interest. I have mostly been well received by them and I have never experienced any obvious threats.

To say that I was calm during the research is, however, an exaggeration. I was constantly under a lot of pressure, and my consumption of alcohol increased during the research as I had to calm down in some way when I came home from research. One of the most pressurizing aspects was that I had to take care of tape recordings and notes from observations in a secure way. I thought in about the same way as Adler:

> At various times we also had to protect our research tapes. We encountered several threats to our collection of taped interviews from people who had granted us their interviews. This made us anxious, since we had taken great pains to acquire these tapes and felt strongly about maintaining confidences entrusted to us by our informants. When threatened, we became extremely frightened and shifted the tapes between different hiding places. We even ventured forth one rainy night with our tapes packed in a suitcase to meet a person who was uninvolved in the research at a secret rendezvous so that he could guard the tapes for us. (Adler 1985: 23)

I can relate to what Adler describes. On one occasion I had done some interviews in which I have been given extra vital information about dealing. I transcribed these tapes really quickly, using assumed names and places, and, after that, went by car 60 kilometres to our summer cottage to burn them. During the days when I had the interviews still on tapes I could hardly sleep.

Another concern was that my informants might die from overdoses. This is due to the fact that key informants become like friends; you start to pay attention to their life situation. On one occasion I heard from a social worker that a young male heroin user had overdosed and died from it. I asked for the name, worried that it may be some of my informants, and she answered with a name that is quite common, the same name as one of my informants. I felt a chill down my spine. I asked to be more sure: 'How old was he?' and the social worker answered: 'Just above twenty-two.' This was the age of my informant. By then I was sure that it was him, one of my closest informants, who had told me that it 'is only the blockheads who OD'. I felt crushed and, directly, called a heroin user who knew him, and he answered: 'No, it isn't him, I thought so too first, but it's another guy with the same name who has been in trouble before.' 'Thank God,' I thought.

Analysis and Theory

The analysis has been ongoing since the day I first set foot in Norrköping with the intention of researching there. Already during the first interview, when I heard words like 'grann' (beautiful/fine), 'stuk' (sprained), 'skruvad' (twisted), the researcher in me began work. Like other researchers in similar disciplines I seek to understand others' thoughts, knowledge and behaviour patterns.

As stated by Agar (1973: 11), 'ethnography is essentially a decoding operation.' This process of decoding can be compared with taking a course in another culture which is run in such a way that you don't find out much about the culture through literature, maps and such. The major source of knowledge is the members of the culture, who tell you how they see existence and what they think about living in the culture in question. The student (the researcher) of the course follows them on a journey through a cultural landscape that is their home environment and takes part in the objects and actions that give the culture content and meaning. After staying with the informants, talking, making jokes, drinking coffee and watching them in different types of situations the researcher's perspective on them changes and new ideas pop up in the head of the researcher.

I would not, however, say that the conclusions of the researcher are like a transparent paper laid on reality, as the researcher always has a theoretical perspective to work from (Kuhn 1970). To use the concept 'culture' means that I had a theoretical perspective in order to systematize the stories and acts of the participants in the culture. The reason for describing them as one culture is that they share a language, most of them know each other and have common friends and counterparts, and so there is a basis to view them as a specific subculture. However, sometimes it is hard to differentiate them from the amphetamine users, and other criminals, and some are closer to these groups than others. Based on age, socializing patterns and view of amphetamine users, however, I have chosen to view the young heroin users as belonging to a different culture than the amphetamine junkies, even if they share certain skills, strategies and problems. In short, I have used the concept of culture in order to understand the young heroin users, and this has naturally affected the text's form, which has a thematic, culture-analytic character.

Working with the aid of different themes is a fairly well proven method in anthropology, ethnography and sociology of culture. The data can be read as if they contain thematic binary opposites, for example: 'action–inaction', 'friend–enemy', 'in–out', 'clean–dirty', 'sophisticated–unsophisticated', 'strong character–weak character'.

I have made a thematic reading of the interviews and observation notes, which is probably obvious from the chapters. Certain themes have been interesting, others less so. Theories have been used to systematize, dramatize and place their stories in relation to society in general. However, if the interviewees' stories had not been contributory to making these theories of interest I would not have used them. The text has been formulated in a dialectic process where I have attempted make the analysis tie together the young heroin users' stories' to the theory.

If I had simply satisfied myself with a description and thematizing from the actor's perspective then my role would only have been to systemize and sort. With the help of theoretical expressions such as society, culture, subculture, and gender code, it is possible to analyse the actors' deeds in relation to the society in which they live. The cultural researcher or ethnographer, in this sense, becomes the interpreter who: (1) tries to describe the perspective and the knowledge from which the actors operate, and (2) tries to place these interpreted perspectives and knowledge in a social and cultural context.

Validity and Construction of Reality

Validity is a matter of whether the research results actually describe what the researcher intended them to. The book's text is in itself a type of validation. The reader can judge how reasonable the conclusions are. Validity can be divided into two aspects, with descriptive validity being about how the interviewees experience the description the researcher has produced. I let six of the interviewees read drafts of my manuscript several times. The most important aspect is that it is in line with their experience of the subculture. One man claimed he could have put a photograph of himself beside the text, which means that he could identify with the text. The text they received was not as theoretically interpretative as it is now, but I received at least reinforcement in that my knowledge of how it is to be in the subculture – to sell and buy drugs and so on – is good. The descriptive validity ought therefore to be good. I have genuinely taken pains to have a good foundation for my descriptions so that I can illuminate general aspects of the subculture.

Texts always involve constructions of reality and experiences of it (Kvale 1996). There are a series of translation problems in every cultural analysis, which involves people.

1. During the interviews the informants interpret their experiences and translate them into speech, which is then conveyed to me. It is often difficult to put words to experiences. This became particularly obvious when they were asked to describe the heroin rush.

2. Their translated experiences were written out and the written word is not the same as speech as it has a different grammatical structure. Also, gestures and tone of voice are lost.

3. Certain of their stories have been chosen and become central in the text, while others have been completely left out.

4. The Swedish text, including phrases from the members of the subculture, was translated into English, and this can't be done without reducing some of the

meaning of the original text. I and the translator have, during the process of translation, worked really hard to make the translation accord with the original text.

The text is also, naturally, an outcome of what I, as a researcher, am interested in. With this I would like to emphasize that this book is not a text about their lives in all their nuances, but rather about aspects of their subcultural lives. For example, I have not discussed their parents or their relationship to people outside the subculture, and this is a conscious choice as I have laid emphasis on the activities that happen in the subculture. Other aspects could have been included and would have produced a different text.

Bibliography

Adler, P. A. (1985) *Wheeling and Dealing: An Ethnography of an Upper-Level Drug Dealing and Smuggling Community*. New York: Columbia University Press.

Agar, M. N. (1973) *Ripping and Running: A Formal Ethnography of Urban Heroin Addicts*. New York: Academic Press.

Andersson, E. C. (1999) *Det extraordinäras lockelse: Luffarturistens bilder och upplevelser (The Attraction of the Extraordinary: Images and Experiences among Backpacker Tourists)*. Lund: Arkiv Förlag.

Aspelin, J. (1999) *Klassrummets mikrovärldar (The Micro Worlds of the Classroom)*. Stockholm/Stehag: Brutus Östlings Bokförlag Symposion.

Baudrillard, J. (1983) *Simulations*. New York: Semiotext(e).

Bauman, Z. (1989) *Modernity and the Holocaust*. Cambridge: Polity Press.

Bauman, Z. (1990) *Thinking Sociologically*. Oxford: Blackwell.

Bauman, Z. (1991) *Modernity and Ambivalence*. Cambridge: Polity Press.

Bauman, Z. (1992) *Mortality, Immortality and Other Life Strategies*. Cambridge: Polity Press.

Bauman, Z. (1998) *Globalization*: The Human Consequences. New York: Columbia University Press.

Bayley, S. (1986) *Sex, Drink and Fast Cars: The Creation and Consumption of Images*. London and Boston: Faber & Faber.

Becker, H. S. (1963/1973) 'Becoming a Marijuana User'. In Becker, H. S. *Outsiders: Studies in the Sociology of Deviance*. New York: The Free Press.

Becker, H. S. (1963/1973) *Outsiders: Studies in the Sociology of Deviance*. New York: The Free Press.

Bejerot, N. (1980) *Narkotika och narkomani (Narcotics and Narcomania)*. Stockholm: Bonniers/Aldusserien.

Berger, P. and Luckmann, T. (1966/1987) *The Social Construction of Reality: A Treatise in the Sociology of Knowledge*. Harmondsworth: Penguin.

Bjurström, E. (1995) Baby you can drive my car. In Bolin, G. and Löfgren, K. (eds), *Om unga män: Identitet, kultur och livsvillkor (Young Men: Identity, Culture and Circumstances of Life)*. Lund: Studentlitteratur.

Bourdieu, P. (1979/1992) *Distinction: A Social Critique of the Judgement of Taste*. London: Routledge.

Bourgois, P. (1996) *In Search of Respect: Selling Crack in El Barrio*. New York: Cambridge University Press.

Bibliography

Brown, B. S., Gauvey, S. K., Meyers, M. B. and Stark, S. D. (1971) In Their Own Words: Addicts' Reasons for Initiating and Withdrawing from Heroin. *International Journal of the Addictions* 6(4) (December) 635–45.

Campbell, C. (1989) *The Romantic Ethic and the Spirit of Modern Consumerism*. Oxford: Blackwell.

Christie, N. and Bruun, K. (1985) *Den goda fienden: Narkotikapolitik i norden* (*The Good Enemy: Politics of Narcotics in the Nordic Countries*). Stockholm: Rabén & Sjögren.

Cohen, S. (1972/1987) *Folk Devils and Moral Panics: The Creation of the Mods and Rockers*. Oxford: Basil Blackwell.

Connell, R.W. (1995) *Masculinities*. Berkeley and Los Angeles: University of California Press.

Douglas, M. (1970/2000) *Natural Symbols: Explorations in Cosmology*. London and New York: Routledge.

Douglas, M. (1966/1991) *Purity and Danger: An Analysis of the Concepts of Pollution and Taboo*. London and New York: Routledge.

Douglas, M. (ed.) (1987) *Constructive Drinking: Perspective on Drink from Anthropology*. Cambridge: Cambridge University Press.

Durkheim, E. (1897/1979) *Suicide: A Study in Sociology*. London: Routledge.

Durkheim, E. (1933/1984) *The Division of Labour in Society*. New York: The Free Press.

Elias, N. and Scotson, J.L. (1965/1994) *The Established and the Outsiders*. London: Sage.

Elsrud, T. (1998) Time Creation in Travelling. *Time and Society* 7(2): 309–34.

Elsrud, T. (2001) Risk Creation in Travelling: Risk Taking as Narrative and Practice in Back Packer Culture. *Annals of Tourism Research* 28(3): 597–16.

Faupel, C. E. (1991) *Shooting Dope: Career Patterns of Hard-Core Heroin Users*. Gainesville: University of Florida Press.

Fiske, J. (1989) *Understanding Popular Culture*. London and New York: Routledge.

Foucault, M. (1972/1992) *Madness and Civilization: A History of Insanity in the Age of Reason*. London: Routledge.

Frykman, J. and Löfgren, O. (1979/1987) *Culture Builders: A Historical Anthropology of Middle-Class Life*. New Brunswick: Rutgers University Press.

Fugelstad, A. & Rajs, J. (1998) *Narkotika: Ett livsfarligt beroende* (*Narcotics: A Life of Dangerous Dependence*). Nora: Nya Doxa.

Giddens, A. (1991) *Modernity and Self-Identity*. Cambridge: Polity Press.

Giddens, A. (1992) *The Transformation of Intimacy: Sexuality, Love and Eroticism in Modern Societies*. Stanford: Stanford University Press.

Goffman, E. (1959/1974) *The Presentation of Self in Every Day Life*. London: Pelican Books.

Bibliography

Goffman, E. (1967) *Interaction Ritual: Essays on Face-to-Face Behaviour.* New York: Anchor Books.

Goffman, E. (1971) *Relations in Public: Microstudies of the Public Order.* London: Penguin Books.

Goldberg, T. (1999) *Demystifying Drugs: A Psychosocial Perspective.* Basingstoke: Macmillan.

Gusfield, J. (1987) Passage to Play: Rituals of Drinking Time in American Society. In Douglas, M. (ed.), *Constructive Drinking: Perspective on Drink from Anthropology.* Cambridge, Cambridge University Press.

Hall, S. (1980) 'Encoding/Decoding'. In Hall, S., Hobson, D., Lowe, A. and Willis, P.E. (eds), *Culture, Media, Language.* London: Hutchinson.

Hall, S., Hobson, D., Lowe, A. and Willis, P. E. (eds) (1980) *Culture, Media, Language.* London: Hutchinson.

Hall, S. and Jefferson, T. (eds) (1976/1993) *Resistance through Rituals: Youth Subcultures in Post-War Britain.* London: Routledge.

Jackson-Jacobs, Curtis (2001). 'Refining Rock: Practical and Social Features of Self-Control Among a Group of College-Student Crack Users.' *Contemporary Drug Problems* 28(4): 597–624.

Järvinen, M. and Rosenquist, P (eds) (1991) *Kön, rus och disciplin – en nordisk antologi* (*Gender, Intoxication and Discipline – A Nordic Anthology*). Helsinki: Nordiska nämnden för alkohol- och drogforskning (NAD).

Järvinen, M. (1991) Berusade kvinnor – ett samhällsproblem ('Drunken Women – A Society Problem'). In Järvinen, M. and Rosenquist, P., *Kön, rus och disciplin* (*Gender, Intoxication and Discipline – A Nordic Anthology*). Helsinki: Nordiska nämnden för alkohol- och drogforskning (NAD).

Kartläggning av narkotikasituation 2000 i Finspång, Norrköping, Söderköping och Valdemarsvik (*Mapping of the Drug Situation 2000 in Finspång, Norrköping, Söderköping and Valdemarsvik*) (2001) Norrköping: Social Service and Police Department of Norrköping.

Katz, J. (1998) *Seductions of Crime: A Chilling Exploration of the Criminal Mind – From Juvenile Delinquency to Cold-Blooded Murder.* New York: Basic Books.

Kerouac, J. (1958/1998) *On the Road.* London: Penguin.

Kristeva, J. (1982) *Powers of Horror: An Essay on Abjection.* New York: Columbia University Press.

Kristiansen, A. (2000) *Fri från narkotika: Om kvinnor och män som har varit narkotikamissbrukare* (*Free from Drugs: Women and Men who have been Narcotic Abusers*). Stockholm: Bjurner och Bruno.

Kuhn, T. (1970) *The Structure of Scientific Revolutions.* Chicago: University of Chigago Press.

Kvale, S. (1996) *Interviews: An Introduction to Qualitative Research Interviewing.* Thousand Oaks: Sage.

Lalander, P. (1997) Breaking Away with Alcohol. *Nordic Studies on Alcohol and Drugs* 4: 33–42.

Lalander, P. (1998) Anden i flaskan (*The Genie in the Bottle*). Stockholm/Stehag: Symposion.

Lalander, P. (2001) Den smutsiga drycken: Om ungdomars konstruktion av klass och maskulinitet. (Dirty Drinking: The Construction of Class and Masculinity among Youth.) *Nordisk alkohol- och narkotikatidskrift* 17: (5–6).

Lenke, L. And Olsson, B. (2002) 'Swedish Drug Policy in the Twenty-first Century: A Policy Model Going Astray.' *The Annals of the American Academy of Political and Social Science* 582: 64–79.

Lindgren, S. Å. (1993) *Den hotfulla njutningen: Att etablera drogbruk som samhällsproblem 1890–1970* (*The Menacing Pleasure: Establishing Drug Use as a Social Problem 1890 to 1970*). Stockholm/Stehag, Symposion Graduale.

MacCannell, D. (1976) *The Tourist: A New Theory of the Leisure Class.* New York: Shocken Books.

Maffesoli, M. (1996) *The Times of the Tribes: The Decline of Individualism in Mass Society.* London: Sage.

Merton, R. K. (1949/1968) *Social Theory and Social Structure.* New York: Free Press.

Nordegren, T., Tunving, K. (1997) *Droger A-Ö* (*A-Z of Drugs*). Stockholm: Natur och Kultur.

Parker, H., Bury, C. and Egginston, R. (1998) *New Heroin Outbreaks Among Young People in England and Wales.* London (Police Research Group) Home Office.

Pearson, G. (1987) *The New Heroin Users.* Oxford: Basil Blackwell.

Polsky, N. (1969) *Hustlers, Beats and Others.* Harmondsworth: Penguin.

Rosenbaum, M. (1981) *Women on Heroin.* New Jersey: Rutgers University Press.

Scheff, T. J. (1997) *Emotions, the Social Bond, and Human Reality: Part/whole Analysis.* Cambridge: Cambridge University Press.

Simmel, G. (1903/1971) 'The Metropolis and Mental Life.' In Simmel, G., *On Individuality and Social Forms.* Chicago and London: The University of Chicago Press.

Simmel, G. (1911/1981) 'Kulturbegreppet och kulturens tragedi.' In Simmel, G., *Hur är samhället möjligt?* (*How is Society Possible?*) Göteborg: Bokförlaget Korpen.

Simmel, G. (1950) *The Sociology of George Simmel.* London/New York: The Free Press.

Simmel, G. (1981) *Hur är samhället möjligt?* (*How is Society Possible?*) Göteborg: Bokförlaget Korpen.

Smith, D. and Gay, G. (eds) (1972) *It's So Good, Don't Even Try it Once.* Englewood Cliffs: Prentice-Hall.

Stewart, T. (1987) *The Heroin Users.* London: Pandora Press.

Sulkunen, P., Alasuutari, P., Nätkin, R., Kinnunen, M. (1997) *The Urban Pub.* Helsinki: Stakes.

Sutter, A. G. (1969) 'Worlds of Drug Use on the Street Scene.' In Cressey, D. R. and Ward, D. A., (eds) *Delinquency, Crime and Social Process.* New York: Harper & Row.

Svensson, B. (1996) *Pundare, Jonkare och Andra (Speedfreaks, Junkies and Others).* Stockholm: Carlssons Bokförlag.

Svensson, B. (2000) 'Speedfreaks, junkies and others.' In Fountain, J. (ed.), *Understanding and Responding to Drug Use: The Role of Qualitative Research.* Luxembourg: EMCDDA.

Svensson, Birgitta. (1998) *Tatuering: Ett sinnligt äventyr (Tattooing: An Adventure for the Senses).* Stockholm: Nordiska museets förlag.

Taylor, A. (1993) *Women drug Users: An Ethnography of a Female Injecting Community.* Oxford: Clarendon Press.

Thomas, W. I. and Thomas, D. S. (1928) *The Child in America.* New York, Knopf.

Thornton, S. (1996) *Club Cultures: Music, Media and Subcultural Capital.* Hanover and London: Wesleyan University Press.

Tolkien, J. R. R. (1959) *The Lord of the Rings.* London: Allen & Unwin.

Trulson, K. (1998) *Det är i alla fall mitt barn: En studie av att vara missbrukare och mamma (It's My Child After All: A Study of Being Abuser and Mother).* Stockholm: Carlssons Förlag.

Turkle, S. (1996) *Life on the Screen: Identity in the Age of Internet.* London: Weidenfeld & Nicolson.

Turner, V. (1967) *The Forest of Symbols: Aspects of Ndembu Ritual.* Ithaca and London: Cornell University Press.

Veblen, T. (1899/1979) *The Theory of the Leisure Class.* London: Penguin.

Weber, M. (1934/1992) *The Protestant Ethic and the Spirit of Capitalism.* London: Routledge.

Whyte, W. F. (1943/1993) *Street Corner Society: The Social Structure of an Italian Slum.* Chicago: The University of Chicago Press.

Williams, T. (1989) *The Cocaine Kids: The Inside Story of a Teenage Drug Ring.* Cambridge/Massachusetts: Perseus Books.

Willis, P. E. (1977/1993) *Learning to Labour.* Aldershot: Ashgate.

Wuthnow, R., Davison Hunter, J., Bergesen, A. and Kurzweil, E. (1987) *Cultural Analysis: The Work of Peter L. Berger, Mary Douglas, Michel Foucault, and Jürgen Habermas.* London and New York: Routledge and Kegan Paul.

Ziehe, T. (1993) *Kulturanalyser: Ungdom, utbildning, modernitet (Cultural Analysis: Youth, Education and Modernity).* Stockholm/Stehag: Brutus Östlings Bokförlag Symposion.

Zinberg, N. E. and Harding, W. M. (eds) (1982) *Control Over Intoxicant Use: Pharmacological. Psychological and Social Considerations.* New York: Human Science Press.

Index

abject, the, 164
acceptability
    heroin use, 43
access, to informants, 173
action, 14, 16, 27, 35, 109, 166
    and heroin use, 46, 104–5, 112–13
    aspect of masculinity, 134–5
    environment and character, 40–1, 82–3
    influence of films, 115–17
    reason for criminality, 21–2
    skills, 158–9, 165
    women, 149–51
    see also adventure; dramatic situations
Adam, 25
addiction, 5, 8–9, 60, 104, 166–8
    blame, 92–3
    invisibility, 99–102
    portrayal in films, 126–8
addicts, 1–2, 42, 43, 98
    self-image, 87–9
    see also drug users; heroin users
Adler, P.A., 23–4, 29–30, 76, 93, 133, 172–4, 177–9
adulthood
    and mentors, 28
    portrayal in films, 121
adventure, 160–3, 169
    blasé attitude, 165–6, 168
    see also action; dramatic situations
aestheticization, of separation, 118, 121, 128
affirmation, 17, 29
Aftonbladet, 3, 5, 171
Agar, M.N., 17, 81, 173, 180
age, 99
    interviewees, 85, 173
agencies, alcohol and narcotic, 3, 171–3, 175
alarm system, 74
Alasuutari, P., 152
alcohol, 4–5, 26–7, 159
    and masculinity, 141, 143

symbolism, 40, 56
alcoholics, 1–2
alienation, 156
altered states of perception *see* perception
alternative reality *see* reality
ambivalence
    research decisions, 174
America, 129–30
    gangster films, 114–17
amphetamines, 113
    addicts, 93, 98
    history of drug use, 2–3, 4, 19–20
anabolic steroids, 34
analysis, of research, 179–81
Andersson, E.C., 156, 160
anonymity
    condition of research, 172, 174
    see also confidentiality
anticipation, 51–2
appearance, 101, 109
    amphetamine addicts, 98–9
    John's friends, 57–8
    overdose, 80
    Roger, 85
    Veronica, 63–4
    see also image
Aspelin, J., 29
authenticity, staged
    influence of films, 118
authority
    and research, 172, 175
    pluralization of, 7, 168
autonomy, lack of
    addicts, 153, 167
avoidance strategies, 68, 69, 71
A-Z of Drugs (1997), 147–8

backpackers
    and experience, 32, 160
    temporary identity, 156